Culture and the University

Also Available from Bloomsbury

Teacher Agency, by Mark Priestley, Gert Biesta and Sarah Robinson
Schooling as Uncertainty, by Frances Vavrus
Peace Education, edited by Monisha Bajaj and Maria Hantzopoulos
A New Perspective on Education in the Digital Age, by Jesper Tække and Michael Paulsen
Subjectivity and Social Change in Higher Education, by Liezl Dick and Marguerite Müller
Hopeful Pedagogies in Higher Education, edited by Mike Seal
Experiments in Decolonizing the University, by Hans Schildermans
Posthumanism and the Digital University, by Lesley Gourlay
Decolonizing University Teaching and Learning, by D. Tran
Utopian Universities, edited by Miles Taylor and Jill Pellew
Transforming University Education, by Paul Ashwin
Changing Higher Education for a Changing World, edited by Claire Callender, William Locke and Simon Marginson
Internationalization of Higher Education for Development, by Susanne Ress

Culture and the University

Education, Ecology, Design

Ronald Barnett, Søren S.E. Bengtsen
and Rikke Toft Nørgård

BLOOMSBURY ACADEMIC
Bloomsbury Publishing Plc
50 Bedford Square, London, WC1B 3DP, UK
1385 Broadway, New York, NY 10018, USA
29 Earlsfort Terrace, Dublin 2, Ireland

BLOOMSBURY, BLOOMSBURY ACADEMIC and the Diana logo are trademarks
of Bloomsbury Publishing Plc

First published in Great Britain 2022

Copyright © Ronald Barnett, Søren S.E. Bengtsen, and Rikke Toft Nørgård, 2022

Ronald Barnett, Søren S.E. Bengtsen, and Rikke Toft Nørgård have asserted their right under the Copyright, Designs and Patents Act, 1988, to be identified as Author of this work.

Cover design: Toby Way
Cover image © James Garman/Unsplash

All rights reserved. No part of this publication may be reproduced or transmitted in any form or by any means, electronic or mechanical, including photocopying, recording, or any information storage or retrieval system, without prior permission in writing from the publishers.

Bloomsbury Publishing Plc does not have any control over, or responsibility for, any third-party websites referred to or in this book. All internet addresses given in this book were correct at the time of going to press. The author and publisher regret any inconvenience caused if addresses have changed or sites have ceased to exist, but can accept no responsibility for any such changes.

A catalogue record for this book is available from the British Library.

A catalog record for this book is available from the Library of Congress.

ISBN: HB: 978-1-3501-9301-7
PB: 978-1-3501-9300-0
ePDF: 978-1-3501-9302-4
eBook: 978-1-3501-9303-1

Typeset by Deanta Global Publishing Services, Chennai, India
Printed and bound in Great Britain

To find out more about our authors and books visit www.bloomsbury.com and sign up for our newsletters.

For Denise

Contents

Preface	viii
Introduction: Whatever Happened to the University *for* Culture?	1

Part I Warring Cultures *and* a Universal Culture   Ronald Barnett

1	The Cultural Crisis of the University	17
2	Culture Wars: Multiplication and (Possible) Re-unification	30
3	A Common Culture: No and Maybe	43
4	For the University and the World: A Culture of the Earth	56

Part II Designing for Cultural Places   Rikke Nørgård

5	Placeful Cultures and Cultural Places	71
6	The Atmospheric University and Cultural Atmospheres	83
7	Cultures for Collective Visioning and Future-Making	96
8	Futurescaping Alternative Universities	109

Part III Within and beyond Culture   Søren Bengtsen

9	Higher Education as Cultural Formation	125
10	Cultural Leadership	137
11	The Indivisible	149
12	Beyond Culture	161

Part IV Dialogical Imaginings

13	University Culture as Force, Coexistence, Endeavour and Entanglement Rikke Nørgård	175
14	A University of One's Own Søren Bengtsen	189
15	An Ecological Culture for a Non-Comprehending World Ronald Barnett	202
	Endnote: Uniting the University and Even the Earth: The Twin Cultures Ronald Barnett	215

Bibliography	217
Subject Index	239
Name Index	247

Preface

My first book – *The Idea of Higher Education* (1990) – was an attempt to institute the philosophy of higher education as a definite field of study. Each of its chapters deliberately marked out points in the field deserving of serious attention, one of which was entitled simply 'Culture'. That was unusual then and has, in many ways, remained so, with its implication that universities and higher education might have cultural purpose(s). Indeed, Bill Readings, in his influential (1997) book, *The University in Ruins*, observed that the university had abandoned culture and had become – we may say – a post-cultural institution.

My sense is that – as the second quarter of the twenty-first century approaches – this is a particularly opportune moment to attend to culture and the university, and to see whether some kind of cultural purpose(s) can be gleaned. On a number of fronts, the world of higher education seems to be becoming more sensitive to matters of culture (the presence of culture wars, the cultures of the Global South as worthy of attention and the responses of different cultures to global crises), and yet the world is also experiencing increasing cultural fragmentation. The matter of culture and the university has become both urgent and global, and a cultural turn is now required in understanding the issue.

My thought was that it would make for a more intriguing and more satisfying book if it was a collaborative production and that the collaborators both had the space to air their own thinking and also engage in conversation together. My two collaborators virtually chose themselves: Søren Bengtsen and I have been collaborating for some years, and there is overlap – but thankfully also difference – between our approaches to the philosophy of higher education; Rikke Nørgård not only is a colleague of Søren's in the Centre for Higher Education Futures (University of Aarhus, Denmark) but also has particular interests both in culture and in university futures and their design. This book is the result of that collaboration.

Ronald Barnett
London, August 2021

Introduction

Whatever Happened to the University *for* Culture?

Starting Points and Questions

The basic intention behind this book is twofold: to show that culture has to be a central matter for higher education and universities and to help in restoring culture to that central place. The idea of culture is foundational for higher education and the university: this, at least, is our contention. To put it formally, we seek nothing less than to institute a cultural turn, both in understanding universities and in helping in the design of their missions and major activities.

For the last half century or so, in policies and practices, and in the literature, in and around universities and higher education, culture has been a topic – perhaps above all *the* topic – that dare not express its name. With rare exceptions (of which Bill Readings' (1997) book, *The University in Ruins*, is the stand-out example), there has been a large void. There is no book in the catalogue that bears anything like the main title of this book – *Culture and the University*. This is doubly bizarre, the silence both within the higher education community and in the academic literature, not least given that the university is a massive social institution that is severely implicated in the matter of culture in all manner of ways.

However, exactly as this book was being planned and drafted, so some green shoots – putting 'culture' and 'university' together in the one phrase – began to appear, at least in high-end online articles and in policy networks (Liyange, 2020; Alt, 2021; EUA, 2021) and in the ways some universities are redesigning their missions; and this development deserves some explanation. Is it just a response to culture wars finding their way onto campuses or is it a deeper phenomenon that now we are starting to see some recognition that universities might have purposes and even *responsibilities* in relation to culture?

Understanding this neglect of the matter and there being indications that it is now attracting attention provide the starting points of this book. Our main target is to identify some ideas and practical principles that may help in developing a new agenda for culture in higher education, so as to forge some strong links between them; in short, to identify *cultural purposes* for the twenty-first-century university. Three questions have stood before us in advancing these more constructive and yet more speculative parts of this book: What concepts and ideas might assist in furnishing a cultural role – or set of cultural roles – for the university in the twenty-first century? What are the difficulties – practically and conceptually – that any such venture might face? Against that background, and in broad terms, how might universities go about forging cultural purpose(s) for themselves?

Self-evidently, the whole project of this book runs quickly into large challenges. First, as major figures have observed (Eagleton, 2000; Williams, 2017/1958), culture is among the most fraught of concepts. Second, we have been using the terms 'higher education' and 'university' as if they are interchangeable but they are each slippery concepts.

'Higher education' is used to refer both to national systems (we speak of *systems of higher education*) and to the educational processes that individual students experience, and so the term has both macro and micro interpretations. Students are *in* higher education (higher education as system), and they have an experience *of* higher education (higher education as a particular set of educational processes). Moreover, universities are large and complex institutions and possess national and global presences, and their activities go well beyond the education of their students including knowledge production and safeguarding (in libraries and databanks), societal memory, symbolic vitality, civic outreach, life enhancement, economic generation, national wherewithal and international soft power. Rather than becoming embroiled in these niceties, we shall generally retain 'higher education' to refer to students and their educational processes and 'university' to refer to the social institution which contains higher education but many other functions besides.

Maintaining this distinction – between 'higher education' and 'university' – is important since we want to show that significant issues and possibilities arise for the advancement of culture *both* for the university as a complex social institution on the one hand – with its local, national, global dimensions – *and* within students' programmes of study and their educational experiences on the other hand. The matter of culture is present and pressing in both domains, that is, the university as a societal institution *and* students' educational experiences.

Why Now?

What give attention to these issues now? Two answers have already been proffered: (i) the matter of culture and the university has been severely neglected for around half a century. However, (ii) having lain dormant for some time, the matter of culture and the university is now being given new energies but without anything approaching a satisfactory understanding of it. One explanation for this resurgence has also been intimated: issues of culture in the wider world, and even culture wars, are finding their way onto campuses. Large issues – abortion, race, state oppression, gender, coloniality, freedom of speech, civil rights, justice, nationalism, identity, the rights of indigenous communities and women's rights and so on – are playing out in universities across the world (with some quite different mixes of issues).

In turn, universities find it difficult to play the part of neutral umpire, not least because the university – whether it wishes it or not – is directly a player. Not far beneath the surface lurks the questions, 'can the university' and 'should the university take sides?' Should it, can it, might it declare a position of its own? So matters of culture are four-square in the university's bailiwick: the university is increasingly being drawn explicitly into engaging – at some level or other – with culture.

However, there are surely deeper explanations for the *joint* matter of culture and the university now beginning to appear in public settings. It is, we suggest, at last beginning to be intuited in the policy domain that major global and societal challenges have a significant vein of culture running through them. The Covid-19 pandemic is illustrative. Although its many features remain unclear, it is evident that culture has come into play at several points, perhaps in food and street market practices, in societal practices (of wearing or not wearing face masks), of deference given or not given to natural science and scientists, of a willingness or hesitancy in being vaccinated, and in compliance with or resistance to the rigours of 'lock-downs'. (Moreover, it seems likely that one factor in vaccine hesitancy is the possession or not of a higher education experience (Soares et al., 2021).)

In short, the spread of the virus, its treatments and their efficacy, and practices among the citizenry and their sustainability delimit explanations drawn from the natural sciences, from economics and from empirical social science. In the end, the phenomena call for the category of culture to be taken seriously. It was always thus but largely invisible. Now, there is emerging – perhaps dimly as yet – a new sense that culture matters.

To put the matter formally, all the entities of the world are entangled (Barad, 2007), such that any entity – in theory at least – can affect any other entity. Culture is not a peripheral phenomenon, but is affected *by* the world and has profound impacts *upon* the world. (In establishing the Reich Chamber of Culture, Goebbels understood very well *both* of these features of culture (Fritzsche, 1934).) Culture hovers between oppression and liberation, between structure and agency and between ontology and ideation.

As remarked, culture wars have found their way onto university campuses, and not only in the public and quasi-public events held in universities. Those culture wars are finding their way into curricula and pedagogies, and beyond the humanities and social sciences. Pedagogies and curricula are being reconsidered for ways in which they might respond to issues of race, gender, coloniality, social class and so forth.

The problem here is not the culture wars as such. It is the more deep-seated *meta*-problem with which universities are now faced, namely that of *culture wars about culture wars*. *Should* the university be seen to be responding to culture wars? Does it have a responsibility, on the one hand, to demonstrate how, rationally, soberly and with little fervour a major social institution – the university – can be seen to taking culture wars seriously? *Or*, to the contrary, does it have a responsibility *not* to be caught up on the moods of the age and hold fast to its essential educational and epistemic callings, whatever they may be?

Some may think that there is opening here for the university an extraordinary opportunity, that of bringing warring factions together into the 'space of reason' (Bakhurst, 2011) that the university, at its best, provides. Culture now becomes central to the university's role in the twenty-first century, that of working at *cultural negotiation* in society and even across the world, rather than endorsing cultural fission. The university can show ways of bringing together extreme positions into the kind of 'ideal speech situation' associated with Jurgen Habermas (1991: 25) – characterized by an interest in truthfulness and of a kind seen all too rarely as the culture wars play out. Others may feel that the university takes up this cultural baton at its peril, for there is – it may be said – no safe space for the university to mark out in teaching, research, its public debates and its societal outreach.

Here is one such domain of culture in which the university is irrevocably a player, where there is no disinterested space available. Prompted especially by suggestions of Boaventura de Sousa Santos in his (2014) book on *Epistemologies of the South*, much interest has developed in the idea of 'ecologies of knowledge', and from that suggestion has come work on 'the epistemologies of the Global South' (de Sousa Santos, 2018; de Sousa Santos and Meneses, 2020). And the university is a major player here. But a key question has yet fully to receive the attention it deserves: Can the epistemologies of the North and those of the South be put together in any coherent way? For universities, there are tricky problems, at once of pedagogy and curricula, of epistemology and positioning.

What is at stake in this debate is a problem of culture but, with few exceptions (e.g. Connell, 2019), culture as such is being given surprisingly short shrift. Just how might the culture(s) of science-driven knowledge of the twenty-first century, which tend to separate knowledge from Nature, live happily with the cognitive cultures of communities that are much closer to Nature? *This* epistemic matter of culture – in which universities are centrally implicated – is surely central if the human species is to find a way of living with Nature.

In embarking into the 'contested and complex sphere of culture in academic spaces' (Peters and Tukeo, 2010), these murky waters – of culture, knowledge, being a university and humanity on Earth (and even *in* Earth (Latour, 2016)) – await us. The matter of culture and the university has both gravity and urgency.

Prepositions and Paradoxes

What's in a preposition? It would be easy to concern ourselves with culture *in* the university or the culture *of* the university. But we can do justice to those matters only on a much larger canvas. Our larger concern has to be that of culture *across* the wider world and the part that the university has been playing and might play in the twenty-first century. In short, our major concern is that of the cultural purposes of the university as a university *for* culture.

There will be nervousness at the voicing of such a quest, but any such nervousness harbours a pusillanimity. Willy-nilly, the university is ensconced in culture, in cultures indeed. To duck the matter of culture, then – as the university has been doing for the past half century or more – is to avoid a set of responsibilities in front of it. Yes, this is a value-laden project that, in the end, must call for the courage not merely to identify issues – although that activity is valuable amid past silences – but moreover to contend for some or other sense of culture with which the university might especially be associated. There has, in other words, to be a recommendatory flavour to what is to come. This is not, however, to suggest a very determinate set of profferings. After all, there are three authors here, each with their own approach; and that is deliberate. But it is unashamedly to indicate that this book must be more than a reconnoitre of the field. Plausible possibilities have to be a goal here.

In front of such a quest, there are thickets to negotiate. There are, first of all, three dilemmas. One is that the university has emerged over hundreds – and even thousands – of years out of culture – cultures of literacy and clerkishness (Gellner, 1991a), of theology (Higton, 2013), of social taste and elevation (Wiener, 1985), and of a life of reason suitable for governmental administration (Ostling, 2018). The significance of universities as laying a cultural veneer upon the administrative class was an important element in its formation in European democracies in the nineteenth century: it enabled the rise of the mandarins (Ringer, 1990) through – as it might be said – *a culture of culture*. And yet, the university came to abandon culture, at least in its self-projection. Few universities in the world publicly attested to their possessing a keen interest in culture as such. Innovation, economy, knowledge, employability, 'excellence' and even service, yes. But culture? *Universities were born of culture but have come to shun culture*; at least, until very recently.

A second dilemma is that in relation to culture, the university has to be both critic and player. The university cannot but be a cultural agent, engaging with cultures and secreting its own cultures. And yet, *qua* university in which all is on the table for scrutiny, culture is a matter for *critique* within the university. Surely, here is one explanation for the university's reluctance to declare its hand in relation to culture. Its critical armoury has shot through the pretences of culture. Culture has been shown to be worthy only of being kept in its place, not of being heralded. It possesses too many difficulties for its explicit advocacy.

Following the work of Ranciere, the idea of 'the hermeneutics of suspicion' gained currency (Felski, 2011), and here we might speak of *a suspicion of culture*: culture is suspect on many fronts. It is accused of partiality, closure, a will to power, exclusion, suppression, stratification, elitism and even ideology. That being so, how might culture gain a *legitimate* purchase in the university? The university, it may seem, can only come at it crablike, eyeing it warily, inspecting it and critiquing it. It cannot be straightforwardly embraced.

The third dilemma is that once the university seriously notices culture, it is faced with a terrible fork. In one direction, it commits itself to some kind of culture but on what basis? Taking *this* path, it runs the risk of endorsing frameworks, ideologies and holds on the world, and is liable to become ideological itself. But if it pauses to critique all cultures that come within its reach, there is no space available on which to assemble a neutral critique: any such critique pretends to a disinterestedness that it doesn't possess (Adorno, 1978). Moreover, culture tends to dissolve in its very critiquing, the pretentiousness of its presuppositions being shot through. A way out of this dilemma is to suggest that the university resides in a *transcultural space*, providing a space in which all cultures can have their day. But this is a sleight of hand, for a transcultural position *is* a cultural position. The challenge still remains to give an account of the kind of culture to be primarily associated with the university.

But What Is Culture?

It would be tempting to attempt to lay out the many ways in which culture has been understood, but such a large task is not one that we intend to undertake, and on two grounds. Firstly, there have been several attempts to chart the idea of culture – earlier, we mentioned Raymond Williams and Terry Eagleton – and, secondly, attempting such a task here would divert us from our main target, that of the relationship between culture and the university. However, a glance at that more general literature on culture is helpful, if only to demonstrate that our precise target – culture and the university – is highly elusive; and even 'baffling' (Eliot, 1962: 27).

We pick out just twelve angles that have particular resonances with higher education and the university, although we make only bare efforts here to specify those links. (Our numbering system implies no hierarchy; and cross-links between – and even antagonisms among – the angles will be discernible.)

(i) *Culture as collectivity*: Culture is a collective form of life, marked out by those scripts, languages, idioms, practices and symbols that provide meaning to a community (de Certeau, 1988; Fournas, 1995; Cassirer, 2000). It is found in anthropological sense of cultures (Ulin, 2001) and is suggestive of members of a community feeling mutually bound in solidarity, and through which the community possesses a unity (Eliot, 1962). It follows that, while culture includes, it also excludes. Not only does the total community of higher education (including its alumni) possess a culture with exclusionary tendencies (towards those who have not enjoyed higher education) but its *internal* academic tribes work to safeguard their epistemic cultures and territories (Trowler et al., 2014).

(ii) *Culture as inward dwelling*: Culture contains a natural tendency in harbouring unreflective elements; and so we may speak of the culture of an age (Taylor, 1992). A reluctance critically to self-examine is wholly understandable since such reflection might lead to fragmentation of a culture. (Prohibitions on critical self-scrutiny *and* fragmentation can be witnessed within universities.)

(iii) *Culture as ideology*: A culture is a carrier of collective interests that form an ideology which systematically represents the world in partial ways (Marx and Engels, 1977; Marx, 1981; Rosen, 1996). Culture is a distorting mechanism, and is easily caught up – for example – in nationalism (Delanty and O'Mahony, 2002). When powerful states start to speak of their universities possessing a cultural role is a moment for wariness.

(iv) *Culture as elevation*: Culture is so taken up with itself that it comes to believe its own ideology. It takes on a normative aspect, conferring status, privilege and superiority upon itself. Those on the outside are clearly culturally disadvantaged (Bourdieu and Champagne, 2002) and even uncultured.

(v) *Culture as power*: In a stratified society, culture takes on the form of a capital and, in turn, can be wielded as a power (Bourdieu and Passeron, 1990; Habermas, 2001). Amid a number of cultures, one culture may be dominant and take steps to retain and even further its dominance. Such tendencies can be seen *within* the academic world, notably in the cultural power exerted by STEM (science, technology, engineering, mathematics) disciplines (Calabrese Barton et al., 2018).

(vi) *Culture as critique*: A culture – cultures indeed – may turn on notions of critique, resistance and emancipation (Eagleton, 2000). A culture may gain its power from its antipathy to another (perhaps dominant) culture and may be a *counter*culture.

(vii) *Culture as instrumentalism*: Although culture has strong self-reproducing (autopoietic) tendencies – still it maintains its own identity and vitality precisely by situating itself in the world. It, therefore, has a whiff of instrumentality in its manoeuvrings, so as to sustain itself. Instrumentalism is evident in universities in their plural organizational cultures, not least in maintaining their survival in treacherous times (Berquist and Pawlak, 2008). Their 'polysemic' character – as an assemblage of cultures – allows universities to be put to multiple ends (Eaton and Stevens, 2020).

(viii) *Culture as endorsement*: With its conservative tendencies, culture has a naturally endorsing orientation. It confers its tacit approval of matters through possessing a set of values (a value background) of its own, and so 'absolving us . . . from moral responsibility' (Eagleton, 2000: 158).

(ix) *Culture as self-realization*: If a culture is to survive, it must contain spaces for individuals to realize themselves (Ryle and Soper, 2002). A vocabulary of flourishing, self-realization, authenticity and becoming may emerge.

(x) *Culture as aspiration*: A culture is always protective of its past but, in maintaining its momentum in a changing world, it often contains an explicit future – or even futures – orientation. It aspires to maximize its values by mobilizing the cultural resources at hand (Bennett, 2013).

(xi) *Culture as repression*: Culture is a means by which one community can exert discursive, linguistic and narrative hegemony over another (Connell, 2019) and constitutes a form of societal repression. Within the academic community, the repressive character of its culture – its judgemental technologies such as rankings, performance measurement and impact scores – is beginning to be scrutinized, both across and within universities. (Utrecht University has recently abandoned impact factors in its hiring and promotion decisions (Woolston, 2021).)

(xii) *Culture as 'excellence'*: A mature culture will be bound to develop its own hierarchy of values. A vocabulary of quality (and qualities), standards and excellence may emerge, and, in higher education, 'world-classness'. It comes to care about those standards that it regards as integral to its way of life, and it may confer honours on those who exemplify its standards. However, as Readings (1997) observed in reviewing universities' modern cultural history, 'excellence' has become a vapid term lacking conceptual content; indeed, an empty signifier.

Every one of these twelve insights into culture has evident expression in higher education and universities, with all their consequent awkwardnesses. The culture of higher education and universities invokes matters of suppression *and* aspiration, of instrumentalism *and* of self-realization, of non-reflexivity *and* critique, of the local *and* global, and of power *and* of care.

Culture Matters

It may be felt that if culture is susceptible to so many meanings, even mutually antagonistic, then it must be an empty concept. It may seem as if it is a nice example of a word with the form that Humpty Dumpty identified in his tutoring of Alice, namely that one can deploy it to mean whatever one chooses, 'neither more nor less' (Hancher, 1981). That being so, we could be forgiven for thinking that the term 'culture' is precisely one from which the university should shy away. With its jelly-on-the-wall character, the term lacks substance and is better avoided.

This is a serious matter. Culture is a large concept, and there surely must be significant ways of attaching it to higher education and universities. After all, it has connotations of collective meaning, community, care, standards, communication, valued way(s) of life, discourse, practices and sustainability over time; and *all* these are significant aspects of universities. But the matter of culture seems ungraspable. Of any position taken up – among the twelve paths of consideration just identified – there is a whole battery of other readings to be brought against it; and some of those readings, with their connotations of exclusion, superiority, narrowness and closure, will be especially discomforting to the university. But this matter – of culture and the university – has landed into the court of the university and decision time approaches. The matter cannot be ducked any longer.

Just what stance – or stances – towards culture are available to the university in the twenty-first century? The good news is that while forlorn positions lurk aplenty, still there are intimations of more positive positions that may assist not only the university in a turbulent age but even the wider world. Moreover, if culture yields so many options for the university, it may be that yet more options can be imagined and new spaces of culture created for the university; and this is the stance behind this book. As well as charting the conceptual and theoretical ground, we seek also to discern new ideas, concepts and principles that are helpful in the shaping of higher education and universities for the twenty-first century.

This book, therefore, can be understood as a set of gatherings of concepts, reflections and suggestions as to ways forward for universities, both individually and collectively. It is a gathering of resources for *future* hard thinking, empirical research, policy formation and sheer practical endeavour. Since this book is breaking new ground – in taking seriously the relationship between universities and culture – we see it as a propaedeutic to work yet to come in each of those domains.

The New Two Cultures

There is a further matter that we must flag in this introduction, that of the *relationship* between culture and the university. We may speak of the culture

– or cultures – of the wider society, and of the culture – or cultures – of the university, but what of their relationship? Is the culture of the university part of the wider society, the wider world even, or does it stand on its own ground? The temptation is obvious, which is to assert that there may be difference – between culture in the wider world and in the university – but there is also overlap. The university occupies a *hybrid space* of culture, a space of its own culture(s) while also participating in the culture(s) of society. There is more to be noted, however.

The university trades on the hybridity of its cultural position, being separate from society *and* being happy at other times to be seen as part of the cultural mainstream: separation *and* integration. For example, in the matter of employability and the graduate labour market, it is at pains to project its students as being employable and yet it also wishes, even if more quietly, to contend for its programmes of study as constituting a refinement, a 'value-added' indeed. The concept of citizenship subtly, too, is enlisted to play both roles, within the dominant culture and also putting into the wider world the culture of the university itself. The university still harbours a sense (if fading or even suppressed) of being a critical and even subversive counterculture, separate from society. But then this cultural separation – between universities and the wider world – may erupt in major political and national crises, when it turns out that graduates seem to be living in their own cultural space. Graduates talk to, communicate with and marry other graduates and form their own cultures.

Much like the church and the monarchy, the university has come to be situated in an awkward cultural space, at once within *and* beyond the dominant culture of society, both closely coupled and so loosely coupled as to set up antipathies to society. Unwittingly, too, the university is playing a major part in the cultural fragmentation of the world. We are facing a reincarnation of the 'two nations' of which a British prime minister, Benjamin Disraeli, spoke in the nineteenth century, but *a division now based not on class as such but on culture*. We face before us, right across the world, *two nations of culture*, between those who have and those who haven't enjoyed higher education.

This is a matter of profound significance. If the world is going adequately to address the large matters in front of it – of climate change, ecological degradation, responsiveness to disaster and risk, of concern for 'the other' – this matter of cultural schism has to be addressed head-on. And, since universities are implicated as one source of this cultural schism, they are obliged to consider their responsibilities in the matter. As stated, universities have traded on their hybrid relationship with culture, both in and outside the dominant culture. *This ambiguous positioning of universities is no longer tenable.*

The moment has come for universities to tackle the matter of culture so as to address this new 'two cultures' challenge, not least to see if connections can be found between the culture(s) of the university and of the wider society. We try, in this book, to assemble some resources to assist this large quest,

This Book's Structure

This book has four parts. The book's three authors each has a part, setting out their own conceptualization of, and suggestions for furthering, the connections between culture and the university. Each of those parts has been compiled *without any conversation between the three authors*, for we wanted to produce three different takes on the matter to hand. If the culture–university relationship lacks a definite framing and if it is both fraught and open, then it makes sense for the three authors not to foreclose conversation by attempting a unified thesis but to come forward separately, each with their own stance and insights. Only in the final part do we construct a conversation, with each of us providing a rejoinder chapter. Even there, we have kept matters open, with each chapter in that final part adopting its own balance between providing a commentary on the other two parts and using that commentary as a springboard for further ideas of culture and the university.

Ronald Barnett's chapters analyse the reluctance of universities seriously to engage with the matter of culture. In turning more to means than to ends, university has become a culture-free zone. (Culture, after all, is precisely a matter of valued ends.) But this is a grave neglect, for life, communication, power, schism and what it is to be human are all implicated. Moreover, culture wars of the wider world have found their way onto campus, and the university is now obliged to be a player in the domain of culture. Matters of racism, concern for indigenous communities, the public good, Global North–Global South relations, the role relationships between the disciplines and their roles (especially the place of the STEM disciplines), *and* collective life on this planet are all matters of *culture*. The question arises: Might there yet be a common culture for the university in aiding the world? The response here is that a culture of the Earth is a plausible *meta*-culture for the university.

Rikke Nørgård's chapters put forward an array of concepts and frameworks for thinking and practice with regard to culture and the university as place, atmosphere, design, network and hybrid. The chapters employ the notions of place-making, atmospheric design, speculative design, future-making, collective visioning and futurescaping to nurture a cultural, designerly and speculative endowment for the university beyond the projected, probable and even plausible. Combined, the chapters indicate how the university can think, be and act as a culturing force in a design- and future-oriented manner that invite for participatory academic institutions and imaginative design cultures, and that can move the university forward in realizing desired values. The chapters take the standpoint that universities and their members, given suitable speculative design frameworks, placeful cultures, cultural atmospheres and methods of visioning, can play a crucial role in opening up both the culture and the future of the university and in turn create infrastructures for more preferable university cultures.

Søren Bengtsen's chapters examine the relation between culture and the university as a relation between education and ethics. The roles of culture and academic formation in higher education curricula go beyond the mere embracing of a culture, or even of a selection of cultures. The ethical imperative in curricula demands that universities, through their knowledge and academic practices, embrace culture as a cohesive force across different values and belief systems. This imperative includes mutual respect, inclusion, diversity, embracing of peripheries and a collective responsibility. Such a stance calls not for cultural assimilation but for being active in forming a culture of interconnectedness, in short an ecological culture. It follows that, while culture is an expression of humanity, it cannot be an anthropocentrism and a human-centred ethics. Cultural formation always includes an understanding of where humanity dwells, its origin and possible futures. Culture should not become a harnessing of sameness but should be a recognition of strangeness around, among and within us. Herein lies the germ of cultural growth.

We conclude with a brief endnote, in the hope of provoking further efforts in engaging with the matters in this book and in identifying yet other issues in the sighting of cultural purpose(s) for the university.

Part I

Warring Cultures *and* a Universal Culture

Ronald Barnett

1

The Cultural Crisis of the University

Introduction

In a recent edition of the *Times Higher Education* magazine, it is suggested that 'The university provides a standardised *cultural* base through which . . . disease is recognized and addressed. It binds together events, separated by oceans and time zones, in Wuhan, Milan and the Bronx. It unites persons suffering [in isolation]. It provides the vocabulary, analyses and anticipated resolutions' (Frank and Meyer, 2020; RB's emphasis). The authors go on to claim that this role of the university – in extending '*a global cultural canopy*' – is now at risk. Populism, a growing fear of strangers, a retreat to one's nation and locality and a mistrust of experts and science cast a pall over such global pretensions. The 'standardised cultural base', which (for these writers) seemed, until quite recently, to be pervasive, and spreading ever widely across the globe – and in which the university has played a key part – is now in jeopardy; indeed, it may be lost irrevocably.

We have here a nice, if rather disquieting, entrée to our present explorations. At one time, perhaps until the mid-twentieth century, a connection between the university and the culture of the wider society was taken for granted. It was not so much to help the world to be more rational, for two world wars had shown where rationality might lead to. The trains would run on time but (literally) to which end? And with what value framework? More than reason as its watchword, many felt that it was a central role of the university to help the world to become more sensitive to life, and to have a care for life, and in all its forms.

Advocates of this viewpoint in the mid-twentieth century – such as Karl Jaspers (1946/60) in Germany, Ortega y Gasset (1946) in Spain and Walter Moberly (1949) in England – pitched their analyses and proposals often against a near-despairing sense of the world, already subject to technological threats. Culture in general was in jeopardy but they felt that university reform was possible and that an explicitly cultural role could be derived for higher education. As late as the 1960s, a major national report (in the UK) – the 'Robbins Report' – could argue, without embarrassment, that 'the transmission of a common culture' formed one of four aims of higher education (Robbins, 1963: 7). There was a common culture still dimly present, and it was a task of higher education to sustain it and even to further it.

Pleas for a tight connection between higher education and culture have long vanished. Even in the 1960s, voices were drawing attention to 'the disenchantment of . . . culture with culture itself' (Trilling, 1967). And, over past decades, we have been left on the one hand with dismal analyses of the situation in which the university is depicted, forlornly, as a *value-free zone*, and on the other hand with sociological analyses, which observe ways in which universities are replete with culture. Here, in this latter perspective, the accounts run in different directions. The university is depicted as tacitly embodying an elite or a closed – *and perhaps even a colonialist* – culture, largely inaccessible to the wider society *and*, paradoxically, is celebrated in being *a site of many cultures* – a multicultural site indeed. And now the university is warily observed to be a site even of antagonistic cultures, as culture wars play themselves out on campus.

Both as a matter of fact and as a matter of value, then, a strong association between the university and culture is problematic, if not completely outré. After all, culture has long been depicted as having been swept up into a culture industry (Adorno and Horkheimer, 1944/89), and now turned into a 'cultural political economy' (Sum and Jessop, 2013). Culture as a resource for meaning in the world has been inverted by its acquiring an economic form. In turn, 'cultural pessimism' (Bennett, 2001), with us for over a century, has lapsed into cultural *neglect*, a lack of interest in culture as such. Against this background, *is* it possible for the university to help in advancing culture in the wider world? Could the juxtaposition – of 'university' and 'culture' – possess any substance in the twenty-first century? These are the questions before us in these first four chapters in this book.

The University as a Culture-Free Zone

In his influential book (1997), *The University in Ruins*, one of Bill Readings' arguments was that culture has been evacuated (not his word) from the university: on his argument, the university had become a culture-free zone. Readings observed that the idea of culture was in difficulty, it having been associated with a dual unity

– as a process of personal development and as a unity of knowledges (64) – *both* of which parts had foundered. That dissolution of the dual idea of culture lay in the further weakening of the link between higher education and the nation state, such that cultivation was defined 'in primarily ethnic terms' (69). The opera house did not need to put 'no admission' notices outside for its audiences were self-selecting.

At the same time as culture had become problematic, so the university had undergone a double shift. In the first place, a technological and bureaucratic society had seeped into the university. Universities had become corporations subject to nostrums of efficiency and had developed massive bureaucratic systems to monitor and to evaluate their own activities and even their own people. This shift was accompanied by national and even cross-national systems of audit and evaluation, the emergence of the empty tropes of 'excellence' – a particular target in Readings' forlorn analysis – and then 'world-class universities' (Rider et al., 2020). In this techno-bureaucratic world, the very mention of culture became difficult for universities, not least as they became international and home to students of *many* cultures. Universities responded both by establishing programmes of cultural studies – at least, 'culture' could be analysed – and by celebrating themselves for their multicultural leanings. This was distinctly a small 'c' set of meanings of culture, cultures rather than Culture.

The upshot of all of this is that whereas, even fifty years ago, the terms 'culture' and 'university' were comfortably and often put together, now they no longer keep each other company in any strong sense. To draw on a concept of Rowan Williams (2003), universities could be said to be in a state of 'cultural bereavement'.

A Culture-Free World?

That universities have, at best, an ambiguous relationship with culture is hardly surprising for this tension is to be seen in the wider world. The very expression 'culture wars' – which we shall come onto in the next chapter – is indicative of contemporary schisms evident in many societies, which can be traced to competing sets of cultural values. And these sets of cultural values – over abortion, gay rights, women's rights, gender identity, national identity markers – are associated with heated arguments and even inflamed passions. Culture seems to be a matter of non-reason better reserved to the private sphere and not to be addressed in the public sphere. Far better to keep one's cultural preferences to oneself, it seems.

We see here a playing out of Ernest Gellner's analysis of culture. In his (1992) book, *Reason and Culture*, Gellner argued that reason and culture fell into opposed spheres of life. Descartes's nostrum *'Cogito ergo sum'* (I think, therefore I am') secreted a distancing of the thinker from culture. It was the individual's own thought processes that furnished a bedrock on which she or he could move through the world with confidence. Everything could reasonably be doubted – there seemed to be little firm ground on which to build a life – but the sheer fact that one could think and reason provided a measure of indubitability.

This amounted to an assault on culture in more than one sense. Culture brought nothing to the party, for modern man or woman could get along very well without it. Even more, modernity and civilization lay in *reason*, and culture was to be shunned as not amenable to reason. Culture invited only a 'take it or leave it' attitude. It was a matter of unarguable taste, not of reason. Moral philosophy in the twentieth century (at least in the analytic tradition) came to a similar conclusion. Cultural utterances were no more than emotional spasms and did not warrant serious attention as if they said anything about the world as such. To utter anything of any substance, one had to produce either analytical or verifiable statements, and, manifestly (Ayer, 1962), culture could generate neither. At best, the cultural sphere was a domain of mere collective opinion. It was a place in which humanity – in the traditions, practices and beliefs of its communities and their separate lifeworlds – wrapped itself up in itself, into a set of non-comprehending imaginaries (cf. Taylor, 2007). Culture held no lessons for humankind in general and could safely be given a wide berth.

Gellner, therefore, could have adopted a much more aggressive title for his book. It could have justly been entitled *'Reason versus Culture'*, for the two realms were embattled with each other. For some, culture provided just a hierarchy-sustaining gloss, conferred by social class, and reflecting questionable good manners and taste; for others, it offered a way of supplying purpose to life through society-wide traditions and lifeworlds. *Either way*, culture was not to be reasoned but was to be lived and *felt*. At best, it was an empty signifier, 'full of sound and fury, signifying nothing'; at worst, a kind of cultural violence was not far away, in dogmatism, ideology and imposition.

Culture and the University, and Life Itself

The juxtaposition of 'university' and 'culture' has been hit, then, by a double tsunami. On the one hand, the idea of culture is in trouble in itself and, on the other hand, that discomfort is multiplied in the university through its own criticality – and its suspicions of a category such as 'culture' – *and* in virtue of its being host to an increasing array of cultures, in multiplying disciplinary cultures and in its public engagements. In the university, culture, it seems, can find a place only as an object of analysis and not of advocacy.

As intimated, there had been a thin line of thinkers who had bravely advocated an explicit role for the university not merely in sustaining culture but actually in advancing it. Perhaps the stand-out representative of that genre was that of Ortega y Gasset. Writing during the Second World War, Ortega – in his (1946/60) '*Mission of the University*' – saw a world suffering from a crisis that was essentially a crisis of culture. 'Culture' was a key concept at the heart of Ortega's philosophy: 'Culture is what saves human life from being a mere disaster; it is what enables man [sic] to live a life' (44). And, for Ortega, 'Culture is the *vital* system of ideas of a period' (44). That emphasis – the italicization of 'vital' – is Ortega's, and its ambiguity is probably deliberate. The ideas in question were those that lay at the heart of a full life; and they were always in motion, having to be kept alive to both serve and lead 'a period'.

And the university? For Ortega, 'the contemporary university' had greatly expanded 'professional instruction' and 'the function of research', but, in the process, 'it ha[d] abandoned almost entirely the teaching or transmission of culture'. It is evident, he added, 'that the change has been pernicious' (Ortega y Gasset, 1946). And so, for Ortega, 'it is imperative to set up once more, in the university, the teaching of culture, the system of vital ideas, which the age has attained'. By the system of vital ideas, Ortega had in mind 'the great cultural disciplines' in physics, biology, history, sociology and philosophy.

Ortega distinguished between an essential 'synthesis' of a discipline and its corresponding science. It was the former on which Ortega was keen, and he even looked to a 'Faculty of Culture' to bring these cultural disciplines together to form 'the nucleus of the university and of the whole higher learning'. The synthesis was to be derived and a curriculum was to be forged on the basis of 'a principle of economy'. In this way, knowledge was to be vitalized. The 'mission of the university' was nothing short of the formation of 'a cultured person' (73).

Thinking of this kind is now passé. Few read Ortega now, and those who do stand out (e.g. Giannakakis, 2020). That whole way of thinking, both of speaking of culture with a capital C as it were and of advocating the university as a major institution in sustaining it, is seldom to be seen. This is an extraordinary shift over the last half century or so. It is not so much that that mode of thinking has been explicitly debunked; rather, it has gradually fallen in desuetude. Subsequent to Ortega, there were one or two rear-guard actions of that ilk – for example, by F. R. Leavis (1969) in England and Bloom (1987) in the United States – but even then, in the 1960s–1980s, the cause was lost. It smacked not so much of elitism but of apartness, specialness and a questionable self-elevation. (F. R. Leavis fought for English to be at the centre of the university; but then he was a scholar of English.)

Pumping up the cultural powers of the university in this way exhibited an unacceptable haughtiness and self-grandeur. This sceptical stance received sociological backing, especially from Pierre Bourdieu (Bourdieu and Passeron, 1990), in whose hands 'cultural capital' came to be seen as a powerful resource by which social classes could maintain their elevated position; and universities were seen as pivotal in this hierarchical process.

But the close association of the university and culture was not entirely over. Attention turned inward, the key idea being that the disciplines of academia secreted their own separate cultures (plural). The innovator here was Tony Becher with his (1989) book '*Academic Tribes and Territories*', which, on the basis of interviews with academics, showed that disciplines could be staked out in virtue of their location on two axes (hard-soft; pure-applied). For a while, that line of research led to more discrete studies into the cultures (plural) of disciplines (Becher and Trowler, 2001; Kreber, 2009), but it rather fell away. After all, it rather ducked key questions. It should have raised the matter of *differential power* among the disciplines. In particular, the place being assumed by the STEM (science, technology, engineering and mathematics) disciplines was becoming evident, even if the acronym was not then in use. The cultures of some disciplines could have been exposed as exerting more *epistemic power* than others (a forensic analysis of which we still await).

This situation poses challenges for teaching and for the university more widely. In relation to teaching, culture becomes an especially fraught category, not least in the wake of flows of cross-national students from around the world. In such a context, talk of 'culture' is question begging for only cultures (plural) are on display. At best, comfort lies in talk of a university as a 'multicultural' space. But this is to disbar culture as such from the pedagogical setting. *There*, 'cosmopolitanism' (Delanty, 2001) seems a much safer idea, the hope being that with a suitably imaginative educational approach, students might become global citizens, able to move deftly among cultures (plural) but presumably devoid of culture in any large sense. On so many fronts, culture seems to produce only nervousness in higher education: a stance of *culture-freedom* has emerged as the dominant position.

In all of this, *the* key issue is being avoided: Might there be a *meta-culture* that transcends the discrete cultures of all academic disciplines? Perhaps, even despite their profound differences (philosophical and societal), the disciplines share some connecting cultural aspects; and if there is any such connecting tissue, it may provide a new way of connecting the university with life itself. That, at any rate, is a matter before us here.

A Power/Culture Relationship

Over the past decade, much scholarly effort has been invested into elucidating the nature of epistemic injustice (Fricker, 2010; Kidd et al., 2017; Nikolaidis, 2021). Several lines of inquiry have opened, and the concept is inchoate. For the most part, it has been deployed to draw attention to forms of injustice in the human world, in the many ways in which beliefs and claims to knowledge of members of humanity have been systematically disregarded (those of women or of people of colour) or explicitly treated as illegitimate contenders for the title of knowledge (especially those in formerly colonized or indigenous societies). From time to time, a link to culture is observed. For instance, Boaventura de Sousa Santos (2014), in his advocacy of 'epistemologies of the South' – which have been undergoing a suggested 'epistemicide' at the hands of the Global North – specifically argues for the protection of cultural diversity and positions it as a critique of cultural imperialism.

In its instantiation in universities, this complex of matters – of knowledge, social justice, epistemic justice, cognitive justice and culture *and* their interrelationships – is only just beginning to receive attention (Walker and Martinez-Vargas, 2020). Key is it that epistemic injustice is to be found *within* the university itself and is, in part, a matter of culture, and of a changing culture at that. Helpful here is a book seemingly unknown in higher education studies, *Knowledge-as-Culture* by E. Doyle McCarthy (1996). Although, in that book, the term 'epistemic justice' is not on show, the concept itself is not far away, not least in the chapter on 'Engendered knowledge'. I want, though, to open up another front that is present in McCarthy's book, that of the intertwining of culture and ideology. Drawing on the French philosophers Althusser and Foucault, ideology may be understood – so McCarthy suggests – *as* culture, as structured 'lived practices of particular groups'.

I now want to couple the idea of ideology-as-culture to the ways in which ideologies operate as systems of power, and to pursue this thought by enlisting

Feyerabend's repeated depiction of science as ideology (Feyerabend, 1978, 1982). That idea of Feyerabend contains – in his oeuvre – a number of elements, which include science having an overblown sense of its purity, there always being a largely unacknowledged gap between the data and their associated theories, that science has come to possess an unjustified prominence in society, and that it is dismissive of the knowledges of other cultures.

We now have the makings of a *chain of links* between knowledge, science, culture and ideology. We see this vividly in the acronym STEM. This acronym *in itself* has standing right across the world, having become a potent signifier across politics, universities, policy networks and beyond. It testifies to the way in which science, technology, engineering and mathematics have come to form a hugely powerful knowledge culture that carries *ideological force*. And, as an ideological force, this knowledge/power/culture cluster continues to sweep up and colonize others around it, even as it is morphing into 'STEMM', with a second 'M' being added for medicine (Cohen, 2021). Emerging here is a *dominant epistemic culture* pivoting around bio-engineering, which includes the engineering of fundamental particles, but is also corralling informatics, modelling and bio-technics and so buttressing the emergence of a 'biocapitalism' (Peters and Venkatesan, 2013).

Other forms of understanding – especially those fields that are allied to medicine and which are sometimes understood as caring professions – have been obliged to subscribe to the scientism of STEMM. This is a cognitive imperialism but it is also a *cultural* imperialism, as a particular cognitive culture becomes dominant. In turn, as this knowledge culture has been accentuated, so other forms of knowledge – which have quite other knowledge interests – have been subject to demotion *as* forms of knowledge. In particular, the humanities are downplayed as not serious forms of knowledge; indeed, they are not even counted as forms of knowledge as such. As such, they are placed in an ambiguous position in relation to culture. If they overtly ally themselves with a cultural mission – and perhaps even see themselves as protective of culture – they reinforce a sense of their being non-serious pursuits; and if they keep silent on the matter, the matter of culture is rendered ipso facto as unworthy of inquiry.

Emerging here is an overbearing *cognitive culture*, and one that is closer to home than is normally recognized. The cognitive injustice that de Sousa Santos identifies is a *transcultural* thesis. It sees cognitive injustice being played out on a grand scale, the epistemic culture of the Global North being depicted as overpowering that of the Global South. Moreover, it sees this – and quite legitimately – as a disturbance in global knowledge ecologies. However, there has been little recognition there that these imbalances in knowledge cultures are present *within* the Global North. More than that, the STEM disciplines have become the dominant epistemic culture not only globally but also *within* universities. The study of sport, for example – central to culture at least since the Greeks – has turned into 'sports science', in which human performance is to be measured, controlled and improved by bio-engineering techniques. The very institution that should be giving a fair wind to all knowledge cultures is now favouring mathematically and bio-loaded disciplines, and other knowledge cultures are relegated, if not actually repudiated.

This situation should not be regarded purely as an internal matter for the university, but has a carry-over into the culture of the wider world. Mathematics has taken over from Latin as the lingua franca that connects the university to the world; and this situation continues to evolve, with the emergence of digitization and computation. In turn, Boolean algebra, algorithms, modelling and risk analyses come to the fore. Cognitive culture is always in motion, but always implicitly down-valuing those forms of understanding that are reluctant or unable to come on board. In turn, such digital hesitancy is liable to lead to the 'not wanted here' door.

Clash of Cultures

Far from the university being a culture-free zone (as Readings was implying), the university is witness *to multiple epistemic culture wars*. (I shall come onto this matter of culture wars more fully in Chapter 2 but it is worth flagging it here, since it serves as a rebuke to the university-as-culture-free thesis.) Culture wars within the university have to be understood as local skirmishes within larger culture wars in the wider society. The wider world is riven with profound cultural schisms over – for example – the value of science, of society and human relationships, of the arts and of education, quite apart from deep splits over concern for the planet, religion, the economy and democracy. To a greater or lesser extent, these external culture wars play out in the university. It cannot be otherwise, for the university is a space in which legitimate differences of view and of holds on the world have their day.

How is the university to disport itself in this swirl of cultures? Is it legitimate for the university to be taking a position among competing cultures, or should it attempt to be a kind of cultural umpire, ensuring fair play between the disputants? This is a serious matter, as cultural debates come to be reflected in both teaching and research. Some will experiment with the educational situation to see how the matter of decolonization might be reflected in pedagogical practices (Bhambra et al., 2018). Perhaps, for instance, students might be asked to debate an incident with decolonial overtones (such as a toppling of a particular statue). Some will seek to import the theme of decolonialization into the research setting, and look to construct a project that addresses the matter head-on, perhaps built around interviews with the residents of a city in which just such a statue has been (unlawfully) taken down.

It will be said that there is nothing untoward in either of the initiatives imagined here. Both hold to a value-neutral line in the actual practices being adopted, a value position being present only in the initial choice of the topic. This is the Weberian (1991a,b) option, that the academy has within it room to keep apart facts and values. But it is disingenuous, for the chosen topic has its place in a worldwide debate which is freighted with values. Colonization is a value-laden term, *as then must be its counter*, decolonization. To conduct research or to set up a pedagogical practice or set out a curriculum on the matter of coloniality is to swim in value-laden waters. *There is no neutral space.* As well as connoting a situation of asymmetrical state power, the concept of colonization is imbued with a sense of the culture of the colonized being placed in a position of inferiority. In this discursive situation, cultural neutrality is impossible since 'culture' has meaning and possibilities within specific sets of language and social practices (cf Laclau, 2000: 83).

It may be countered that to engage with culturally sensitive matters is not in itself to take up a position. A pedagogical practice, a research project, can be pursued disinterestedly. There is an alternative beyond tearing down a statue and placing it, with suitable 'educational' material, in a museum. But this response misses the point. For to engage in this way is to commit to and to be part of the enveloping discourse. It is to be drawn into the culture war of coloniality. Once the university has moved into this discursive and febrile setting, the university becomes a player, however nuanced it considers its stance to be.

The university cannot but be a player in a whole set of cultures. The more it allows itself to engage with the wider world, the more it forfeits its independence. This is not a matter of regret, but it should be understood that the university cannot both be an actor in the world and remain immune from cultural entanglements. The discourses it moves in alone are testimony to its being culturally ensnared. For this reason alone, the matter of culture and the university has taken on a new significance, and it should now, therefore, reclaim our attention.

A Cultural Pharmakon

The term 'pharmakon' was introduced into philosophy by the French philosopher Bernard Stiegler. By it, Stiegler sought to indicate that the situation of the world presented both malady and therapy (2014a: 19). Matters are serious but they also contain possibilities of remedy. Stiegler went even further, and applied this idea to his presentation of technology, especially computer and internet technologies. Stiegler (2015: chapters 2 & 3) saw in modern technologies the makings of a world 'stupidity' but yet also glimpsed the possibility of a 'spirit' (Stiegler, 2014b: 65 et. seq.) that offers a route to enchantment in the world.

Stiegler's idea of pharmakon and hopes of, and indeed faith in, computer-based technologies need to be treated with caution – as did he – but there are two points for our present purposes. The first is this. Although the term 'crisis' is overused in connection with the university, worldwide the university can fairly be said to be exhibiting a *cultural crisis*. The university knows neither whether to shun or to embrace culture, to give it a wide berth or to neutralize it. It declines to say anything of substance about culture as such. It is not just diffident on the matter but is positively squeamish about it.

One area in which the matter of culture in the university is positively embraced is the dubious matter of institutional culture. It is dubious because the matter is usually treated antiseptically, as a matter of technical analysis, the so-called institutional or managerial cultures shorn of a deep sense of the structures of human meaning they impart (Berquist and Pawlak, 2008). As a result, the university has turned into a cultural hotchpotch. Worse, the university has fallen prey to cultural takeovers, by science (especially in some universities in the world) and by faiths, and to uncritical 'critical' pedagogies and scholarship. 'Culture', as such, has become a concept that dare not speak its name on campus, and so the campus has fallen prey to culture wars, both internal and imported from the wider society. The university is in poor cultural health, with some cultures suppressing others within it.

But then the question arises as to whether the university possesses resources that just might make it possible for the two concepts – university and culture – to seriously be put back together. This is a momentous issue, and not only for those concerned about the place of the university in the world and its future but also for the whole world.

I said a moment ago that there are two points to be made in the wake of Stiegler's insistent analysis, and I have just made a very general point (that the university is confronted by its own cultural crisis but may yet possess resources to address that crisis). A more particular matter is that of the digital age. We observed that Stiegler adopts a relatively optimistic position. While the internet is contributing to a worldly 'stupidity', it also – for Stiegler – contains possibilities of enabling a new spirit to be released. And perhaps there is here a seed of cultural possibilities for the university. The internet and the digital revolution are presenting terrifying prospects of an algorithmic age, a robotic culture, an internet of things in which the human as such is down-valued and manipulated; but perhaps, too, it affords the university new powers to assist in ushering in a new kind of democracy, not least through the possibilities that it opens for massively wider connectivity with the wider world.

There is an ambivalence here, which is reflected in the idea of the post-human: some see in posthumanism a brave new world in which, with technological prostheses of various kinds, human being extends itself into new life forms (Herbrechter, 2013). For others (Braidotti, 2019), posthumanism is a concept that draws attention to the anthropocentricism inherent in human engagements with the world and that seeks to displace humans as just one set of beings on Earth. We take up these matters of culture in the digital age in the next chapters.

Conclusions: Living with the Crisis

In the 1940s, with the world in turmoil and a general loss of stability and agreed ways of going on, it was recognized that universities collectively were in crisis, and a cultural crisis at that. As the twenty-first century unfolds, a similar situation presents: alongside ecological, economic, health and societal crises, the world and its universities face a new cultural crisis.

So, our starting point now has even more point: Was Readings right, that culture and the university are irrevocably separated? There are two options: (i) Readings was right, for the university has been evacuated of culture; (ii) Readings was wrong – and *this* is the argument I shall advance in the next three chapters. Far from the connection between the university and culture being severed, the connections are multitudinous. And therein lies a problem: the university lacks cultural integrity, even while it is awash with cultures.

Indeed, the university is beset with culture wars, those that are more specifically internal *and* those that flow into it from the wider world. *Internally*, it is faced with *cognitive* cultural wars, as the disciplines vie with each other (with the STEMM disciplines often sweeping aside all others). But it is also faced with internal culture wars of more *pragmatic and operational* kinds, where decision-making cultures seek to dominate the conduct of universities, with their 'smart' regimes of risk averseness and performance management. In its engagements with the wider world, the university is plunged into culture wars of the most severe kinds, both beyond the campus – and not least with its battles with the state – and, nowadays, on the campus, for the university has become a fluid space where the rivalries of worldly debates play out (where they are allowed to do so).

Our starting question *was* (in effect): '*Can the concepts of culture and university be re-united?*' However, against the horizon of this initial analysis – to the effect that the university is saturated with cultures (plural) and power plays between them – the question *now* becomes: 'Can there be a sustainable way of uniting culture and the university such that re-unification does justice to and even enhances the integrity of the university?' This matter deserves to be addressed as a matter of urgency. Unless it *is* addressed, the university will be rudderless, caught in a swirling sea of clashing and idiosyncratic cultures. This new question, therefore, is the question before us in the next three chapters.

2

Culture Wars

Multiplication and (Possible) Re-unification

Introduction

Is the university a site of culture wars or not? The tea leaves may be read in different ways. It can be observed that most universities in the world have been ensnared in networks of global higher education, in which science is globalized, and across the world nations are literally buying into this agenda. We might use terms such a 'cognitive capitalism' or 'knowledge capitalism' but they fray at the edges in doing justice to this extraordinary phenomenon – this globality of higher education – which is only two decades in duration or so. After all, this tidal wave is witnessing major increases in science production not just in the usual suspects (China, the United States and Europe) but also in places such as India and Indonesia (Marginson and Xu, 2021). Culture in the university, accordingly, can be adjudged either to be at an end *or* simply to be a single dominant culture, that of science and technology (now already morphing into bio-technology). On either view, it is a misreading to think that the university is a site of culture wars. The war is over: science and technology have won.

However, a quite different reading is plausible. Across much of the world, in a context of populism, social movements around ecological matters and social and personal rights, clashes around institutional autonomy and academic freedom, and the role of the university as part of the public sphere in which societal debates are played out on campus and on local streets, the university is *increasingly* a site of culture wars. Cultural schisms in the wider society have found their way into, and are being fought out deep inside, the academy.

So culture wars are at their end or only just beginning? But, in any event, perhaps culture wars are more widespread in universities, and so *more insidious*, than are commonly recognized. Those are the issues in front of us in this chapter.

Just Like Ideology

Culture is much like ideology, with both being caught up in parallel societal movements. In the 1960s, we were told that we were at the end of ideology, and, now, it is glaringly evident that we were never at the end of ideology. The 'end of ideology' thesis was itself an ideology (Zizek, 1999: 2). A parallel situation holds with culture. The world of higher education can be forgiven for believing that culture is a category that can be repudiated and that there is no longer any link between the university and culture: the two categories have been sundered. Just like ideology, however, we are entitled to say that the university has not witnessed the end of culture, far from it.

The end of ideology thesis was given its major public expression by Daniel Bell in 1960 – in *The End of Ideology* – and the thesis was reinforced by Francis Fukuyama three decades later (in 1992), in *The End of History and the Last Man*. It was argued that there was a growing consensus across the world in favour of a social-democratic capitalism; there was debate to be had only around the edges as to the balance of the priorities.

In both cases, however, we were given an endnote which qualified the argument. In his Afterword (in the 1988 edition), Bell (2000) worked through criticisms levied at his book, claiming that he had been misunderstood. His thesis had been one of the exhaustion of political ideas, not of economies or social orders. Some of his critics had pointed to the upsurge of radicalism in the 1960s as disproving the end of ideology thesis but, for Bell, this was 'not a political phenomenon but a cultural phenomenon. . . . In all [that] turbulence there were no new socialist ideas, no ideologies, no programs' (432). This was not to say that modernity – in the United States at least – lacked the capacity to develop public ideas. On the contrary: there was a 'receptiv[ity] to ideas' to be found in the major universities ('Harvard, Colombia, Berkeley, and other large centers'). This was a 'liberal culture', sustained by a 'cultural elite', which was 'receptive to ideas, critical in its outlook and encouraging of dissent', such that 'even dissent [was] an accredited member of that culture' (314).

Bell, then, was very comfortable in seeing strong connections between universities and culture, especially in the academy's receptiveness to ideas. Culture at least was alive on campus (even if political ideologies were not). And it was a 'liberal culture' sustained by a 'cultural elite' in the most prominent universities. There is, we may note, something of a tension in Bell's argument. Bell acknowledged the radicalism of the 1960s and would have been aware that much of it was driven by university students. He states that it was bereft of ideas but yet he had also drawn attention to the elite culture of the leading universities as being 'receptive to ideas, critical . . . and encouraging of dissent'. This tension is important for it is suggestive of the university as a space of ideas and as possessing a culture of debate.

Francis Fukuyama (1992) also made a pitch for ideology being 'in the past', given 'a general consensus' in favour of liberal democracy (211), and makes much play with culture, albeit rather differently. For Fukuyama, the liberal democratic state possesses its own culture, with its values of participation, rationality and secularism. Overtly, it pressed no particular world view of its own: it was a reticent culture, refraining from taking sides. What was important was debate in itself, and careful, measured debate at that. However, for this culture to develop, earlier traditional and 'variegated' cultures had to be overcome (214).

There is here a complicated set of relationships between culture and liberal democracy. Culture – 'understood as a set of factors such as national identity, religion, social equality, the propensity for civil society, and the historical experience of liberal institutions' (219) – can impede or galvanize democracy. Culture is neither a necessary nor a sufficient condition of democracy. Accordingly, 'the realm of politics remains autonomous from that of culture' (220). But still, in Fukuyama's view, the state and culture swim in each other's waters; and both continue to change. While culture is important in its own right, 'cultures are not static phenomena like the laws of nature' (222).

Taken together, these two narratives open intriguing lines of consideration. The central issue in these four chapters is that of the possibility of a normative relationship between the university and culture. My thesis is that not only can we sensibly put the ideas of university and culture together but that the university has responsibilities *towards* culture. However, Bell and Fukuyama are posing awkward questions to that thesis. *Does* it make sense to speak of the culture of society? Is culture in the wider society even significant?

Implicitly, both texts can read as giving an affirmative answer to the first question: the liberal democratic society *does* possess a dominant culture. Certainly, that culture has *several aspects*, even if they present varying weightings in different places. Liberal democratic societies are more or less open, more or less secular, more or less open to public reasoning, more or less generous to strangers (both individually and collectively), more or less characterized by genuinely public spaces, more or less open to critique and *self*-critique, and more or less governed by the rule of law.

Precisely because this liberal culture has a strong vein of purposive tolerance within it (Oberdiek, 2001), it is prey to infiltration by usurping currents: forces lurk that would take advantage of its openness and seek to bend an open society to their advantage. This culture, therefore, is prone not only to internal conflict (as its various subcultures are embattled with each other) but is also prone to takeover by malevolent forces. But if this is a fragile culture, it also possesses strength, which it gains from its complexity: being composed of so many different elements, it possesses an agility that allows it to flex with its times, according differential weight to its elements (enshrined in a three directional slogan such as 'equality, fraternity, liberty').

Our second question – whether culture is really significant in modern society – opens to two readings. The first reading has to be 'not much'. Culture is only a minor player in the grand scheme of things. Fukuyama is – as noted – clear on this. Culture is neither a necessary nor a sufficient condition of the presence of a liberal democracy. Indeed, culture could *impede* the liberal democratic order. The second reading is to the contrary: culture – or, rather, culture of a certain kind – can aid the development and the sustaining of a liberal democratic society.

Cultural Dissolution in the Academy

The implications for the academy are several, and come in the form of questions: If we are to look for ways in which the academy can strengthen and aid culture in the wider society, where might we turn in the first place? Is it that, just fortuitously perhaps and even if hardly recognized within itself, the academy contains granules that could be helpful for culture in general? However, that phrase 'culture in the wider society' has first to be cashed out.

In the twenty-first century, society is not characterized by an absence of culture but, to the contrary, 'we have a panoply of subcultures with multiple crossovers' (Huyssen, 2020). (The university exhibits a similar pattern, a matter that we shall come to shortly.) This is a situation in which the same event is seen in opposed ways by different communities with their own subcultures: the police are seen to be 'heavy-handed' *and* as 'defending law and order'. Opposed communities, with their own sets of meanings and values, talk past each other, with few if any points of contact.

It is on the basis of there being multiple cultures that much angst arises over their relationships, as well as debate over multiculturality. Nevertheless, it can be assumed that there has to be some meta-cultural glue, so to speak, to which a fair number of these cultures can give their allegiance and in sufficient intensity so as to provide some degree of societal unity. Liberal democracy, it may be said, provides just such a *meta-culture*: it is not really a culture as such but provides an umbrella – at once institutional and discursive – under which many cultures can shelter.

In the last chapter, I drew attention to Ernest Gellner's book, *Reason and Culture*, which set off 'reason' and 'culture' against each other. Culture came to be understood as the antithesis of reason; and reason could get on very well without being buttressed by culture. Here, however, in these reflections on liberal democracy, we are glimpsing the opposite prospect. Reason might become so powerful that it becomes the dominant culture of society: reason *as* culture, in other words. Moreover, this culture of reason can precisely serve as that umbrella culture of society under which other cultures can shelter. Indeed, *any* culture can shelter under it providing that it is prepared to conduct its affairs in a reasonable manner and is – on occasions – willing to subject itself to reasoned inquiry.

With the relationship between reason and culture understood in this way, the phrase 'culture wars' becomes something of a misnomer. Abortion or pro-life, religion or atheism, meat-eating or veganism, equality or freedom, public or private, transgender as a constructed category or as a natural category: providing that adherents in these antipathies are willing to conduct their disputes with a readiness to hear opposing views and to respond to the other, all such subcultures can live under the banner of the culture of reason. Unfortunately, we have witnessed a disavowal of this principle and an abandonment of the hope that lies within it. Consequently, a closure and an antipathy to strangers has entered disputes so that the culture of reason is fraying at the edges.

In the previous section, it was observed that culture is like ideology: just as we have frequently been told that ideology is at an end, so too with culture. Again, the two arguments go in parallel directions. *Ideology* was claimed to be at an end because it had dissolved, there being no large ideas – no grand narratives indeed – to fill in the gap. Only separate forms of life or paralogies (Lyotard, 1984: 60–1) were available. *Culture* is at an end because reason as an overarching culture has dissolved to be replaced by *countless smaller cultures*. Instead of a grand culture (of reason), now we have a proliferation of warring cultures; and little to keep them in check.

It is a bit like the case of Yugoslavia. Tito was a strong authoritarian near-despot, exerting power and control over states of different ethnicities and religions, holding them together in a binding state totalitarianism. Once he had died, however, the states broke away from each other, fragmenting into warring entities, with massacres and terrible injustices quickly following. Iron cage or mayhem: those may seem to be the cultural options in front of us.

This, however, would do an injustice to liberal democracy. Indeed, it is a strength of liberal democracy that it is able, as noted, to flex itself this way and that so as to provide space to variegated religions, ethnicities, social classes and so forth. Like a skyscraper that flexes in the wind, this flexing of liberal democracy supplies a resilience in withstanding its internal stresses. It is only when one culture becomes dominant and another feels subjugated that the stresses threaten political order. And we are surely witnessing just this pattern among liberal democracies across the world, where populism has emerged, sustained by a sense of neglect of some communities, not to say disparagement, in some quarters; and those tensions are very much cultural in their character.

Do we not see parallels between the matter of culture and the university? Whereas once it made sense to speak of the culture of universities and to suggest a definite link with culture in the wider society, now we have only the dissolution of the academy as a culture, being replaced by multiple wars between contending cultures.

Culture Wars on Campus: Difficulties of Peace-Making

The term 'culture wars' is familiar enough, though seldom explained. In higher education, it conjures a dual sense of cultures clashing and that the university is caught up in those conflicts. Typically, debate polarizes positions. Is the university for 'excellence' or for 'access and fairness'? Is the university to be a defender of 'free speech' or is it, in advance, to shun certain positions as 'illegitimate'? How are sensitive matters of ethnicity, religion and gender to be treated in the university? 'Political correctness' is often invoked and becomes a cudgel in these disputes (Lea, 2009). Some consider that all views are legitimate, providing that they subject themselves to interrogation, while others consider that some views are otiose in the university.

Such questions prompt a yet-deeper set of matters, which we can call the 'Eagleton/ Scruton' debate. Terry Eagleton and Roger Scruton are heavyweights who have had much to say about culture but they approach the matter from fundamentally different perspectives. In one corner is Terry Eagleton, a radical and left-oriented cultural and social theorist, and in the other corner is Roger Scruton (albeit recently deceased), a conservative philosopher.

For Eagleton (2000), culture is a set of phenomena to be analysed and critiqued but on the lookout for its *future* possibilities. The pretensions of culture are to be exposed, not least so as to clear the ground for prospective sightings. For Scruton (2016), quite to the contrary, culture is heralded as containing the finest (and mainly past) achievements of humanity, and the task of the cultural analyst is to ferret out the highest forms of culture – now understood as high culture – despite the angst that it brings (so powerfully displayed in T. S. Eliot's ([1922] 2001) poem 'The Waste Land', to which Scruton refers). One critic pokes at the mighty, demonstrating the power and privilege that so often lies behind what counts as culture; the other is in part a buttresser, and a fierce defender, of culture.

To generalize these two stances, with one, culture is *ended*; or, at least, there can be no facile subscription to culture, it having been revealed as an emperor often without clothes. With the other, culture is propped up and even heralded, but with what legitimacy? On the one side, culture is to be critiqued and placed in its marketized, economic and class settings – and now even in its imperialist and colonialist settings. If culture *is* to be heralded here, it is the culture of the impoverished, the marginalized and the invisible. On the other side, severe judgements have to be made, and only limited forms of culture are given accolades.

The university is severally implicated in this. Is it itself part of high culture, even if it dare not speak its name? Mystique lies in its arcane and – for many – unfathomable vocabularies, symbols, practices and holds on life. However, precisely as an open discursive space, the university lets in many voices, many cultures: no cultural uniformity here! It is a multicultural site – *and* an intercultural and even a post-cultural site (Welikala and Barnett, 2021) – in which cultural attachments are, at best, ephemeral. 'Individuals may [even] operate in multiple cultural spheres and belong to them all' (Peters and Tukeo, 2010).

But then arises the thorny matter of standards of debate. Can the university be a space of cool, dispassionate reasoning and keep the passions of culture wars either outside its gates or, if they be let in, find a way of neutralizing them? Does the university not have a right to insist on a certain decorum, of turn-taking, respecting attested authorities, sticking to evidence and following a line of argument? Of insisting, in other words, on its *own* culture?

These are far from hypothetical matters. In the pedagogical situation, public events, the academic seminar and even the pages of a journal paper, pleas are heard not to be discomforted, or denigrated, or critiqued or morally injured. Individuals and states take umbrage at being impugned or made to feel awkward. Resort is sometimes had to J. S. Mill, the English liberal philosopher of the nineteenth century who – in his essay 'On Liberty' (1969) – deftly argued in favour of an open speech situation (as we may put it today); in this respect, he was an early Habermassian. Mill's position contained a sophistication worth noting. Not only does the speaker who is liable to be convicted of a heresy deserve to be heard but the participants, too, have a right both to hear his (or her) argument *and* to hear the rebuttal, if there be one. Participants can learn from both the opponent *and* the proponent.

However, the liberal's dilemma is still with us: 'Are there *discursive* limits to what can be said?' Is there space within the university to express racist or gendered views or views that are critical of religions? How narrowly or widely is the circle of tolerable claims to be drawn, as the university flexes in the wind? Some wish to ban even particular words (even pronouns) in a university setting. The descendants of Mill, on the other hand, would prefer to see the university as the widest possible space of dialogical reason. The counter-view has two concerns. One is that an open space would allow in those who would close off space to others: they would deny to others the very freedoms that they seek to profit from themselves. Excommunication would, therefore, be justified on grounds of *self-contradiction*. But there are also moral and pragmatic concerns that a totally open space would allow the opinionated or the dogmatist to shout down the quiet voice of reason.

It will be said that there is no difficulty here. For peace to break out, all that has to be instituted are the conditions of a balanced dialogue, of give-and-take, of turn-taking and of a valuing of truthfulness, sincerity and a sensitivity to context; in short, a Habermassian ideal speech situation 'plus plus'. The problem here is that to which feminists in particular have drawn attention, that the argumentative game is being played on a field that is already tilted: 'the assembly is already speaking before it utters any words' (Butler, 2015: 156; see also Benhabib, 1994). This is the ground on which Miranda Fricker's influential book (2010) on 'epistemic injustice' is pitched: some voices are simply not allowed onto the pitch ('hermeneutic injustice') or are disregarded even if they are on the pitch ('testimonial injustice'). An implication is that the context in which debate is being held has to be taken into account. However, the context is seldom defined and it can be narrowly or widely drawn. Are white people to be condemned because of their racist forefathers? Is abortion to be denied because a human being is felt to be present from the moment of conception?

It may be said that these are matters in the wider society and can be left at the door of the university, but that is short-sighted and for two reasons. First, seminars and discussions are held under the aegis of the university where controversial issues are addressed. *Cancel culture* is present on campus but it was ever thus, for all cultures are in the business of cancelling – or disbarring – those not abiding by their special rules. More insidiously, the matter shows itself deeply within the academic community; and here culture wars can be seen starkly, and with even the loss of academic reputations and livelihoods. In social theory and critical theory, cudgels are drawn and heatedly so at times. Positions are taken up, and reputations are traduced. The idea of a university as a space of reasoning is in the dock as an apologia both for an indefensible status quo *and* for an unquestioning radicalism.

There are now many different cultures *within* the space of the academy, but a major fault line has opened between those who believe in hurling the university into society and those who believe in attempting, however impossibly, to retain a semi-detached space for the university to be able to inquire into and reflect upon the world. That there are all kinds of gradations between these poles – of separateness and engagement – only underscores the point being made here as to the presence of many cultures in the university.

The other reason not to accept that culture wars in the wider society can be kept outside the walls of the university is that they are finding their way into its educational processes. This is a matter that is still largely hidden and would be a matter for delicate empirical research. The matter, however, has been with us for over half a century.

Little Cultures: Divide and Rule

In the UK in the 1960s, in an infamous and heated *'Two Cultures'* debate, the question was posed as to whether all of the university's disciplines came up to scratch as forms of culture or whether it was just some. Was it just the humanities – especially English – wherein culture was to be found (this was the position of the Cambridge academic and literary critic, F. R. Leavis (1979)) or, in order to be a cultured person, did one not need an understanding of the second law of thermodynamics? (This latter was the position of C. P. Snow (1978).)

En passant, Snow did not need to have been so concerned since the position of the humanities was already weakening, and it was science that was well on its way to triumphing, even if it did not acquire the status of 'culture' (which just dwindled as a trope in the public sphere). The humanities did not undergo any *manifest* crisis – despite the hand-wringing that has gone on (Plumb, 1964;

Bérubé and Nelson, 1995; Nussbaum, 2010) – but rather just very gradually withered on the vine, punctuated by the odd expulsion.

If that debate was to be held today, it would surely take the form of 'a plague on all your houses': *both* the sciences and the humanities should be a little more modest in their cultural pretensions. It would be observed that the social sciences now constitute a large set of inquiries of some significance (Kagan, 2009), not least because they seem in some quarters to offer a prospect of steering human behaviour; and they have been joined by professional and performative studies. But more deep-seated issues remain. Believing so much in themselves, academic disciplines fight among each other instead of deploying their cognitive capital collectively. As it is, the divide-and-rule strategy, with the ensuing cognitive-cum-cultural wars within the academy, suits the state rather nicely. The academy fails to harness its collective epistemic resources in addressing major issues of the day.

For over forty years, through the work of Klein and others (Frodeman, Thompson and Dos Santos Pacheco, 2019), the matter of interdisciplinarity has been a matter of scholarly interest; and that idea is now being superseded by the resuscitated idea of transdisciplinarity, now being given an ontological twist. It is observed that the different aspects of the world are themselves entangled, and, so, epistemologies are entangled not only with each other but also with the world as such (Code, 2006; Bhaskar, 2010b; Gibbs and Beavis, 2020). However, while there have been sporadic attempts to do some justice to these ideas in curricula initiatives, they have yet to be grounded in practical principles that an astute institutional leadership could take on board. As a result, the separate cognitive cultures remain the markers of the academy's tribes and territories (Becher and Trowler, 2001), and the potential collective cultural capital of the academy remains unfulfilled.

Another line of argument would be to critique academic disciplines as rather unreflective *little cultures*. They should not be judged too harshly on this account for *all* cultures are inwardly disposed. Cultures include and they exclude; and their exclusions not just keep out others but envelope those within with their own local imaginaries. But just how might academic disciplines widen their orientation? What might be the wider context within which they could – and even should – place themselves and their work? Picking up the previous point, just which transdisciplinary themes might serve as overarching umbrellas under which the disciplines might be brought together?

Candidates for a wider context are multiplying. Simmering over the past half a century or more has been the voice of economic 'reason', a voice that has grown stronger with the advent of cognitive capitalism (Boutang, 2011), now morphing into algorithmic capitalism (Peters, 2013). Whether this digital economy amounts to a culture or an anti-culture – or even a post-culture – is a moot point. However, that voice is being joined by others that would lead the academic life in the direction of cultures with various mixes of social and inclusive sentiments. In response to the claims of the dominant economic culture, suggestions are coming – from quite different directions – that the academic world should take on more of a public spirit (Marginson, 2007; Levin and Greenwood, 2016; Grant, 2021). Its culture should contain a sense that the university is a public institution (whatever the source of its funds) and that it should seek to deploy its resources in favour of the public good, howsoever understood.

A second prod is one that is implied by ecofeminism, which is that the academic life should become an intellectual arm of an ecological culture, with a profound care for the total human-natural environment (Plumwood, 2008; Hourdequin, 2015). Yet another contemporary voice, of even more recent origin, is the advocacy of the Global South in general and of indigenous cultures more particularly (de Sousa Santos, 2014). Here, the implicit charge is that the cognitive cultures of the Global North are more restricted that they would deign to admit. They plead a cause of universalism but they are, as implied in the charge sheet, cognitive cultures of, and in the interests of, the West (Wood, 2015; Zaman, 2021).

Multiplying Cultures: Tensions Both Long-Lasting and New

All this amounts to an unsettling of the university's cultures. As noted, over the last two centuries, the university has split into *multiplying* cultures. We are alerted to there being 'six cultures of the academy' (Bergquist and Pawlak, 2008) but it is far more than that, as the 'multiversity' becomes a site of multicultures, across both its academic and its administrative arms. Indeed, that division is passé, as 'third-space' roles abound, neither specifically academic nor administrative but being something of both (Whitchurch, 2012). *Hybrid cultures* offer the university a cultural flexibility, finding their centres of meaning variously (e.g.) in money, control, human values, efficiency, disciplines, teaching, professions, religious traditions, ecology, sustainability, national identity, particular industries and even academic development.

As intimated, these cultures do not always live happily together. There is tension even *within* them. Sometimes, one of the tribes descends into a civil war and even (as noted, with philosophy in the University of Sydney (Critchley, 2001: Preface)) with subcultures breaking off to mark out and defend their own new territories. There is not yet total cultural anarchy: the epistemic cultures of the university more or less find accommodations with each other. And management tries to bring all of a university's cultures together by imposing institution-wide regulations and insignia: the university's power point template acts as a unifying signifier. However, there is a certain amount of cultural violence to be seen, and cultures with power (the managers, the natural sciences) will turn on the weaker cultures (the staff developers, the humanities). There may even be evictions and excommunications.

Culture wars are to be seen, therefore, in the wider society which are throwing themselves into the academy and adding to those already in the academy (Edgerton et al., 2005), which now has both internal and extramural culture wars with which to contend. The academy is now witnessing fighting being waged on both fronts simultaneously.

One matter here is so old that it is easy to overlook it, having been present for the last 200 years. It is that perennial issue of higher education seen as a matter of human cultivation, whether as a form of liberal education or '*Bildung*' (Løvlie et al., 2003) or as a matter of preparation for the world, and preferably for the world of work. It is not simply a matter of culture versus utility, for the doctrine of utility is so entrenched that it constitutes itself a very large and pervasive culture. *This* culture war is better understood as a clash between those who see inherent value in human being and consider higher education to be an educational process intended to enlarge that inherent value and those who see value lying in the university's productive capacities in the wider society, and preferably economic profitability at that. Understanding or skill, mind or economy, knowledge-as-its-own-end or knowledge-as-means: these are the antinomies of this culture war, which continues to be potent, at least in the more market-driven economies.

Conclusions

Culture wars are present in the academy, and many are being fought with vigour and even hostility. However, for all the press headlines, only occasionally are there raised voices: the academy conducts its culture wars in a restrained way. Individuals are just denied a hearing, or are quietly asked – by email – to pack their bags.

These culture wars are intensifying and multiplying. They are *intensifying* as resources are coming under pressure (even if those resources remain, *in real terms*, undiminished): consequently, each epistemic field has to fight its own corner. They are *multiplying* through the university's public engagement, its walls having become porous to the culture wars of the wider society. Culture wars are being fought not only on the battlements of the university but within the keep.

At least, it can be firmly stated that culture is not at an end in the university. To the contrary, the university is replete, if not overrun, with cultures. The end-of-culture thesis should be despatched. But then the question arises as to whether there might be a meta-culture that could serve as some kind of cultural glue, under which most other cultures can shelter and each might have its day. That issue lies ahead of us.

3

A Common Culture
No and Maybe

Introduction

My two previous chapters have mounted critiques of the idea that the concepts of culture and university can be put together with any serious intent. By culture, I mean here an upper-case sense of culture, Culture with a capital 'C', as it were. And by 'serious intent', I have in mind the possibility of evolving a quasi-normative conception of the relationship; that is, universities generally might justifiably see themselves and promote themselves as playing a part in enhancing culture in and of the wider society, and that they may take on cultural *purposes*.

The first chapter critiqued Readings' observation that the university is a culture-free zone. However, the chapter observed that, now, the university is actually awash with cultures. The second chapter went further, observing not only that cultures are thick within the university but also that they are – to a significant degree – mutually antagonistic. The university is a site of culture wars, wars that are endemic between the disciplines and within the university as an organization and wars that have been imported into the university from the wider world. It is now part of the function of the university to demonstrate to the world how organizations might live with civil war – *in the form of culture wars* – permanently in their midst.

On the story of either chapter – the end of culture as an idea *or* the warring among multiple cultures – the prospects for the university in enhancing the wider culture of society seem forlorn. At best, the university is a site of mini cultures; very much a lower case 'c' presence of culture, but its cultural openness is questionable. Except in a few universities across the world, an Inuit or aborigine or other indigenous person who wandered into a university could not count on finding a ready welcome. The typical university has limits to its readiness in welcoming strangers into its midst.

We have, therefore, *the worst of all cultural worlds in the university*: a disinclination seriously even to speak of culture, let alone to engage head-on with the issue; a myriad of minor cultures vying with and sometimes trampling on each other; a lack of boundaries to what is culturally permissible; and an absence of any large idea of culture that can do justice to the university as a site of culture, which it *has* to be. As a result, the university is ripe for cultural takeover by dominant cultures, both within and beyond the academy; and it has come to pass. What was once felt – within the academy's culture – to possess *inherent* value has come to possess value only insofar as its activities are 'commodities' with an (extrinsic) economic return. In this respect, universities are merely aping the fate of culture in the wider world, which has turned into a 'culture industry' (Rebentisch and Trautmann, 2020: 21).

If this analysis holds water, then 'culture [is bound to] share an uneasy relationship with education' (Peters and Tukeo, 2010: 277) and the idea of the university as a kind of engine of culture is in difficulty. It embodies even an excluding culture as an agent of colonialism, imposing a dominant culture (of the Global North), or state capitalism or even scientism. The challenges in locating a sense of cultural purpose within the university seem insuperable.

On the Nature of the World

If we are to think about the kind of culture that might be associated with the university in such a way as to be of assistance to the world, we should start by identifying pertinent key features of the world; and 'the world' has to include all the entities of the Earth including Nature and the Earth itself. We can illustrate implications of this suggestion by reflecting on the nature of the Coronavirus.

The Coronavirus shows vividly that the world is more or less *totally* interconnected. Entities in the world implicated by the pandemic *include* viruses, health systems, cultural practices, human bodies and the organs and structures of those bodies, transport systems, social institutions (such as schools, families), work practices, human psychology, the internet, political systems, communication systems, ideas, myths, religions, animals, agricultural practices (which may have disturbed animal habitats), economies, universities, science systems, business practices, ethical evaluations, states and their relationships with their citizens, self-understandings and knowledges as such. This is only an indicative list and could be *much* extended. The point is that the virus shows dramatically that the entities in the world are interconnected: human and animal, organic and inorganic, formal knowledge and practices. *Moreover*, knowledge systems play a particular part in these interconnections.

Knowledge is a set of cognitive cultures that are affected by the world and yet can themselves have effects *upon* the cultures of the world. It may even be the case both that knowledge bequeathed the virus – perhaps it initially 'escaped' from a laboratory – *and* that knowledge, of many kinds, will help to suppress the virus. Knowledges can endorse the dominant cognitive cultures of the world – of globalism, instrumentalism and neo-capitalism – and can help in critiquing those very phenomena and even redressing their worst features. Sinner and saviour – that seems to be the situation of knowledge.

A battery of concepts is on hand in identifying this interconnectedness. They include complexity, indeterminacy, open-endedness, fluidity, emergence, contingency, entanglement, inequality, relationality and unpredictability. This is a world that is in total motion (Nail, 2019), with its entities acting haphazardly on each other. Other ideas come quickly into sight too, including a sense that good and harm swim together, and that the world – even the natural world – is malleable to some extent. A little more formally, epistemology – understanding the world – and ontology – how the world is constituted – swim in each other's waters (and so we see such rather awkward constructions as 'onto-epistemologies').

A cardinal doctrine of the recently emerged *realist* philosophies is that the entities in the world are on a level with each other, that no entity possesses a higher status than any other entity. The world exhibits – as we are told in 'object-oriented ontology' at least (Harman, 2018) – a *flat* ontology. The problem is that Harman and his fellow travellers in the new realisms downplay power relationships between entities in the world, between natural and human entities and within Nature. The virus graphically points up these aspects of ontology. First, it is evident that the entities in the world have causal properties and have influence on other entities. Second, while there are reciprocal relationships – the virus affects transport systems and transport systems affect the virus – still there are dominant *hierarchies of entities*. Life chances *are* affected by the economic order and one's position in it.

This situation plays out in *knowledge-as-culture*. Increasingly, we hear much from statisticians, modellers, bio-engineers, virologists, immunologists, epidemiologists, genomic engineers and others in the biomedical fields but of the philosophers, political scientists, anthropologists, sociologists and ethicists we hear rather little. In understanding the world, therefore, we are presented with a *hierarchy of knowledge cultures*. Some forms of meaning bequeathed in knowledge production are more equal than others.

Roy Bhaskar's philosophy of Critical Realism (2008) is helpful here. Not only does it give prominence to the way the world is – its ontological character – but it plays up its layered character, the causal effects that entities can have on each other, and the open-endedness of natural situations and the qualities of emergence that they possess. It also insists on ontology and epistemology as residing in different regions but notes that knowledge can have effects on the world: *reasons can be causes* (Bhaskar, 2015: 80–97; Singh et al., 2020). And we see this in our example: the reasonings of scientists and public health experts may lead to roll-outs of vaccines, so constituting a *cause* of the subjugation of the virus. Causes exist both in the world and in our knowledges *of* the world. Cognitive cultures are very much entities in the world and act *on* the world, a point that is crucial for this inquiry.

Culture: No Longer a Fringe Affair

Culture is in a doubly ambiguous situation. Characteristically, culture is a set of enduring collective meanings that bind a group or community together, such that its members feel that they possess a unity. All four aspects are crucial, namely that (i) culture is enduring and (ii) collective, and enable the members of a community (iii) to feel bound to each other through (iv) a common set of meanings, to recognize oneself in the other. However, if the entities of the world are in motion and take on unpredictable formations as they collide, then each of these four aspects of culture is in difficulty.

In the world, (i) nothing endures, (ii) collectives are fragile (they are always splitting and re-forming, and their inner connections are always being tested) and (iii) individuals feel increasingly less bound to each other, not least since (iv) a common set of meanings seems difficult – if not impossible – to come by. This is a world in which the category of culture, in the strong form being proposed here (with its four aspects), is deeply in trouble. It may even be said to be passé. That the university feels queasy in the presence of the idea of culture is understandable: as an idea, culture seems ephemeral; as a social form, it is illusory.

We developed a form of this *culture-as-passé* thesis in the previous chapter, in a comparison with ideology. Both ideology and culture could be said to have been overtaken by a global attachment to a socio-economic *Weltanschuung*, in which bureaucracy, organization, STEM, efficiency and now digitalization have swept culture aside. It is economic capital that counts or, to summon another neologism, *instrumental* capital, *not* cultural capital. *If* the dominant way of life is to be construed as a culture, it is a soulless culture. *Meaning has no meaning any more.* The place of the humanities as a constituent of academic life falters and is even supressed as the STEM disciplines cement their unchallenged place (and which now, as remarked, have become STEMM, to include medicine (Cohen, 2021)). This is a dynamic terrain with a jockeying for position even among the favoured disciplines. Now, it is not just science, mathematics and technological disciplines that are in the ascendancy but that, within that group, the digital, the bio-informatic and bio-technical disciplines are being accorded special preference (Peters and Venkatesan, 2013).

There is much talk of epistemic injustice and even epistemic violence (Fricker, 2010; Kidd et al., 2017). In large part, this language has its place amid issues of the relationships between the so-called Global North and the Global South. Much less noticed is that epistemic violence is to be found *within* the Global North, the level of such violence being directly related to the distance of a field from the dominant epistemic form, namely that of being empirical, mathematical, producing vast databanks and digitization, income generating within a university, linked to economic power beyond the university and likely to lead to publication in 'world-class' journals. Inevitably, in such a cognitive culture, work that is scholarly, reflective, based on the word, oriented towards interpretation and understanding and perhaps more local in character, or that may be critical of current hegemonic orders (whether political, social, ideological, economic or epistemological) is bound to have a thin time of it.

There is, admittedly, an ambiguity here, reflected in the following proposition: the dominant cognitive culture shuns cultural capital. More simply: culture shuns culture, an apparent inconsistency that can easily be resolved. *The new cognitive culture disparages and suppresses the old cognitive culture.* The king is dead; long live the king! The new cognitive culture can get along very well without the old culture – literally so, for money and riches flow to the upstart. Moreover, the new culture can project itself as all-pervasive: it holds the secrets of the world, if not the universe. If the ecological crisis is to be solved, it is science and technology that will achieve the goal; and if life is impossible on this planet, well, there is always the prospect that science and technology, aided by the powers of digital resources, will be able to get us to another planet.

This is a form of culture wars with nuclear cultural warheads. Nothing short of the future of the whole Earth – and not just humanity – is in question. Far from being a matter of superstructure, of an epiphenomenon, of an adornment on the fringe of society, now the matter of culture takes – or should take – centre stage.

Just what is it to be human, to be a society, even to be Earth? What part does culture have and how is it to be construed?

Rent Asunder

Laments over the splitting of the disciplines have been voiced for at least a hundred years. However, the matter is still not well understood. At one level, it is straightforward: the evolution of universities, the greater attention being given to research and scholarship, the rise in the numbers of people involved and the emergence of academic publishing: all of these were bound to lead to a differentiation of the disciplines. Of the formation of subdisciplines and even new disciplines, there shall be no end. The matter has the form of a fractal, repeatedly subdividing and splaying out into web upon web of intricacy, a cognitive structure with a common set of roots and now with an amazing pattern, but with its parts so far apart that they have little or no apparent common elements.

The key question is, 'How has it come about?' That deeper story has yet fully to be told but it would surely have to include the emergence of a technological society in which its processes came to be founded on formalized knowledge, a knowledge society, increasingly dependent on cognition and understanding of many kinds but giving increasing prominence to science and technology, and, most recently, the emergence of a digitized world, depending on data and data processing which is already morphing into an algorithmic world. Other strands in the story would be the ever-closer interest in knowledge production on the part of the state and the massification of higher education.

This complicated story is important for two reasons. First, as implied, we see a continuing proliferation of epistemic cultures (Knorr-Cetina, 1999). The fundamental split remains that between science and the humanities, the latter having been all but vanquished. (Which nineteen-year-old would speak proudly of taking a degree in the humanities?) And the story just sketched indicates why that debate became so intense. One of the major trunks – the humanities – was felt to provide the pathway to Culture, if not to happiness. Science felt belittled, and it wanted to be appreciated. It should not have worried for it came to supplant the humanities as the dominant cognitive culture, even if not yet as fully accepted *as* Culture. But the general point is that there is no single cognitive culture. Discrete cognitive cultures form such that almost any group can establish its own academic journal and annual conference, and secure a hallowed place for itself within the academic world.

Second, *how* we know is bound up with *what* we think we know: epistemology implicates ontology. It is not just that we are in the presence of profoundly different epistemologies, with their different readings of the universe and relationships to it and their fundamentally differing languages and modes of experience; it is even more that the cognitive cultures have within them quite different presuppositions about the world and its possibilities. Science is now entangled in the world, and sees in it profit and problem solutions. Science is like a huge iceberg: much of it lays beneath the surface. With the humanities, however, what you see is largely what you get; and for many, given the dominant culture of technique, of valuing means to ends, and of power in the world, the humanities do not amount to very much. The humanities have few friends at court, the world being much less interested in them.

In being entangled in the world, science is distorted by money and power, for example in the relationships between universities and pharmaceutical corporations. In having no such entanglements, the humanities not only remain untainted but also adrift from a changing world and so largely ineffectual. The options for cognitive cultures seem be either a Faustian bargain with money-making and political influence or a desert-island impotence.

The Lure of General Education

Against this background of a splitting of cognitive cultures, many have sought for nearly a hundred years to bring them together into a coherent educational project. It has had a chequered history: as Gramsci noted (2005: 26), there had long been 'a question-mark over the very principle of a concrete programme of general culture'. Two points should be noted. For a long time, one intention – though naturally not loudly voiced – was that of humanizing the scientists. The scientists were felt to be without culture and were in need of a cultural veneer. Alternative curricula were forthcoming: on the one hand, a diet of the 'Great Books' of Western civilization, a programme that begged all manner of questions, not least since the canon picked out was that of white Western – and mainly American – men, and, on the other hand, courses in communication and presentational skills.

Now, the boot is entirely on the other foot. Today, the issue is that of students in the humanities understanding something of science and technology and preferably having some adeptness in that direction. For some years and across the world, ministers of higher education – especially in market-driven higher education systems – have voiced concerns as to the value of an education in mediaeval history or classical civilization or even the humanities as such. The implication is that the cultured are not so cultured after all. At least, their students should learn coding skills, or so the debate often seems to suggest.

The other point is that the idea of general education is an educational project, having purchase only in relation to students and their education. It never seems to occur that their teachers and professors might also be in want of a general education. It is true that, at least since the 1960s, calls have been heard in favour of interdisciplinarity but those suggestions have been concerned to find ways of bringing the disciplines into some kind of connections. It was rarely on the cards that those academics themselves warranted a broadening of some kind. Their identities were contained within the disciplines they made themselves within those boundaries (they were indeed disciplines in a Foucauldian sense), and their being was just that – as physicist, or geologist, or historian, or economist or whatever it may be.

The prospects for general education seem to be bleak, therefore. The epistemological landscape is too heterogeneous and too disparate, and is a setting in which ideas of 'alterity' or otherness (Levinas, 1999) or 'recognition' (Honneth, 2005) gain little purchase. The world of the cyclotron, of nanotechnology, graphemes and the fluidity of quantum mechanics is far from the world of mediaeval manuscripts or the messiness of inquiries into democracy and racism. Against such a horizon, 'culture' can be an umbrella term for pedagogical efforts that seek to bring fundamentally different forms of *being* into some kind of relationship with each other. But how might that be?

A number of possibilities suggest themselves. Ortega y Gasset, it will be recalled, proposed the collocation of forms of understanding, grouped together under the principle of economy (or parsimony) so as to provide a curriculum of the 'vital system of ideas' of the time. As noted (Chapter 1), Ortega was not afraid explicitly to associate this project with culture; indeed, his proposals were driven by a keen sense that culture was being lost from the university. Even if the collective will had been present, the project was doomed from the start, for it seemed to demand of every student that she or he would become a Renaissance person, able to form an understanding of the universe of knowledge.

A second idea was that a common curriculum be derived built around the Great Books. We have already observed that it was a question-begging strategy: On what basis was the canon to be chosen? The criteria were seldom set out for the Great Books were assumed to be self-evident; they just turned out to be an excessively narrow selection which told one more about the cultural prejudices of the selector than it gave insight into a justifiable educational project.

A more plausible option is that of the student as a global citizen, an idea taken up by both educationalists and philosophers (notably, by Martha Nussbaum (2010), a representative of both clans). The links with culture are evident but again are question begging. In an interconnected world, so it is reasoned, the student should come to have an empathy with others. Michael Peters (2018) has pointed out that the idea all too easily lends itself to a global entrepreneurialism: the student-as-global-citizen is able to do business all across the world. On the other hand, the idea also harbours a Kantian leaning towards universality; but this could be the makings of a subjectivity without a keen sense of difference.

A further possibility is more of an emerging imaginary, namely that of multicultures, which is implicit in a number of intellectual currents. One lies in concerns over transnational cognitive injustice. Perhaps the leading exponent of this movement is de Sousa Santos (whose work we met in Chapter 1), and who points to the invisibility of knowledges of the Global South (within the practices of the Global North) and argues for an 'ecology of knowledges' to be formed. Precisely the manner in which different and even opposed epistemologies are to come together, we are not told. Aligned to this proposal is the welter of pedagogical initiatives in the Global North being played out under banners such as 'Rhodes Must Fall' and 'Why is My Curriculum White?' A quite separate strand in this skein is that of an interculturality to be found in the epistemic communities concerned with language, culture and communication. A hope within the idea of interculturality is that some common ground can be found for communication across borders of language and culture.

This grouping of ideas and ventures has both a negative and a positive element. A common thread is a determination to combat any kind of cultural hegemony. *No one culture is presumed to be superior as against any other*, but it is assumed, in *inter*culturality, that some connectivity can be found between cultures (Welikala and Barnett, 2021). The difficulty about this project is illustrated by the very laudable practice in one of the leading journals in this field – *Language and Intercultural Communication* – which presents the abstracts of its papers in two languages. The very practice that is supposed to effect a bridge across cultures is testimony to the gap *between* cultures; texts emerging from different cultures are characteristically unintelligible to other cultures, hence the dual-language abstracts, which in turn only confirms the cultural gap.

A last option is emerging in the wake of new incarnations of the digital age. Many are observing, correctly, that we have here a global tsunami, sweeping across the world and, moreover, not just that higher education is being swept up in this tidal wave but that it is also – through the knowledge production and knowledge exchange efforts of universities – a motivating force behind the new digital forms. The option here takes a weak and a stronger form. The weaker option is 'go with the flow'. It notes the tsunami, and says that this is the way the world is and that, therefore, it is incumbent on all to become digitally literate (it is not enough to be digitally 'tethered' (Savin-Baden, 2015)), and that it is a duty of the higher education system to help to bring about that state of affairs. This would amount to a *digital culture*, in which human beings merge with digital systems, even if attempting simultaneously to hold on to qualities uniquely possessed by those same human beings.

The stronger version is a form of 'posthumanism', as it is termed. This variant places the digital age in a wider perspective, suggesting a new kind of human being. It notes digital interactivity and sees potential for being in this world of total connectivity. A number of intellectual strands come together: the 'flat' realist ontologies and Bhaskar's layered critical realism (noted earlier); critico-feminisms, which are searching for an interconnected humanity that takes the part of the other (Braidotti, 2019); the idea of the Anthropocene and – even more recently – of the Ecocene (Boehnert, 2018), in which humanity accepts that it has overreached itself for 300 years, placing itself at the centre of the world. The juxtaposition of these movements is prompting thinking about what it is to be human. Humanity has to displace its old self into a new self, hence '*post*humanism'.

To what extent are there glimmerings here of a culture for the twenty-first century, and one in which higher education can reasonably be enlisted in the endeavour?

A Logical Problem

There is a logical problem facing attempts to put the concepts of university and culture together. Culture necessarily both includes and *excludes*. The concept of culture has application in the context of a set of meanings, activities, values and interpretations held collectively. There can be no Robinson Crusoe cultures (Gellner, 1969: 105–6). Cultures bind the people of a community together. No culture, no community, *and vice versa*. However, cultures also exclude. Indeed, a latent function of culture is precisely to draw a boundary around a community and to exclude those not within the boundary. A culture marks out an in-group and all others, who are not members of the clan. Culture breeds otherness, *but* of a disparaging kind: the other is positioned as a stranger, and even as alien.

All this being so, a problem arises for the university. The idea of the university has universal pretensions. A university that is marked only by particular interests – of a region, a polity, a form of knowledge, an ideology, a religion, a race or gender – puts in question its right to be termed 'university'. In principle at least, a university should be open to all knowledge: it should have a right to pursue its inquiries wherever they may lead. A researcher cannot be forbidden to read a particular paper; a student cannot be told that her or his question is ultra vires. Neither inquiry nor critique can be curtailed, for otherwise we are in the presence of ideology and/or dogma. The world exerts its claims not discretely but in toto: 'The universal exists' (Serres, 2018: 89). This, at least, is a legitimation of what it is to be a university.

That being so, if there is a universality within the idea of the university – even if we cannot be sure what it is and even if, in fact, each university is a bundle of particularities – how might culture gain a grip? Universality and particularity: the university is being asked to ride both horses at once; and the two horses are moving in opposed directions. We should note that this conundrum has long perplexed scholars (Butler et al., 2000). We see it in debates about colonialism, in relation to identity in a world of difference, about global social and cognitive justice, as to whether there is any universal glue in a world of contingency, and around the matter of citizenship. This is a matter that has plagued the liberal mind, which both wants to be sensitive to difference and to ways in which difference has been occluded and yet wishes to find ways in which the peoples of this tiny planet can recognize and speak to each other.

In their different ways, luminaries such as Kant and – contemporaneously – Zizek, Butler, Nussbaum, Lyotard and, most recently, Honneth (with his theory of recognition) has each moved in these waters. I suggest, however, that we can still find especially helpful resources in Habermas. His (1984, 1987) theory of communicative ethics stands out, with its project of discerning 'validity claims' – originally four and then reduced to three, of truthfulness, sincerity and appropriateness – that lie within any human interaction with an interest in reason. In a magisterial essay, Habermas reflects on this project of his, positioning it neither as a Kantian reason secured by self-realizing human beings nor as the ultra-globalizing Hegelian spirit. It is an intersubjective reasoning that stands not as a utopia but is to be 'approached in a sufficiently sceptical manner', and it is a project that has to be 'historically situated' (Habermas, 1995: 144, 146).

If we now take up this framework into our interest in the university and its link to culture, perhaps there is the embryo of an idea that we can develop. The university, after all, is a social institution with a history that contains the development of reason and reasoning. It is, though, a specific kind of reasoning. Moreover, that reason is far from being fixed: reason in the university is always on the move, and options are opening. Universality and contingency: perhaps the circle can be squared after all.

Conclusions

Might there be a common culture that stands as a foundational plank of the university *and* provides a resource for the wider society? Such a quest is fraught but it should not be abandoned prematurely. The difficulties, though, are considerable and they are ontological, epistemological and ethical. *Ontologically* (especially in Bhaskar's critical realism), not only are the entities of the world interconnected but they are layered and characterized by differential power exerting force between them. *Epistemologically*, efforts to understand the world have shattered into fragments, which again stand in relations of power among them. And this pattern can be seen within universities and across the universities of the world, as a dominant epistemic order of instrumentalism, science and biopower has taken shape. And *ethically*, we are faced with a situation of (global) ethical pluralism, with no obvious universal framework behind them. Differential force within the world *and* fragmentation in ways of understanding and in living in this perplexing world: in such a setting, that the university might attach itself to the idea of a common culture seems fanciful at best.

Efforts have been made to bring the different epistemic cultures together but all such attempts have foundered, not least because those cultures stand in different relationships to the world. Epistemic culture was a gloss, a veneer: to be cultured was a mark of distinction, of cultural superiority indeed; and the humanities did well on this score. Over the last hundred years, those tables have turned. Science has come to be prized because it offers power over Nature. We can depict this situation either of a *repudiation* of culture *or* of science and the digital world as providing a *new kind* of culture. *Either constitutes a cul-de-sac for our purposes*, both being devoid of meaning except that of power (over Nature and human beings).

However, two shafts of light have opened for us: (i) the Habermassian project of intersubjective reasoning, which extends the possibility of human reasoning as culture with its inner ethical values, and (ii) Bhaskarian critical realism, both in (a) its idea of confronting the impairments in the real of the world – by absenting absences (Bhaskar, 2008b) – and (b) in its later incarnations, which saw possibilities of redemption in an impoverished world (Bhaskar, 2010). In my final chapter, I want to bring these two sets of resources together and do so against an ecological horizon. In this way, we may just be able to eke out a new way of holding the concepts of culture and university together, and in a way that is fitting for the interconnectedness of the twenty-first century. A common culture may yet be within our reach and in which the university has a particular role to play.

4

For the University and the World
A Culture of the Earth

Introduction

The previous three chapters assessed the prospects of a common culture that the university might advance and which might be of value to the wider world. It has been a largely dismal story, and the charge sheet contains two sets of charges. Commentaries provide pictures of there being a *culture-less* world, shot through with soulless technicism, economicism, algorithms, mass digital media, bureaucracy and state power. Culture has turned not just into a 'culture industry' (Adorno and Horkheimer, 1989) but even into a 'culture economy' (Sum and Jessop, 2013; Bennett, 2013). *However*, others draw attention to the world being replete with ever-proliferating and non-comprehending cultures (plural). These disparate cultures are held to be social, discursive, material and epistemic, and contain strains of gender inequalities, coloniality, hostility to difference and resistance to open debate.

The same situation, therefore, is viewed in entirely different ways – an absence of culture *and* of multiplying cultures. However, *in both cases*, the upshot is that there is no grand unifying culture and the very idea of a common culture that may assist the world can make no sense.

If that is the case for the wider world, it is also the case for the university, it being such an all-encompassing institution. Some (notably Readings) observe that the university has had the cultural air drawn out of it such that it presents as a culture-free zone. And since Readings' book appeared, the university has become digitized and become a direct force of production within cognitive and informational capitalism (Peters, 2013). It is a culturally barren landscape. Alternatively, others observe that the university is par excellence replete with cultures. Its epistemic communities are now, like the universe, expanding and moving apart, non-comprehendingly of each other, both horizontally *and* vertically.

Horizontally, the disciplines, with their epistemic cultures, contend against each other, splitting apart, and erecting barricades, tightly policing any who seem to stray on their territories. (One journal forbids diagrams; another expects it.) *Vertically*, the disciplinary cultures negotiate with the organizational cultures, of metrics, demonstrable outcomes and income streams, of decision-making and collegiality. And there are criss-crossing subcultures. A single university cleaves into a research culture and a teaching culture, with identities and communities marking out their territories, and with tensions both endorsed and challenged by management policies and actions. So culture-free *or* culture-saturated: both are legitimate readings of the university.

The Great Schism

How is this possible, that the wider society *and* the university can be plausibly read in such opposed and legitimate ways – overrun with cultures *and* devoid of culture?

We may explain the matter through a social theory of ideas (of epistemic cultures indeed) – as a dispute between the philosophers and the sociologists. Those of a philosophical bent are prone to countenance a *universalist account*, the idea that there can be a culture characteristic of the university as such. What is interesting is that there are several candidates for the role, the university being looked variously to sustain a culture of *reason, being* (or *becoming*), *inquiry, life, concern* or '*otherness*'. Each could be said to be *the* culture of the university. Their adherents could fairly suggest that a university not in possession of any such culture – say, the culture of reason – was not a university at all. It might be achieving worthwhile ends in some sphere, but it could not count as a *university*. It would not be fulfilling the *idea* of what it is to *be* a university.

On the other hand, the *land-of-a-hundred-cultures* account arises from a sociological interpretation, which picks out assemblies of meaning, activities, material aspects and identity held by identifiable groups. For instance, an interest in the disciplines as major formations in academic life will lead to an inquiry into ways in which academic subcultures form around *differing* cognitive framings of the world *and* their attendant practices. It is implied that there is just no way of arbitrating between the epistemologies of disciplines with their tacit sense of the make-up – the ontology – of the world and their related ways of going on. This sociological orientation begins, therefore, from a sense of cultural differences in both beliefs and practices, a sense of *cultural relativism*.

It seems, then, that the matter of culture and the university is *legitimately* open to two fundamentally opposed approaches, one that hankers after a single, grand and universal account (the philosopher's gambit) and one that starts from a sense of difference, and even difference built around power structures, with multiple, contending and even proliferating cultures and their forms of life (the sociologist's opening). *Universality* and *relativism*: this is *the great – and deep – schism* in understanding culture and the university. Both perceptions possess legitimacy, and there seems no rational way of choosing between them.

My argument, however, is to the contrary, and I shall suggest another image, that of the Moebius strip. Far from the two accounts being quite separate, with no way of preferring either, I suggest that each runs into the other and that they each owe something to the other: they are *inseparably* joined together. And I shall propose a meta-culture – founded on the large theme of ecology – that does justice to both positions, universality and relativism.

Ways of Approaching the World

So as to make progress, we may pick up a discussion in the last chapter concerning the relationship between our understandings of the world and the way the world is, that is, putting it formally, between epistemology and ontology.

Building on Habermas's (1978) theory of 'knowledge constitutive interests', different disciplinary cultures may be seen as containing contrasting epistemologies that correlate with different perceptions of the ontology of the world. At one time, the natural sciences perceived the world to be whole, uniform, relatively stable, external and available to empirical investigation. However, over the past hundred years or so, that dominant *Weltanschuung* has been displaced *within science itself*, the whole universe at micro and macro levels being seen as in motion and unstable, *and* that perceptions seem to be able to alter the way the world is and one's relationship to the world. It is a world of utter contingency and a situation in which the being of human beings is entangled with the constitution of the world (Barad, 2007). There is no world-independent view of the world for human being is inserted in the world. We learnt this from Kant more than 200 years ago, that we do not have unalloyed access to the world, but that thesis has been radicalized by the recent revolution in science. There simply isn't a stable world waiting for us even if we could shed our social and psychological selves and the spectacles they bestow.

I want now to put this picture of *ontological instability* into the company of Roy Bhaskar's Critical Realism (which we encountered earlier). Even though it went through several stages in his lifetime (Bhaskar, 2010), two features (among others) were durable throughout. The first is that Bhaskar held to a separateness between the way the world is (ontology) and our knowledge of it (epistemology). Whereas the world is as it is, we understand it in different ways. Building on this distinction, Bhaskar was able to propose a Holy Trinity: a stratified ontology, an epistemological relativism and a judgemental rationality.

By means of this schema, Bhaskar was able to mount a severe attack on constructivism, while accepting the radical variation in accounts of the world that constructivism implied. There could be infinite number of constructions of the world, hence 'epistemological relativism'. However, Bhaskar's schema both insisted that there is a world beyond our accounts of it and there are, via 'judgmental rationality', legitimate ways of understanding the world. Bhaskar did not accept – à la Popper (1975) – that knowledge resided in a third world, independently of thought and action. Human beings 'do not construct their knowledge: they reproduce it or transform it' (Bhaskar, 2008: 195). Knowledge is dependent on there being a world that we are trying to understand *and* where there are already prior understandings.

Let us now put these ideas together, of a world in motion that is always beyond our understandings and of our efforts to understand it. Human beings are not separate from the world, but they nevertheless try to understand the world; and this is so whether we have in mind quarks, glaciers, nations, ideologies, organizations, knowledge itself, human beings or poems or ourselves. And in trying to understand the world, human beings may disturb the world. They may even corrupt the world, whether the natural or the human world; and the human world includes knowledge *of* the world *and* of knowledge and understanding itself.

In these reflections, we have a way into the conundrum of culture in the university as universal *and* as multiple. It just might be the case that we can speak of there being a culture that is seriously determined to understand the world *and* there being many legitimate ways of approaching the world: the one and the many; a single culture and multiple cultures; culture as universal *and* as relative and multiple.

A Distant Culture

Let us raise the stakes even more with some dogmatic assertions. The world is in a mess, and just one of the causes of this situation is the epistemology that was formed in Northern Europe in the seventeenth and eighteenth centuries. Among the leading emissaries of this philosophy were Descartes, whose (1966: 20) aphorism '*Cogito, ergo sum*' ('I think, therefore I am') posited a human being as separate *from* the world and able to form judgements independently *of* the world, and Kant (1982: 266–75), for whom the human world was a 'phenomenal' world, unable to penetrate the real ('noumenal') world and cut off from it by dint of the structures of the human mind and the categories intrinsic to it. In short, the dominant philosophy of Northern Europe portrayed a distance between human beings and the world in which they lived. Culture, accordingly, was distant from the world.

This sense of culture – in what came to be known as 'the Global North' – as built around a distance between humanity and the world-in-itself came to have a profound impact. In it, human beings saw themselves as apart from the world *and* as having knowledge *of* the world, and it was a further short step for humanity to believe that the world was its to act upon, control, manipulate and extract from it. Here lay the seeds of the instrumentalism that developed in the nineteenth century and gathered pace in the twentieth century.

It was on the basis of this idea – that humanity could go it alone and that enquiry could be pure and independent of the world (Gellner, 1991b) – that Western knowledge was established, and in which the university played such a signal part. It was there that the disciplines emerged, each with a sense of a world independent of human reason and waiting to be grasped by human reason, and each increasingly unable to engage with other disciplines. This is the situation that Nicholas Maxwell (2014) has sought to depict in his forty-year quest, in charting a loss of wisdom in thought. The university has been reduced merely to engaging with discrete problems, and unable to address 'what is of value in life'.

We have here a dual-problem situation: a belief that humanity stands off from the world and can establish objective understandings of the world, independently of it; and a splitting of the different forms of knowledge that have developed, which are separate not only from the world but from each other. *Both* aspects of this situation share *a tacit sense that culture is a kind of magical expression of human beings in the world and offers no path to understanding*. It is hardly surprising that universities came eventually to have no explicit truck with culture.

It would not be right to see this is as a situation devoid of culture. On the contrary, this outlook has come to form itself into perhaps the most powerful culture that the world has ever seen. It is the basis of what came to be known as Modernity, that shrugging off of superstition, of dogma, of religion and all else that smacked of non-reason (even if, as Latour (1993) observed, 'we have never been [completely] modern'). From it stemmed control over Nature and then control over humanity itself. It is against this background that we can make sense of Zizek's (1999) suggestions that 'culture' is never far from 'evil', totalitarianism and, of course, ideology.

Two Options and Their Sources

The story here has gone on becoming ever more dismal. It will be recalled that two counter-readings have been identified: on the one hand, the university has lost contact with culture, and has become a culture-free zone; on the other hand, the university is overrun with cultures, plural. And the question was posed: How is this possible, that two entirely opposite readings of the situation are not only plausible but legitimate? We have ventured an answer, in distinguishing between two cognitive modes: a philosophical *universality* and a sociological *relativism*; but we can now develop that suggestion.

Philosophy rings its hands over the loss of a link between culture and the university (especially in the Frankfurt School of Critical Theory and particularly so in the case of Adorno, for whom 'culture ha[d] failed' (2014: 366)). Philosophy holds this view because it has in mind Culture with a capital 'C', as it were. Living in its transcendent space, it hankers after a culture for the whole of humanity (Serres, 2018). However, for philosophy, culture is not only a universal but is also a critical concept: culture is reflexive and creative (Jessop, 2017). Through thought and reason, the gaps between the potentialities in concepts *and* the ways in which the world fell beneath those potentialities could be exposed; this, at least, was Adorno's (2014) position.

We may note that Readings – who pressed the line as to the university being culture-free (which he lamented) – drew upon German philosophers (from Kant onwards), who had in effect espoused the Reason-as-Culture line. Readings' lament contains tacitly an image of Reason-as-Culture as a *Weltanschuung* for the world. That idea had become untenable – for Readings, at least – the university having been reduced to a bureaucratic, instrumental and performative institution, serving the interests of cognitive capitalism (to which the empty notion of 'excellence' bore witness). Not even culture-free, the university was culture-*less*.

Sociology sees the matter quite differently. What sociology notices is a proliferation of mini cultures; and the university is now overflowing with them. Three sets of cultures are apparent: (i) disciplines and intellectual fields constitute epistemic cultures; (ii) students exhibit overlapping cultures, of race, ethnicity, religion (or none) and nation, but they also quickly disaggregate themselves into their own cultures (of sports, politics, ecological concerns and so on); and (iii) the university exhibits several organizational cultures even within a single institution (of collegiality, metricization (a belief in management-by-numbers), digitization and large imaginaries (of nation, sustainability or whatever it may be)). These cultures are proliferating, fluid, criss-crossing and interconnecting, and with tensions between them. Some are internal to the university, and others are imported, aligned to projects and interest in the wider society.

Culture and the university, therefore, may be understood through two opposite vantage points: on the one hand, as an exploding universe of cultures moving ever apart from – and often in conflict with – each other; and on the other hand, as a universal culture in and across humanity as a whole *or that might plausibly be mooted for it*. Since both positions have legitimacy, a question is this: Might there be a way forward that could do some justice to both positions, of a universal culture *and* of cultural relativism? To make that question operationalizable: *Can a universal idea of culture be found that might act as an umbrella for a variety of academic subcultures and that could be said to have a* particular *resonance with the university?*

The Obvious Candidate and Its Deficiencies

The obvious candidate – to address the questions and their conditions just posed – is that of Jurgen Habermas's *Theory of Communicative Action* (to which we alluded earlier). That 800-page two-volume work (1987, 1991) has – I think – nothing to say about higher education as such (although he does touch on the matter of schools (1987: 371)), but it has a number of planks that can bridge culture and the university, which include the following ideas:

(i) There being implicit in human speech acts an *ideal speech situation* (1991: 25), that participants are not just exuding mere grunts but are attempting seriously to communicate; that such communicative action presupposes

certain validity claims, namely those of truthfulness, sincerity and appropriateness (1991: 278).
(ii) That culture is 'the stock of knowledge from which participants in communication supply themselves with interpretations as they come to an understanding [of] the world' (1989: 138).

These two planks are sufficient for our purposes, but we should note two further points that Habermas makes:

(iii) The 'lifeworld' – where 'culture' is to be found – is liable to colonization by instrumental reason (1989: 354–5).
(iv) The rational life is guided by 'the force of the better argument' (1991: 25).

Collectively, these four points offer reasonably sturdy foundations for a *universal* theory of culture and the university. There is a universal link between culture and the university, and it is right in front of us, it being embedded in the idea of the university as an institution that institutionalizes reason through its inner ethical core. In practice, it may fall away from grace but – as an idea, at least – the university is an institution founded on communication guided by universal principles of truthfulness, sincerity and appropriateness. This set of *ethical* norms is not just to be found in the deep structure of the communicative life of the university but is the narrative that the university and its members tell of themselves. The principles of rational and ethical communication are emblazoned in the flag that flies over the university. *The culture of the university turns out to be none other than a universal set of ethical foundations to collective reasoning.*

The university, then, is the institutionalization of ethically rooted reason *and* is, thereby, a space of reason within the wider society. As such, this culture – of ethically based communication – becomes a field of 'social action' (Honneth, 1993): despite its fissiparous and warring tendencies, its inner critique has the extraordinary quality of binding it together, through the commitment to the ethical values inherent in that communicative framework.

But is there not more to the matter? If this is all there is to the issue of university and culture, surely it would have been noticed before now. What was the basis of Readings' concerns, and before him the quite different voices of Nietzsche (for whom universities were 'forcing houses for . . . spiritual instinct-atrophy' (2003: 73)) and Ortega (1946)? Were they misguided, in failing to notice what was there all along, and that the dominant culture of the university is the bringing into institutional form the universal and ethical substrate of human interaction?

Their concerns were really real, for they were pointing to actual deformations: the university was and *still is* falling short of its self-understandings.

Certainly, this falling short has taken different forms. For Nietzsche, it was a failure of will, a desiccation of spirit, a barrenness of life. For Ortega, it was a loss of vitality that had accrued with the professionalization of the university and its disintegration into separate disciplines. For Readings, it was the incorporation of the university as such, having been bound into the machinery of the state, and the bureaucratization that had ensued. And further such critiques can be sighted among yet more recent commentaries, for example in Virilio's (2010) *University of Disaster*, bewitched by the speed of the internet, and Stiegler's work (2014b, 2015) detecting a loss of spirit, as the university has allowed itself to be co-opted into a non-thinking 'stupidity'. All these critical commentaries – and others could be cited (such as Heidegger and Derrida) – are proffered by those who are on the side of the university but who sense that it has lost its inner spirit.

The Habermassian option, then, of a discourse ethics lying universally within language, has to be declared insufficient. First, it is counterfactual in that the university, the very institution that might have been held as being the institution of reason, has been undermined, or even could be said to have undermined itself. But note the nature of this undermining. It is not that the university has become an institution of anti-reason as such. Rather, it is that reason in the university – especially over the last three-quarters of a century – has turned on the fulcrum of *instrumental* reason. This point is central in Habermas's oeuvre, which is that instrumental reason has colonized communicative reason. Reason is merely a means to an external end, no longer guided by the force of the better argument but by its likely 'impact'. But this critique may be extended.

Our quest is that of a universal idea of culture that can both sensibly form a strong link to the university and that will be appropriate to the twenty-first century. The problem of the university, in cultural terms, is not only that it no longer has a sense of the value of knowledge as its own end (Newman's (1976) position), or that knowledge is being put to purposes beyond itself (Habermas' position). Rather it is that reason is not being put to ends that generate *spirit* (Stiegler's position). The university is a desiccated institution.

We have encountered a profound turn in our inquiry. The instrumental reason that has come to characterize the university has put the university into a state of *entropy*. It is gradually being drained of spirit and is literally declining. How might we explain this situation? It is that the instrumentalism to which the university has aligned itself is leading to a gradual loss of energy *in* the university itself. This instrumentalism posits an end that is separate from knowing. It is an extrinsic end that cannot retain a will to know indefinitely. This is not a universal situation. In specific cases, this will to know can be motivated by an external end. One seeks to know in order to produce a cure for a cancer. But, as a general principle, inquiry in the hope that there may be solely a material end lacks motivational power.

Initially, in the forming of an academic identity, not least in a competitive career setting, there can be motivational power. But as one's career and position are secured, and as pressing problems are 'solved', so this instrumentalism loses its hold and a state of entropy ensues. The situation that Stiegler so correctly diagnoses (the university falling into a state of entropy) is, therefore, entirely explicable. There is a rupture between the drive to understand and its end. Moreover, the end may not be linked to human beings as such. The scientist seeking a cure for cancer can identify with its end. But that is a contingent association and is not always available. Fundamentally, we are faced with a situation – given the incorporation of the university into cognitive capitalism (Roggero, 2011) – in which the academic or the student is separated from finding personal meaning in their cognitive labours.

Readings was right but not for the reason he supplied. The university has become an institution that is not just separated from culture but is *anti*-culture. Its instrumentalism is a repudiation of culture, for its instrumentalism separates the knower from ends. Academic life becomes – to use an old category – a species of alienated labour. No wonder that so often one hears laments about the academic work being lifeless, dull, predictable, formulaic and lacking in originality; and one hears too of a loss of morale. If culture is an internalized system of value, and one that supplies inner meaning, then the present system of academic labour is *devoid of culture* and malevolently so. Lyotard (1984) implied as much in observing that what mattered was not the (internal) truth value of a claim but rather whether a truth claim possessed an (external) value: 'what use is it?' (p51) has come to be the dominant question.

A Culture of the Earth

The fundamental question is now even more complicated: *Is there a way of attaching the idea of culture to the university so as to provide (1) a universal umbrella under which the university's myriad of specific cultures can sit that might also generate (2) a positive spirit, able to nourish and provide meaning to, and sustain energies in, (3) the university and (4) its members that also (5) link the university ethically to the whole world?* Within this question, therefore, are *five conditions of a suitable meta-culture* for the university in the twenty-first century.

The answer – and it is *the* answer – is in front of us, and yet we do not see it. It is the Earth. Over the past sixty years or more, the Earth has turned into a cause, and has taken off with considerable velocity. The cause is evident in the ideas of Gaia, the Anthropocene, autopoiesis (or self-reproduction), sustainability and the Ecocene, and also in global green movements and transnational political agreements. Prompted by a sense of 'global warming' and 'climate crisis', the time of the Earth has come (Latour, 2019). Universities are responding around the world, in teaching, research and scholarship and in their outreach; and their corporate strategies display a keen interest in the United Nations' Sustainable Development Goals, a heightened sensitivity to indigenous peoples (in a region), and a determination to exhibit a 'greening of the campus'. And in all of this ideological and practical fervour, it is often students who are the driving force: after all, their future is at stake.

We have here the makings of *a culture of the Earth* or, to put it less poetically, an *ecological culture* (cf Bendik-Keymer, 2006; Plumwood, 2008; Descola, 2013). Whereas instrumentalism leads to entropy and a dissolution of energy, this ecological culture can constitute – to use a term of Bernard Stiegler's (2014a) – a *negentropy*. It can *negate* the present entropy and supply a new – and positive – spirit to the university and a spirit, at that, that *ethically* connects the university not just to society or even just to the world, but to the whole Earth. This ecological culture is already demonstrating its capacity to catch fire. It is an emergent culture for it is always opening and widening, and taking on new forms, as it leads to new interpretations, and sightings of new possibilities (in teaching, learning, research, scholarship and outreach). Now unleashed, it is never quiescent.

The university is a natural home for this ecological culture. The care for the whole Earth that lies at its heart can find expression in research, teaching, assessment, academic writing and the university's forays into the wider world. It can show itself across the *eight major ecosystems* with which the university is entangled – of knowledge, learning, social institutions, the polity, the economy, the natural environment, individuals as such and culture itself (Barnett, 2018). It can be present in policies and projects that the university pursues, both on a transnational basis *and* in the smallest crevices of its activities. Accordingly – in its universality, positive spirit, institutional potential, identity formation and ethical Earthly reach – this ecological culture is a culture that can meet *all five* of the conditions of a suitable meta-culture just adumbrated.

In this specification of an ecological culture for the university, two linked points should be made. First, the natural environment cannot be privileged, urgent though its claims are. For the natural environment seriously to become a major focus of the university's attention (as it should), all the other seven ecosystems have to come into play too. Second, *if* any of those eight ecosystems are to be favoured, it is those of knowledge and learning, for it is especially through knowledge and learning that individuals and institutions will come to possess the wherewithal through which a culture of care for the whole Earth can find expression. Opening here, therefore, is a call for an institutionalized 'ecoliteracy' across the universities of the world, as part of a wide 'ecopedagogy' movement (Kahn, 2010).

Against the background of these first four chapters, there are elephant traps in front of the idea of a culture of the Earth as an overarching culture for the university. It may have lots of energy imparting momentum to it but that very energy can easily turn into an ideology, a totalitarianism on campus, assured of its own righteousness (Charbonneau, 2018). A separate danger is the reverse: this culture will be tolerated by the big powers and channelled into non-dangerous and limited spaces, where it simply has to fend for itself amid the myriad of other cultures on campus. The two cautions are connected for the first possibility may lead to the second: undue fervour may lead to impotence. A culture of the Earth has it within itself to become a universal culture of the academy but it will need, therefore, considerable academic-political nous. Admittedly, it is not at all clear that matters will allow it to move in that measured way.

Conclusions

The story of culture and the university has had two different plots but they formed a single impression: any sense of there being a culture that can unify the university and higher education *and* also help to sustain a broad culture in the wider world is now passé. *On the one hand*, the forlorn (Ortega-Readings) thesis that the link between culture and the university is now severed, the university having been swept up into the apparatuses of the world, and so become devoid of culture. *On the other hand*, the democratic vista espies dozens of cultures on campus, across students, the faculty and the administration. The university is a site of multiple, small, introverted – and often mutually hostile – cultures. Culture wars are evident on campus and are growing in their range and intensity.

I have suggested that *both* viewpoints – cultural universality and cultural relativism – have legitimacy. Placed together, however, they produce a cognitive illusion, in one moment one depiction, and another moment the other, and no way of adjudicating them. However, if we deploy the Moebius strip as a metaphor (cf. Zizek, 2009: 4), the ambiguity dissolves. The human reason within the university naturally opens to *multifarious* frameworks of understanding, but to secure their legitimacy, each framework has to submit to the tribunal of collective reason and the *universal* discourse ethics within it. One depiction runs into the other, and so on in a continuing cycle. The two positions are not counter *to* each other: we do not have to choose between them. They can be held together, even if uncomfortably.

We are, though, left with the question that these chapters have provoked, particularly by the parallels in Chapter 3 between culture and ideology: *Is there the possibility of an ideology – a cultural ideagy as we may term it* (Barnett, 2003) *– that might catch fire across universities and provide them with a worldly spirit*? My suggestion has been that just such a culture is at hand, namely an *ecological culture*. At its centre would be a strong sense of the claims of the Earth in toto. This culture of the Earth would be sensitive to the (eight) major ecosystems with which the university is entangled, not only those of the natural environment and the economy but also those of knowledge, social institutions, learning, individuals, the polity and culture itself. Each university is intertwined with all of these ecosystems.

There are the makings here of a *five-way universal culture* for universities across the world: it respects the discourse ethics universally within human communication; it straddles all universities and their internal cultures; it is sensitive to the deep structures of universities in the world; it is sensitive to the cultural potential of higher education as a process of personal human development; and it reflects a universal interest (of all peoples) in this Earth. This is utopian but it is an eminently feasible utopia (Barnett, 2018), with many movements in these directions being seen across universities, and across their students, faculty and administrators and the wider cross-national higher education environment. In this culture of the Earth, a set of universal connections between universities and culture may just be glimpsed. Only one question remains: Is it too late?

Part II

Designing for Cultural Places

Rikke Nørgård

5

Placeful Cultures and Cultural Places

Introduction

Culture is a central pillar in our lives; we live through and *do* culture in every moment and wherever we go. Culture frames our thinking, doing and being as university scholars, students, researchers, teachers or leaders. And, in turn, the thinking, doing and being of these diverse members of the university creates its culture. When a new student or leader sets foot on a campus for the first time, a reciprocal relationship of affecting culture and being affected by culture is established. The culture of a particular university as well as the culture of the university as a conceptual whole impact how we communicate, act and interact as academic collectives and communities.

This is true even when it comes to the architecture and the buildings of the university, which stand as cultural expressions of the way the university exists, engages and relates to people, society and the world. That is how the university lives in and sees the world. However, the study of culture, especially relating to the construction industry is nascent, and so cultural processes and the consequences of culture, or the consequences on culture, are paramount but not, as yet, very well understood (Fellows and Lui, 2013: 401). This lack of understanding of how architecture, place-making and culture are deeply intertwined is problematic, as we become unable to critically comprehend the cultures that are created in and through the design and architecture of the university and the places for academic cultures they offer. Hofstede stresses that what binds successful organizations, institutions or corporations together – or, here, the idea of the university – is not a unified 'corporate culture' but, rather, shared cultural practices (Hofstede, 2002: 6). Accordingly, some scholars have proposed treating 'culture' as a verb (Street, 1993; Wax, 1993), while others propose the adjective 'cultural' to allow for more multifarious, diverse and heterogeneous understandings of how cultures are created and shared (Appadurai, 1997; Fellows and Lui, 2013). The university as an institution of *culturing* as well as a place for the *culturing* practices of academics, then, becomes a cultural actor through its practices of places and place-making. This implies that the university 'has no existence apart from the succession of practices that instantiate, reproduce, or – most interestingly – transform it' (Sewell, 1999: 47). In this way, the university becomes a cultural and culturing institution through the spaces, sites and places it offers as a lifeworld for its members. And, conversely, the members of the university are culturing it as a particular place and lifeworld through their practices of thinking, being and doing.

From this intertwining of, on the one hand, culture as an institutional sphere devoted to the making of *place-bound* meaning and, on the other hand, universities as places for the cultural practice of its members, emerges the *placeful cultures* of the university. According to Sewell, culture as an institutional sphere is devoted specifically to the production, circulation and use of meanings: 'The study of culture, if culture is defined in this way, is the study of the activities that take place within these institutionally defined spheres and of the meanings produced in them' (Sewell, 1999: 41). Conversely, culture as academic practice highlights culture as something emerging from the various practices of the members within an institution or community and is characterized by wilful action, power relations, struggle, contradiction and change. Seen through the performative term of culturing, culture is not a coherent or stable system of symbols and meanings, but a means for the performance of meaning, action and place-making (Sewell, 1999). In this intersection between the institution as culturing place and the members as culturing agents, the university as space, site and place of and for culture emerges.

This chapter will, through theories and philosophies of place, approach the university as socio-material culture and placeful concept. Importantly, this does not imply that culture is *built* or made up of architecture and buildings. Rather, the university is a cultural *place* for the academic being and becoming of students, teachers, researchers, managers, leaders and everyone else living within the university. Concrete and conceptual at the same time. From this follows that specific university sites, such as campuses, research centres, department buildings, libraries, lecture halls and canteens, are not culture, but sites *of* and *for* culture. As a whole, they constitute the many spaces within which the university and its members take place:

> This much is true for place: we are immersed in it and could not do without it. To be at all – to exist in any way – is to be somewhere, and to be somewhere is to be in some kind of place. [. . .] Nothing we do is unplaced. (Casey, 1997: ix)

A somewhat similar perspective on universities is found in Nixon (2008), Strain et al. (2009) or Temple (2019), who, in different ways, highlight that universities embody certain ethics as institutions or places and express them as virtuous academic culture. Viewed from a place-based philosophical perspective, the university as a *site* for culturing, then, constitutes an inextricable material link between universities, members and culture. To be or become an academic and to take part in academic culture, one needs a place of belonging that merges thinking and doing, architecture and articulation, individual and culture, by inviting institutions and members to dwell *place-fully* within each other.

However, at present there seems to be a disconnect between the conceptual and concrete dimensions of the university. On the one hand, accounts of the university as a built environment describe in detail the concrete campus, the university as space and site, its architectural styles and layout, building materials and concrete learning environment, but hardly mention the university as cultural place for thinking and becoming (Temple, 2019). On the other hand, theories and philosophy of higher education and the university seldom consider the university as space, site or place beyond conceptual ideas, frameworks or models (Temple, 2019). That is, the question of how culture becomes embedded into the university by way of spatial layouts, architectural design, geographic locality and place-making is left in the dark. Such disconnect between the conceptual and concrete realms of the university runs the risk of turning the university into a *non-place* (Augé, 1995).

Both a university constructed as a functional space devoid of placeful cultures and a university conceptualized as imagined space without cultural places put both institutions and members in danger of being *unplaced* (Casey, 1997). The university as a cultural place and placeful culture needs to connect the conceptual (thinking) and the concreteness (site) of its being into a *lived place* (Lefebvre, 1991) in order for its members to feel connectedness and care for the university itself (Temple, 2019).

The University as a Place for Culture

From a perspective of culture and the university as the intertwining of conceptual idea and concrete site, the university as a place for culture emerges from the intersections of conceptual space, concrete site and cultural place to form a lifeworld for its members. Importantly, neither place nor culture exist outside the members of the university, but is produced through the culturing entanglement of emplacing, place-making, emotional attachments and imbued sites of affiliation. Humans pass through space (non-place), but inhabit place (Augé, 1995; Creswell, 2004; Tuan, 1977). As space, the university functions much like a map of a campus, a collection of coordinates to navigate or a row of numbered rooms. The university as space is like corridors one passes through to move from one site or lifeworld to another. In this way, the university is not where life or culture happens, but a space of traversal. If we position *real* life, *real* work or *real* culture as something that takes place outside or away from the university, it becomes nothing more than a temporal or spatial corridor one passes through in order to get an education, get a job, go home, manage a project, go to a meeting or carry out teaching. The university as space is not a cultural place, but, rather, a means to other ends.

The university as place, on the other hand, is defined by being an inhabited environment, much like a home: 'Enclosed and humanized space is place. Compared to space, place is a calm center of established values. [. . .] When space feels thoroughly familiar to us, it has become place' (Tuan, 1977: 54). If the university does not materialize itself as a place for its members, it runs the risk of being a space where its members are *people out of place* or *persona non locata* much like refugees, passers-by, expats, displaced or other people without place (Cresswell, 2004: 13). For the university to become a cultural place and a place for culture, it needs, first, to be transformed from immaterial space (concept) to inhabitable site (world). Second, it needs to become a vitalized and vibrant heterogeneous place for culturing (cultural place).

Here, Lefebvre's *The Production of Space* (1991) comes to mind. Lefebvre called for the decolonization of places to reclaim the places of everyday life and culture. For Lefebvre, this could be accomplished through insurgent counter-discourses based on new practices of and in cultural places. Cultural or concrete places, for Lefebvre (1991), signifies a bottom-up reaction to those institutional systems whose dominance have degraded *smooth* sensed place to *striated* abstract space. To (re)vitalize university space and transform it into cultural place, it and its members need to challenge the striated space through counter-discourse and recapture the university as smooth place or placeful culture:

> Places have power sui generis, all apart from powerful people or organisations who occupy them: the capacity to dominate and control people or things comes through the geographic location, built-form, and symbolic meanings of a place. The array of building-types is, on this score, also a catalogue of how places differently become terrains of powers [. . .] spaces become the focus of

government [or institutional] development policies, and control of territory is one measure of effective state sovereignty. Place enables power to travel, to extend its reach over people and territory. (Gieryn, 2000: 475–6)

Following from this, the place-making of heterogeneous cultural place becomes vital for our thinking, being and doing at the university. The university must make the values of inhabited culture evident through materializing places of and for culture. To inhabit the university as cultural place is to experience being in the centre of culture without necessarily being placed in the centre of the university: 'Just as I am in the dwelling that is also in me, so I feel *centered* by being within the dwelling in which I reside – orienting myself by what is around me – while I am also *centering* insofar as I give direction to things and rooms in that same dwelling' (Casey, 1997: 293–4). In this way, the intertwinement of place and culture has an intricate existential effect on the academic lifeworld of the university. It is a more complex relation than the relation between university space or architecture on the one hand and the idea of the university and university culture on the other hand.

The connection between culture, place and the idea of the university, points towards the creation of *placeful cultures* through which all three are united and transformed. Temple (2019) suggests that we consider the ways in which university space becomes university place, through the transformation of space into site and site into place leading to the creation of cultural place and placeful culture. Similarly, Foucault points towards exploring institutional practices that embed and express culture through the entanglements between 'private space and public space, between family space and social space, between cultural space and useful space, between the space of leisure and that of work' (Foucault, 1986: 23) as a way of encountering universities as heterotopic places, counter-sites and placeful cultures.

Taking central philosophies of space and place (Creswell, 2004; Casey, 1997; Tuan, 1977; Lefebvre, 1991 and others) as a point of departure, we come to appreciate the connections between culture and the university and apprehend the university as cultural place and placeful culture.

Understanding the University as Space, Place and Site

When we think of space, we often think of coordinates, geometry, areas, volumes, spatial layouts and so on. Such abstract space is transformed into place as it acquires definition, value, meaning and culture (Tuan, 1974). That is, when people invest meaning in a portion of space and become attached to and invested in it (culture is one such way), it becomes a place: 'What begins as undifferentiated space becomes place as we get to know it better and endow it with value' (Tuan, 1977: 6). Places are what people make out of spaces (Temple, 2019). While we *observe* space or *use* sites, we *live* in (cultural) places and create them through the production of culture. In this way, places also connect us with the world and each other – they are places *for particular someones* and *for particular somethings*. They are cultural lifeworlds. Space on the other hand is extrapersonal and abstract: 'space has no trodden paths and signposts. It has no fixed patterns of established human meaning; it is like a blank sheet on which meaning may be imposed [...] humanized space is place' (Tuan, 1977: 54).

Whether we approach the university as space (abstract idea, geometric grid or spatial layout), site (architectural or localized space) or place (experienced or liveable world) has crucial implications for the formation of culture. One current challenge comes from the tendency for space to conquer or abolish place (Friedman, 2005) that turns the university into a non-place and makes its members unplaced. From this perspective, placeless universities such as the global online university or the purely architectonic campus become a void (space) or vessel (site) to its members, in effect dissolving the university as place and placeful culture. Here, the university as placeful culture is being lost at the expense of an increasingly homogenous and displacing sameness, where the university come to have affinity to other non-places such as airports, shopping malls or global corporations. Through this assimilation of place into space, its members are transmuted into visitors or travellers finding themselves subjected to what Augé (1995) calls 'a life in nowhere land'.

In *Place and Politics* (1987), Agnew puts forward three fundamental dimensions of space/place: location (space), locale (site) and sense of place (place). First, the university can be said to be located in space. That is, it has fixed objective coordinates on the Earth's surface. The university can be found on a map; it has an address and it is a specific localizable *where*. Second, the university is a venue or material setting for culture in the form of architecture within which people conduct their lives as members (Cresswell, 2004) – the university has a material form through its buildings and campus and is in this way an occupiable *site*. Third, the university can be or become a place for people to experience and produce culture. Here, the university becomes a habitat or lifeworld through its ability to create meaning, culture and belonging. By *sense of place*, Agnew points to the experiential, emotional and cultural attachments people can form with places (Agnew, 1987). Consequently, when people move from an experience of the university as a *where* (space or site) to a *being there* (place), the university is transformed from placeless to placeful (Nørgård and Bengtsen, 2016).

Place, then, is not merely a backdrop or a context for culture to unfold, but, rather, place becomes an agentic participant in culture – a culturing force with decisive and form-giving effect on the culture that takes place there. Place saturates cultural life and is a medium through which culture takes place: 'places are made through human practices and institutions even as they help to make those practices and institutions' (Gieryn, 2000: 467). Places can make or break culture and the university through the cultural practices, meanings and values people integrate in and deduce from place. In this way, we can have places – and, hence, university cultures – that are racist, misogynist, threatening, sexist, class-divided, colonial and oppressive (or the opposite). For better or worse, *remarkable* places make for *remarkable* culture through giving form and expressive force to the idea and experience of the university: 'Architectural space reveals and instructs' (Tuan, 1977: 114). The university as a site for academic cultural being is ideologically informed by ideas of how a university should appear, the ideas its architectural style ought to stimulate in the observer, the behaviour its organizational or hierarchal style should evoke as well as the relative (un)importance of different academic activities and so on (Temple, 2019).

The university as placeful culture shapes, mutates and grows thinking into a certain kind of cultural being. As such, intimate connections exist between the places we inhabit and our thinking, doing and being within them. Academic cultures interlink with architecture and architecture interlink with academic cultures. The university as cultural place has – through this architectural emplacement of thinking, doing and being – the capacity to dominate and manage people and culture. As such, the university as cultural site becomes a *terrain of power* resulting in either cultural engagement or cultural estrangement (Gieryn, 2000) where the architectural importance of the university as cultural place resides in its ability to invite for cultural transformation through careful agencing of place and event (Tschumi, 1994). The construction of the university as cultural place is at the same time the execution of a community (for better or worse) that epitomizes a place-sensitive perspective on the university as placeful culture and cultural place. The architecture or built environment of the university (site) intervenes in the culturing of the university as well as its collective idea and identity. Like police maintaining order by patrolling neighbourhoods or restricting access to them, so too can the university maintain bureaucratic control by monitoring and determining culture through designing *policing sites*, deciding who and what properly belongs. It is the culturing power of this *taking place* that makes the university as space or site come alive and become a placeful culture for thinking, doing and being together. The university needs to carefully *produce place* (Lefebvre, 1991) in order to *have* culture.

Beyond Buildings: The University as Placeful Culture

Architectural sites such as universities could, according to Foucault, produce positive effects only when the *liberating intentions* of architecture coincide with the real practices of people in the exercise of their freedom (Foucault, 1986). To achieve this, universities need to be transformed from indifferent *any-where*, *any-thing* and *any*-body abstract space to heterogeneous places filled with qualitative multiplicities. Universities as places of and for culturing are intimate contact points between *some-where*, *some-thing* and *some-body*. Becoming a placeful culture is the enactment of a 'polyvocality of directions' (Casey, 1997: 303–4). For the university to acquire or have placeful culture, it must provide site-specific and placeful *vitalizing academic events* of culturing to its members. This can be in the form of academic festivals, student-owned squares or buildings, experimental and co-constructed classrooms or co-operatively run research centres. Through this, the university not only takes place but also gives place by creating room (metaphorically as well as literally) for things to happen through culturing practices.

Taken together, the university as placeful culture carries with it a particular open-ended cultural world and moral order (Tuan, 1974). Through this, the university as placeful culture executes certain virtues, holds sacred purpose and defines *fields of care* with which collectives and communities identify and distinguish themselves from (cultural) others (Tuan, 1974). Through culturing the site and turning it into an inhabitable liveable place, the university simultaneously opens its members up to the culture of the university and opens itself up to be cultured in return. Through this, the university as a cultural place and place for cultures is a prerequisite for subsequent cultural belonging and academic communities. As such, university culture is a *place-making* project where place provides both the cultural setting and site within which new academic ideas, thinking and being develop.

Beyond buildings, the university as place impacts what and how we think as well as what we do and how we act practically as well as academically. The loss of place, it follows, has devastating implications for individual and collective identity, action, sense of belonging and culture (Gieryn, 2000). The challenge then, for the university, is the difficulty of (re)generating place and (re)producing cultures to manifest itself as a placeful culture for academic belonging, cohesiveness and togetherness. Or, as Temple (2009: 218) puts it: 'The creation of a community and its culture turns, I suggest, the university space into a place.' The built environment of and the idea of the university oscillate into a certain cultural and culturing place that is put forward as an invitation for people to interact with and within the university in certain ways. Through this practice of oscillating place-making, university sites are transformed from traversal spaces to cultural places (Creswell, 2004; Tuan, 1977; Nørgård and Bengtsen, 2016).

Following Creswell (2004) and Tuan (1977), the university has the potential of becoming a lifeworld beyond bricks and buildings, through the ways it offers itself as a lived place:

> [P]lace is also a way of seeing, knowing and understanding the world. When we look at the world as a world of places we see different things. We see attachments and connections between people and places. We see worlds of meaning and experience [. . .] To think of an area of the world as rich and complicated interplay of people and the environment – as a place – is to free us from thinking of it as facts and figures. (Creswell, 2004: 11)

Lived places, such as universities – when they constitute placeful cultures, encompass cultural values, resonances and history that enable members to co-construct individual and collective meaning (Temple, 2019). The university as a cultured and culturing place can be likened to Lefebvre's (1991) concept of *perceived space* which is revealed through the everyday life and practices that go on in a place as well as Deleuze and Guattari's *smooth space* (Deleuze and Guattari, 1988) or Amin and Thrift's notion of *flesh and stone in interaction* (Amin and Thrift, 2002: 10). Placeful cultures in smooth places stand in opposition to striated space governed by fixed schemata and organized through determinability, linear striation, monofocal perspective, recognizability, controllability and homogeneity. Such striated architectural spaces are simultaneously *nowhere* and *anywhere*. (Deleuze and Guattari, 1988; Casey, 1997). Here, the university as heterogeneous placeful culture becomes eradicated through the totalitarianism of uniform striated space which in turn diminishes or eradicates the particular cultural spirit, virtue, thinking or being that is living within the campus, department, discipline or academic collective. The university as non-place, striated space or pure architectural site vanquishes the university as placeful culture. Conversely, cultural smooth place is irregular, heterogeneous, polyvocal, particular, tactile, multifaceted, unruly and *something somewhere* for *someone* to be lived through. Such heterogeneous liveability is 'the very basis of the constitution and experience of smooth space [. . .] one moves not only efficiently but intensely' (Casey, 1997: 305). The sense of place, the university as placeful culture, arises from the synthesis of the living body of its members and the salient cultural thinking, being and doing of that place. The cultural place of the university must be experienced at close range and through a deterritorialization of *the space of sites*.

While the university as architectural site 'sell "style" that – when built-in – becomes the look or feel that people associate with a place [. . . Place] arranges patterns of face-to-face interaction that constitute network-formation and collective action [. . .] fundamental social classification take on an imposing and contrasting force as they are built into everyday material places' (Gieryn, 2000: 471–4). To emerge as placeful culture, the university must move from the idea of architecture as style and striated space towards the idea of architecture as placeful event or *happening* that continues to take place and give place even after it is built (Derrida, 1997). To create place for culture in architecture is to create sites for culturing to take place through architectural *spacing* (Derrida, 1997). To open the site for its members to engage the university as culture and allow them to take over the university as place through culturing and to be taken be over by the university as culturing place. In this way, a festival, a co-operative or a co-constructed campus square is something simultaneously culturing the university and its members.

The university beyond buildings, then, does not occupy place but provides place for culture to happen. And in so doing, it creates a placeful culture for its members to be *spaced out* in it (Derrida, 1997; Casey, 1997). Rather, than being confined by a site or building, cultural places (or architectural event-making) is expansive: 'The subject spaces out in the very building that, in the course of its own *espacement*, "makes place for the event". In so doing, building and subject alike let the event take place: they bring it to eplacement, find place for it' (Casey, 1997: 315). Through allowing for architectural spacing out beyond buildings the university as placeful culture can emerge as a place that bears the signature of both culture and its members in its design, construction and practice. The aim for university as culture, then, is to move towards place in all its heterogeneity, jagged imperfection, polyvocal locality and deterritorialized espacement. Place is not a building; it is somewhere *to be* and *to be found* through an excess of spacing out (Casey, 1997). Consequently, the university as placeful culture is *eventmental* (Casey, 1997), in process and unconfinable to a building or site.

Through placeful culture, the university comes into being all over the place, not just here or there, but as a somewhere everywhere. And, so, to live through the university as cultural place is to be in and of that place. Through taking up place by way of place-making, university culture becomes revalorized. But, the university as cultural place and place for culture can easily be lost. When places become appropriated or expropriated as striated space or closed-in closed-down managed sites, place evaporates into geometrical, functional, bare locational or traversal space destitute of depth, life and culture. The university closes in on itself and regresses back to being a building. Its spirit – placeful culture – is lost.

Conclusions: Cultural Place/Placeful Cultures

This chapter has argued that the university needs to be a place for and of culture – a placeful culture – through integrating individual and institutional, architectural and ecological as well as conceptual and concrete cultural spheres for culturing thinking, being and doing. This interweaving creates a place for culture as a value-saturated and place-making *event*. The university as placeful culture needs to *give place* for culturing and *take place* through culturing in order to materialize itself as a vibrant and vitalized lifeworld for cultural academic being. Place-making – the becoming of place – makes culture manifest itself through dialogical integration of people and places. Here, the university as smooth sensed place becomes a being *of* culture and *for* culture. Through shedding striated functional space and opening up its terrain of power for its members to engage in cultural processes of place-making, the university can be the place through which culture happens.

The university as cultural place is not a building but a purposeful lifeworld for a heterogeneous collective of people to drive culture and the university forward. Here, the university is in itself a lived purpose, a cultural place-making entity that creates a place for culture through becoming a something for someone somewhere – a place worth living. It is a humanized place that shapes, transmutes and grows heterogeneous thinking into a certain kind of university being and opens itself – as place – up to its members so they can form emotional, experiential and existential bonds with it. Such place-making, spacing out, decolonization and deterritorialization, as presented in this chapter, offers opportunities for the university to exist, do and think as culturing and cultural being.

This is in contrast to the *hegemony* of striated institutional space – a system's exercise of managerial power over the idea of the university and its members – that grows from the instrumentalization, homogenization, compartmentalization, colonization and functional systematization of university space. This hegemony weighs down on academic life and university culture – it systematizes, uniformizes and rationalizes on the backdrop of neoliberal institutional logic – in effect flattening the academic sphere, diluting university thinking, doing and being and transforming cultural place into a number of sites, buildings and rooms (Arndt et al., 2021; Lefebvre, 1991).

If people's place-making activities are rejected by the university as managed space and site, they end up experiencing themselves as *persona non locata* – homeless and unplaced without or outside both culture and the university (Gieryn, 2000; Augé, 1995; Casey, 1997). Consequently, the university as place is meaningful to the extent that its members can dwell in it, have a sense of (co) ownership of it and feel agency in relation to it. Or, as Lefebvre puts it in *The Production of Space* (1991):

> It is within place that time consumes and devours living beings, thus giving reality to sacrifice, pleasure and pain. Abstract space, the space of the bourgeoisie and of capitalism, bound up as it is with the exchange (of goods and commodities, as of written and spoken words etc.) depends on consensus more than any space before it [. . .] So long everyday life remains in thrall to abstract space, with its very concrete constraints; so long as the only improvements to occur are technical improvements of detail (for example, the frequency and speed of transportation, or relatively better amenities); so long, in short, as the only connection between work spaces, leisure spaces and living spaces is supplied by the agencies of political power and by the mechanisms of control – so long must the project of 'changing life' remain no more than a political rallying cry to be taken up or abandoned according to the mood of the moment. (Lefebvre, 1991: 57–9)

To nurture and sustain more liveable universities and vitalized academic culture – and counter the overall effect of losing cultured and culturing academic place to abstract institutional non-place – the university, however, needs not only a culture of place-making but also a cultural and culturing *atmosphere* that affects and inspires both universities and members to immerse themselves in what it means to think, do and be as and in a cultural university. The concept of atmosphere and atmospheric design in relation to culture and the university will be the main focus of the next chapter.

6

The Atmospheric University and Cultural Atmospheres

Introduction

In 'The concept of culture and higher education' (1996) Maassen highlights the analysis of organizational culture as a critical element in the study of higher education institutions. This implies a focus on the non-rational, symbolic and what Maassen calls the *atmospheric design* of university life. In a similar vein, Hardy (1990) argues that when it comes to the cultural life of universities, higher education research tends to take an atheoretical, quantitative, functional or objectivistic approach. Both suggest that studies addressing culture and the university needs to be more thoroughly grounded in the existing literature on culture as well as better to account for the affective, symbolic and bodily dimensions of culture. Before investigating and describing dimensions of culture and the university such as organizational culture, educational culture or academic culture, we need first to indicate both the concept of culture and its theoretical underpinnings as well as a particular philosophical or theoretical approach to culture and the university.

In the present chapter, the approach taken to culture and the university is based on theories of atmosphere, atmospheric design and cultural atmosphere. This particular perspective helps us to see culture of the university as something that, on the one hand, envelops and affects the experience and existence of everyone that comes in contact with it (like an atmosphere), and, on the other hand, can be intentionally produced and designed in such a way that it forms a cultural atmosphere that safeguard the attitudes, principles and values of the university and its members. This is in line with Maassen's (1996: 158) definition of academic culture as 'the set of attitudes, beliefs, and values that integrates a specific group of academics [which can be used] to analyze the impact of governmental policies or steering strategies, disciplinary aspects, the academic profession at large, or the institutional context on the academic culture'. But, before unpacking the conceptual framework of atmosphere, atmospheric design and cultural atmosphere, we will first, in adherence with the above caution, pay closer attention to the notion of culture in the context of *the atmospheric university*.

The University as Cultural Atmosphere

Culture is a complex whole, something experienced by all people in all social groups, organizations or communities. In the context of the atmospheric university, it is related to the so-called affective turn that has been 'extremely fruitful for understanding affective and emotional aspects of human lives as they unfold through space' (Bille, 2018: 1). Here, atmosphere is positioned as that which radiates culture and lifeworld to the members of a certain place or organization. Atmospheres are world shapers through emanating the culture of an institution (Bille, 2018; Böhme, 2017). The members of the institution experience the cultural atmosphere as 'the collective programming of the mind which distinguishes the members of one group or category of people from another' (Hofstede, 1994: 5). The university as cultural atmosphere, then, constitutes an atmospheric design that radiates assumptions, attitudes, values, orientations to life, beliefs, policies, procedures, conventions and so forth to its members and influences each member's thinking, behaviour and being in that space, institution or group (Spencer-Oatey, 2008). In this way, each university posits its own cultural atmosphere that in turn affects the experience, existence and practice of its members in distinctive ways. The cultural layer that new members of an institution, such as a university, get in contact with is its atmospheric design:

> When one enters an organization one observes and feels its artifacts. This category includes everything from the physical [or digital] layout, the dress code, the manner in which people address each other, the smell and feel of the place, its emotional intensity, and other phenomena, to the more permanent archival manifestations such as company records, products, statements of philosophy, and annual reports. (Schein, 1990: 111)

In the context of atmosphere and atmospheric design, cultures should be thought of as integrated wholes or organized environments that come together to constitute a specific atmosphere wherein its members breathe, feel, think and exists. Consequently, the introduction of a new university strategy, the integration of new technologies, the construction of a new building, the redesign of a lecture hall or the implementation of a policy on gender might set off a cascade of interrelated changes transforming the whole atmosphere and culture of the institution (Ferraro, 1998).

Cultural meaning is constructed through socio-material interactions, and leaves atmosphere-generating traces in the form of artefacts, designs, organizational structures and institutions that then come to constitute an atmosphere for future interaction, thinking and culture. Culture becomes an atmospheric experience and 'embedded [. . .] in objects and organizations' (Lechner and Boli, 2005: 16). Here, the atmospheric design of the university becomes a blueprint of past cultural constructions and for future cultural interactions, meaning making and academic culture (Andersen-Levitt, 2012). Importantly, Hofstede (1994) highlights that it is not the corporate culture values and the visions hype of the early 1980s that nurtures and scaffolds university cultures. Rather, it is a deeper atmospheric, affective and affectionate culture of academic thinking, doing and being which emanates from and shapes the core of the university. Each institution possesses its own cultural atmosphere that emanates from its atmospheric design which is

> a relatively enduring quality of the internal environment of an organization that (a) is experienced by its members, (b) influences their behaviour, and (c) can be described in terms of the values of a particular set of characteristics (or attributes) of the organization. (Tagiuri and Litwin, 1968: 27)

According to Ferraro (1998), the three basic components of culture – things, ideas and behaviour patterns – can undergo gradual alterations, deletions, inventions that in effect change the atmosphere and culture of an institution. This implies that the atmosphere and atmospheric design of something such as a university needs constant and careful attention. In considering the culture of the university, it is therefore important to avoid the negligence of the placeful and embodied nature of things, ideas and behaviours: 'the here-suggested atmospheric turn can help to rebalance the perspective while keeping the new methodological variety introduced during the design turn' (Volgger, 2020: 140).

The purpose of such an *atmospheric approach* to culture and the university, then, is to consider and reflect on how the notion of atmosphere and atmospheric design may support cultural, affective and spatial endowment (the essence of a place) that in turn nurtures particular environments and experiences of the university (Volgger, 2020). The intrinsic link between, on the one hand, a distinguishable spirit, placefulness and the culture of an environment and, on the other hand, the experience and existence of humans in such an environment has led to studies of how to produce authentic cultural atmospheres and experiences, with authenticity often linked to specific local conditions (Volgger, 2020; Ram et al., 2016). This intertwinement of place, atmosphere and affective experience positions culture and authenticity as relational concepts which connect a place's cultural identity, intensity and atmosphere with the identity and experience of its members (Rickly-Boyd, 2012; Volgger, 2020). Accordingly, the present chapter can be read as continuing the last chapter's discussion of the university as cultural place and placeful culture.

But, what then is *atmosphere* and *atmospheric design*? And what does it hold for the university as atmospheric *culture*? In order to answer these questions, we need to begin by ascertaining how atmosphere is conceptualized from a non-instrumental, affective, somatic and experiential perspective, so as to see culture and the university through an 'atmospheric mode of presentation [...] which also points in evocative fashion to something beyond rational explanation' (Böhme, 1993: 113). University cultures, by way of atmosphere, is 'perceived by the way in which they make a resonating body vibrate' (Böhme, 2017: 129). Atmospheric culture is made up by the voices of environments and institutions that make bodily existence and experience vibrate. Culture becomes a phenomenon of resonance that tinges the thinking, doing and being of everyone that comes in contact with it (Böhme, 2017).

Understanding the University as Atmosphere and Atmospheric Design

Some institutions are more culturally powerful than others, partially due to the expressive force and cohesion of their atmosphere. Almost immediately, when entering the institution, you catch on to the cultural atmosphere and particular style of the place and let yourself become absorbed within the ether of the things, life and persons who live there. But how can we come to grasp and design for such elusive notions as atmosphere, atmospheric cultures and the atmospheric university? Philosophers, scholars and designers within the field of atmospheric design 'have argued that atmosphere constitutes a fundamental aspect of the human experience of the world and that it thus is an important part of the identities and conceptualisation of landscapes, architecture and homes' (Bille et al., 2015: 31).

> Our general theme, *making atmospheres*, has a provocative character. It sounds slightly perverse, even paradoxical. Making – does that not have to do with something tangible? With the world of the concrete things and apparatuses? And atmosphere – is that not something airy, indefinite, something which is simply there and comes over us? How is one supposed to make atmospheres? (Böhme, 2013: 1)

Gernot Böhme, the most influential philosopher on atmosphere and atmospheric design (Böhme, 1993, 1995, 2013, 2017), describes atmosphere as the way things strikes us, tunes us and alters our mood or dispositions (*Befindlichkeit*). Approaching the university through the concept of atmosphere positions it as something that speaks to us as and through atmosphere, which, in turn, opens up an existential terrain of thought, affect and experience resonating with and within it (Böhme, 1995). Atmosphere is the *speaking face* and the *breathing body* of culture (Böhme, 1995). It tinges the culture of the university and unifies its members into an affective state of being (Böhme, 2013). Atmosphere, according to Böhme (2017: 70), becomes a fundamental fact of human experience and existence: 'the way in which people sense at once where they are, through their disposition. Seen in this way, atmospheres shape a person's being-in-the-world as a whole: the relationships to environments, to other people, to things [and the university as culture].'

The university consists, essentially, in the twin production of cultural atmosphere and atmospheric cultures which is accessed through the bodily being of its members. The culture of the university is inscribed into its very structures: 'the most important aspect of architecture is how people feel in and around buildings' (Böhme, 2017: 75). The atmosphere of a university is the *cultural spirit* that strikes visitors and members alike as characteristic of that particular place, or as the manner in which they are existentially positioned by it and carry out life within it.

Overall, the concept of atmosphere and atmospheric design points towards the sensuous, emotional and cultural *feel of a place*. Böhme (2017: 69) views atmosphere as 'the sphere *of felt bodily presence*' that creates the very conditions for life in that place. Approaching the university through the concept of atmosphere positions the university as *Gefühlsraum* (felt space) (Böhme, 2017), and its culture is accessed through notions such as ambience, sense of place, attunement, tuned space and other concepts pointing towards the ways that culture of a designed place can move, impact, transform or enchant people who come in contact with it:

> The character of an atmosphere is the way in which it communicates a feeling to us as participating subjects. A solemn atmosphere has the tendency to make my mood serious, a cold atmosphere causes me to shudder [. . .] In general, it can be said that atmospheres are involved wherever something is being staged, wherever design is a factor. (Böhme, 2013: 2)

According to Böhme, there is at our disposal a rich vocabulary to describe the atmospheric design of places such as a university, for example, serious, sombre, serene, oppressive, uplifting, commanding, inviting, inspirational, intellectual and so on. Members of the university *inhale* and *exhale* the cultural atmosphere of the university on a daily basis, meaning that they absorb it bodily, affectively and existentially. We find similar 'cases where the serenity of the valley or the melancholy of the evening strike us when we are in a quite different mood and we find ourselves seized by these atmospheres and even correspondingly changed' (Böhme, 1993: 119). Likewise, the atmospheric design of a university can seize and change its members. Its culture is experienced as an affective sphere of attunement in relation to the members' bodily being and existence in the presence of the university and how it feels to be *here* (Böhme, 1993).

Culture, through the notion of atmosphere, becomes a disposition (*Befindlichkeit*). This implies that cultural atmosphere of a university can be depressing, uplifting, expansive, restrictive. And through this, members enveloped by the atmosphere will find themselves in a depressed, uplifted, expansive or restricted mood. This draws attention to the cultural actuality and agency of architecture and cultural places in relation to the experience and existence of affected members: 'One can feel the atmosphere in one's disposition towards a particular mood. One is *tuned* by an atmosphere. Each atmosphere has its own distinctive character' (Böhme, 2017: 118).

Importantly, the concept of atmosphere focuses on the *in-betweenness* of place and people, subject and object, as atmospheres are always located in the interactional connection between environment and experience (Bille et al., 2015; Böhme, 1993). While a place's ambience can be positioned as primarily oriented towards the object, design or environment and a person's mood (or *stimmung*) as primarily oriented towards the subject, person or experience, atmosphere is the bridging of the two. This positions atmosphere as a *hybridizing* concept or phenomenon that fuses or dissolves traditional boundaries between cultural subject/experience and cultural object/environment. Accordingly, atmosphere exists in the in-betweenness of people and places and points towards a productive intermingling of experience and environment in cultural life (Böhme, 1993; Bille et al., 2015). Here, culture materializes as an atmos-*sphere* that creates intimate resonance and vibrancy between them.

Approaching culture as atmospheric design entails the translation of inchoate impressions (atmosphere) into articulate speech (design) as 'it is only by conversing about atmospheres, and the physical things and places that produce them, that we might reach agreement on how to reshape our environment with a view to enhancing our collective well-being as bodily beings among others, human and otherwise' (Rigby, 2011: 277). Arguing that atmospheres can be made, produced and staged also implies that they can be anticipated and intentionally designed for (Böhme, 2013).

The Design of Cultural Atmospheres

To design cultural atmospheres, then, is to create a nurturing atmosphere for imaginative thinking, doing and being within academic cultures, to design for the arrival of events in experience and environment that *tunes* and *tinges* culture and the university. Atmospheric design 'does not relate to the determinations of things, but to the way in which they radiate outwards into space, to their output as generators of atmospheres' (Böhme, 2013: 5). In this way, atmospheric design is concerned with the expressive and affective power of places and things, their *ekstases*. A university with and of culture is, then, constituted by having an atmospheric design that radiates with culture in ways that are immediately felt by visitors and members alike. In short, atmospheric design is the art of bringing something like culture into being and making it speak with a clear and strong voice.

Specifically, Weidinger (2018) presents a five-step approach for creating atmospheric designs that capture the spirit of a particular place such as a university. The first step is to find the atmospheric theme for the university based on its particular virtues, values and cultures. The second step is to transform this intangible theme into tangible compositions of cultural atmosphere. The third step is to shape and guide the tangible spirit of the place in ways that captures and envelops its members in an articulate atmospheric culture. The fourth step is to engage the members in the culturing practice of the place through becoming co-creators of atmospheric design that bridge environment and experience. The fifth step is to accentuate the cultural atmosphere of the place through design details that strengthen the atmosphere and *tune* the mood of visitors, newcomers and existing members so that it resonates with the unique spirit of that particular place. Weidinger (2018) emphasizes that atmospheric design decisions must be based on the cultural context and *genius loci* of the place in question to summon and amplify the spirit living in the place, not the other way around.

To achieve this, Volgger (2020) points to three core traits that enable designers to capture the spirit of a place and integrate it with an atmospheric design: (i) acts of empathic listening to the existing spirit and culture of the place which often expresses itself as a particular environment and existential terrain; (ii) acts of redesigning and amplifying the atmosphere in ways that respectfully emphasize the spirit and culture of the place so it becomes discernible to all senses; (iii) acts of bridge-building between environment, experience and existence through designing the place in such a way that it connects place and people through its atmosphere (Volgger, 2020).

The notion of atmospheric design, atmospheric architectures (Böhme, 2017) or staging atmospheres (Böhme, 2013) might seem paradoxical at first – intentionally to design for something as ephemeral, vague and ambiguous as atmosphere. However, 'architects and designers intentionally shape the experience of, and emotional response to, a place through the material environment, seeking – with various degrees of success – to affect people's moods and guide their behaviour for aesthetic, artistic, utilitarian [cultural] or commercial reasons' (Bille et al., 2015: 33). That is, they work to materialize the university as cultural atmosphere by way of conjuring the *genius loci* of the university.

The University as Cultural Atmosphere

Employing the concept of *genius loci*, we move from the notion of place and placefulness in the previous chapter, to the notion of the spirit or atmosphere of a place. *Genius loci* highlights the unique feel, mood or spirit that radiates from a specific place and encompasses the interactions between the atmosphere of a place and its members (Auret, 2018). To invoke the university as cultural atmosphere is to see the university as an institution of intense and intimate feeling, touching us like a living creature. Christian Norberg-Schulz (1980) reintroduced the concept of genius loci into architecture, requesting architects to consider the construction of buildings as simultaneous the construction of atmosphere. After all:

> Atmospheres can be considered as one, specifically emotional means through which *genius loci*, that is, the cultural interpretation of space, is delivered if not constituted. While genius loci concerns the cultural – or some might argue 'spiritual' – dimension of places (identification space), the concept of atmosphere starts with the emotional dimension (emotional space). (Volgger, 2020: 143)

Fostering and nurturing the university as cultural atmosphere by *staging genius loci* (Volgger, 2020) consists of place-based interventions to create an *intended atmosphere* (Kotler, 1973). As such, atmospheric design through the act of *staging* (Böhme, 2013) points to the intentional and reflective creation of a particular meeting between a place (institution) and its members focused on imbuing the place with culture, atmosphere and character. 'The making of atmospheres is therefore confined to setting the conditions in which the atmosphere appears' – it is setting the stage for the 'imaginative idea the observer receives through the object' [or atmospheric design] (Böhme, 2013: 3–4). Considering culture and the university, atmospheric design, then, assumes the crucial task of strengthening the symbolic links between individual elements and the comprehensive whole of the university in order to nurture cultural socialization and create a consistent atmospheric culture. To support genius loci-sensitive design approaches in the context of university culture, it is therefore crucial to ensure that the university's particular spirit or atmosphere is integrated in and emphasized through the design (Volgger, 2020). That is, atmospheric design should be the mouthpiece of the particular cultural spirit inhabiting the university – 'Which means that the term atmosphere presents itself to us as a response to a question: how to attend to collective affects [or culture] that are not reducible to the individual bodies that they emerge from?' (Anderson, 2009: 80).

Through atmospheric design, the university comes to possess a cultural atmosphere and is simultaneously possessed by it. The totality of the cultural atmosphere that lingers in a university and within its places, practices and members often hesitates at the edge of the inexpressible. Yet, the atmospheric qualities that are ascribed to this *something* are remarkable for their particularity: serene, homely, imposing, intellectual, welcoming, depressing, uplifting, inclusive, hostile, moving, collegial, sublime, open, closed, to name a few (Anderson, 2009; Böhme, 1993). In this way, it is possible to speak about the atmospheric qualities we encounter in the form of the cultural atmosphere of the campus square, an empty room before a meeting, an exchange between teachers and their students, in the ways a discipline is practised, in the signature of an institution's academic practice or within the being of an individual academic or an academic collective. By articulating and connecting specific atmospheric qualities to the particular places, practices and people of an institution, their cultural atmosphere surfaces can be approached with designerly practices of framing and staging.

The atmospheric design of a university is the designerly invocation of a cultural atmosphere that comes into being as a 'certain quality which words cannot translate but which communicates itself in an arousing feeling' (Dufrenne, 1973: 178). Atmospheric design is the creation of an *environment of intensity* that overflows the built architecture and spatial layout of the institution and opens the university up to being apprehended as a cultural atmosphere through feelings and emotions. The cultural atmosphere of the university envelops its members through the way it simultaneously expresses a certain lifeworld and designates particular ways of existing in it. In this way, the university exists as a cultural *atmos-sphere* for its members that not only occupies space but also permeates it and surrounds its members through the way its atmospheric design enhances, transforms, intensifies, shapes and in other ways intervenes on the experience and existence of its members (Anderson, 2009; Böhme, 2017).

Framing culture and the university through the notion of atmos-sphere enables critical examination of the university in relation to how it attunes its members to a particular academic culture. But it also enables inquiry into how members of the university through their thinking, practices and way of existing within the sphere attune the cultural atmosphere of the university. In terms of the members' attunement to and attuning of university culture, 'the deliberate staging, orchestration, or manipulation of atmosphere, also becomes a way of performing what the world both *is*, and *should be*. A space may for example potentially feel safe, comfortable, or exciting, but it *should* also feel that way' (Bille et al., 2015: 34).

Some atmospheres seem to envelop, resonate with and move people more than others. This can depend not only on the skill of the designer but also on the cultural qualities of the spaces, designs and practices of the institution. Nurturing a culture worth experiencing and existing in, through atmospheric design, requires cultural attunement between environment and experience, institution and members, people and places: 'designers depend upon their acceptance of the feel of an atmosphere, but can never be sure whether a crowd [or institution] will charge the atmosphere with unwanted or unexpected tones or play the roles envisaged' (Edensor and Sumartojo, 2015: 252). Consequently, particular universities are atmospherically charged by both designers and members in the service of the idea of the university. Overall, the university as cultural atmosphere 'radiates as it were into the environment, takes away the homogeneity of the surrounding space and fills it with tensions and suggestions of movement' (Böhme, 1993: 121). The cultural atmosphere constitutes, through atmospheric design, an environment within the university that is culturally *tinctured* through the presence of buildings, people, spatial constellations, organizational frames and so forth. In this way, culture and the university emerge as 'something thinglike, belonging to the thing [or design] in that things articulate their presence through qualities – conceived as ecstasies [. . .] A valley is this not called serene because it is in some way similar to a cheerful person but because the atmosphere which it radiates is serene and can put that person into a serene mood' (Böhme, 1993: 122). According to Böhme and others approaching the world through the concept of atmosphere, creating culture in the university is a question of *staging atmospheres* through design work on an object such as a university. The wisdom and knowledge of the designer thus consists in both understanding how such design work is best carried out and how desired cultural atmospheres of the university is produced (something that will be addressed in the next chapter).

Conclusions: The Atmospheric University/ Atmospheric Cultures

Atmospheric design is one way for universities to bring about the materialization of placeful and spirited cultures that connect with the emotional, experiential and existential dimensions of academic life and, in so doing, create a cultural atmosphere: 'Architecture is so influential on the mode of movement that social [and cultural] exclusion and inclusion becomes orchestrated through atmospheres, and hence becomes a way of allowing ideals of social [and cultural] norms to come into being' (Bille et al., 2015: 36). Obviously, such a harmony might not be obtained, since there may be a disconnect between the members' disposition (*Befindlichkeit*), experience or cultural values and the atmospheric design of the university. In this way, 'atmosphere may play a role in [cultural] power struggles' (Bille et al., 2015: 34) between the institution and its members.

Universities with powerful atmospheric designs tune people to their culture and genius loci so they cannot help to hum along. Designers can, through atmospheric design, help to bring about a (re)enchantment of the realm of the university, kindling a sense of cultural wonder through which the university is made 'newly-present' to its members so that they attend more intently to the atmospheric culture they find there (Edensor and Sumartojo, 2015). Such atmospheric design of the everyday university forges a collective experience of identity and culture that are attuned to one another and to the affective-aesthetic-concrete designs at hand (Carlson and Stewart, 2014; Edensor and Sumartojo, 2015). Acquiring an atmospheric culture, the university becomes a spirited place where personal and professional experience and existence willingly merge with institutional and academic environment and lifeworld. Atmospheric cultures position members, not as passive recipients or loyal servants of a brand, but as participants participating in the co-constructing of cultural atmosphere. Not because they are employers, employees or students, but because they resonate with, thrive in and feel empowered by the atmospheric culture of the place.

Accordingly, the university as cultural atmosphere and atmospheric culture is not to be confused with the architectural or aesthetic branding strategies of the neoliberal university that aim to increase the commodification of the space and position the university as part of the experience economy or service industry (Edensor and Sumartojo, 2015). Here style and intensified aestheticizing of the space highlight a brand rather than create culture. Such a brand-strategic aesthetic intensification, instead of creating atmosphere or culture, signifies an intention to bedazzle the 'customers' of the university and constrain members' ability to perceive the real atmosphere that underlie their enslavement as workers and users (Edensor and Sumartojo, 2015). Rather than an atmospheric university, it is a *university of spectacle* in which spectators, customers and users passively and at a distance behold seductive, stylized, controlled and clean spaces organized by capital and those in power that have colonized and replaced atmospheric cultures and messy life with branding strategies and neat buildings. The neoliberal university becomes a *designscape* – a collection of brand design, architecture, urban planning, events and functional spaces that produce uniform taste and *aesthetic consent* (Julier, 2005). The university as designscape becomes a way for the university to express power, exert control and manage the space, its members and the university brand.

If institutions are not vigilant in avoiding such shifts towards designscapes, the consequence might be a diminution of atmospheric qualities and practices, of culture. To nurture atmospheric cultures for academics to thrive in, the university must be receptive to the cultural ties that form its foundation – the genius loci or spirit of the university – that, again, produce affective belonging, togetherness and otherwise. Like the atmosphere (good or bad) *gets inside* its members and envelops them, so must the members be able to *get inside* the university and envelop it through their academic and cultural practices. Consequently, the atmospheric university requires a willingness to think together, do together and be together by way of co-creating and co-owning atmospheric culture. In the atmospheric university, the members form a sense of *cultural communitas*, rather than being passive figures, mutely attuned and uncritically receptive to the culture of the university (Edensor and Sumartojo, 2015).

Herein lies also the promise of atmospheric cultures. They make members come alive and feel touched by the university and the culture that emanates from it as atmosphere: 'To perceive atmospheres means to open oneself up emotionally' (Böhme, 2017: 121). For universities and their members to open themselves up to one another through producing atmospheric cultures, is, according to Böhme (2017), tantamount to wanting to participate and expose oneself to the culture of a place – 'Producing atmosphere, is one step out of slavish consumerism [. . .] To learn to engage with atmosphere enables each individual to participate critically and to contribute to this world in which we live today.' Producing and staging cultural atmospheres by way of design is one way to regain a voice for both university and its members. This will be the focus of the next chapter.

7

Cultures for Collective Visioning and Future-Making

Introduction

Culture is by its very nature a collective and communal phenomenon that 'must be abstracted from the complexity of human existence' (Sewell, 1999: 39). We find ourselves and each other – as similar or different – in and through communities and collective cultures: perhaps in a study group with different students studying similar subjects; in an interdisciplinary research team coming together around a project; at a staff meeting connecting multiple campuses; or stumbling across colleagues attending the same conference in a foreign country. A feeling of communality and the companionship of the collective in different ways enable us simultaneously to get over ourselves and find ourselves: suddenly feeling an intimate belonging to one's discipline by working together in a shared project space beyond its culture; understanding the reasons for why you want to study and the person you aspire to be through year-long personal and professional discussions within a study group; or realizing the institutional cultural bond that is shared across faculties and departments in the ways colleagues reflect on the presentations and approach of the themes within a conference.

Culture, as a communal ecology, may be thought of as an intricate meshwork of values, meanings, relations and spatialities cast across a university, a department or a research programme or scholars sharing the same office space. By thinking, being and working together over time, they come to inhabit and participate in a shared culture.

Following Sewell (1999), the conception of a collective culture of the university implies particular notions of cultural practice. To engage in a cultural practice is to engage in a collective and to think, do and be something in the world as part of a collective – thereby changing both the world, the culture and the self. Importantly, this does not entail that collective cultures are homogenizing, harmonious, unified or univocal. Rather, they are characterized by being inherently contradictory, loosely integrated, contested, subject to constant change and weakly bounded. Such conceptions of culture, pointing towards collective cohesion, open up new vistas for cultural practice as decentred but collective, communal but heterogeneous and simultaneously value-based and value-contested.

The culturing work of universities becomes not so much about establishing collective consensus as it is about organizing and offering spaces for collective difference and different collectives: 'Struggle and resistance, far from demonstrating that cultures lack coherence, may paradoxically have the effect of simplifying and clarifying the cultural field' (Sewell, 1999: 57). Academics at a staff party might find themselves in heated discussions about what counts as science and the use of methods in research. Department leaders suddenly find themselves in deep and prolonged debates about how the future institutional strategy should be worded in order to capture the spirit of the disciplines the department represent. Educational developers at the university's pedagogical centre encounter great resistance from both teachers and students as they present the new learning management system because they say it is in conflict with the pedagogical values and practices of the institution. Or, institutional leaders find themselves in a situation where they have to come together and form a joint position on research integrity and academic freedom due to public debate and governmental encroachment in the country.

From these observations arises an important distinction between collective cultures as adaptation or incorporation *and* collective cultures as enculturation or participation that points towards 'the changes that an individual experiences as a result of being in contact with other cultures and participating' (Berry, 1990: 460). The proposal here is that the university as a collective culture signifies enculturation to a cultural identity characterized by contradiction, resistance, changeability, heterogeneity and polyphony. Collective culture is 'shaped by agency and power, but cannot be created by fiat' (Weeks and Gulunic, 2003: 1315). It requires acts of what in this chapter is called *collective visioning*. The main factors that influence the nature of collective culture are goals and objectives, history, critical events, ownership, size, technology, environment and people (Wilkins and Ouchi, 1983; Handy, 1985; Moran and Volkwein, 1992; Schein, 2004). This in turn forms a cultural meshwork of multifarious norms, values, beliefs, ways of behaving, visions and so on. From processes of collective visioning emerges possibilities for deeper participatory cultures engaged in meaningful enculturation in accordance with the spirit of the university. And, subsequently, the *translation* of that spirit into materialized preferable futures for the institution, its members and the many cultures binding them together.

The University as Collective Culture

This chapter, considering the university as a culture for collective visioning and future-making, builds upon the notion of culture as contested processes of meaning making: 'The notion of culture as contested meaning making implies that people, not faceless forces, create world culture and make globalisation happen, and that what happens is contingent rather than inevitable' (Anderson-Levitt, 2012: 451). What values, visions and actions should shape and drive the culture of the university is always open to question and change both from outside and inside of the collective. Particular people in particular places and situations construct and *contest* culture together, opening up manifold futures for the university in the form of an array of possible and unbounded pathways. However:

> actors who have been in a position to influence past meaning making and to shape past institutional practices, or whose allies or predecessors have been in that position, enjoy a great advantage in shaping future meaning making. We can ask, for example, who are and who have been the school superintendents or high-status education professors or other decision-makers and opinion leaders who have had a stronger hand than other people in shaping institutions. (Anderson-Levitt, 2012: 449)

From this, it follows that universities and people with the power to shape culture and the future of the university should make sure 'that their institutional cultures reflect these central aspects of humanity' (Waddington, 2019: 242). According to Waddington (2019) and Worline and Dutton (2017), the university needs to notice and listen to the cultural suffering that is present in its organization and institution in order for its members to thrive, and for culture of the institution to flourish, and then approach this suffering with genuine empathic concern and take action to make meaning of and alleviate such suffering.

Culture, concern and compassion go hand in hand, and involve both listening and responding through transformative or future-oriented changemaking processes. Compassion, here, *is* culture in the form of an organizational process that involves both engaged listening, committed care and culturing change. Here, value-based, vision-driven and future-oriented compassionate action motivate

'A commitment to working together to shift cultural patterns and behaviours at individual, group and organisational levels' (Waddington, 2017: 67).

Increasingly, universities and their leaders, academics, students, staff and other members are coming to recognize the significance of sustaining and developing the university as a compassionate culture (Gibbs, 2017; Kanov et al., 2017; Waddington, 2019). In order to nurture such cultures of collective compassion, universities must, on the one hand, ask their leaders and managers to embody institutional compassion, care and concern when leading and shaping cultural practices (West et al., 2017), and, on the other hand, as compassionate cultural institutions make sure to provide processes and practices for all members of the university to participate in the idea of the university through being active leaders and shapers of university culture themselves by actively welcoming, promoting and nurturing collective speculation, visioning and actualization. This implies opening up the university, its culture and future to active cultural debate, critical interrogation of taken-for-granted ideals, value-contestation, culturing practices and value-based premises, as well as shifting away from top-down leadership or management perspectives towards bottom-up collective visioning and future-making processes (Pässilä and Vince, 2016).

Adopting an approach to university culture as caring and critical-creative worlds under constant collective dispute, discussion and construction requires a sense of both culture and future as something emergent and enacted, rather than stable and established: 'When we do this, it brings organisational culture and change *theory* closer to organisational culture and change *practice*' (Waddington, 2017: 246).

The values, cultures and futures of the university are not given. To speak of futures, cultures and values being imposed upon the university is not without point. Universities work out their future under the imprint of powerful forces – of the state, of cross-national agencies and of the economy acting on their culture and impacting their future. But universities have some room for practising their own institutional and cultural agency. Accordingly, the values, cultures and futures of the university have 'continually to be worked at and eked out, practically, laboriously, and with some political astuteness' (Barnett, 2019: 58):

> Some universities around the world are beginning to seize the opportunities of these new spaces and relationships to explore quite new activities both within the university and with their members and with the wider world. Collective imaginings are being developed to form new imaginaries of the university, in some universities at least. Will other universities follow? (Barnett, 2019: 58)

One issue is, then, how to foster and promote participatory cultures of collective visioning and future-making that can move the university towards desired values, preferable cultures and alternative futures. Speculative design with its focus on *desiderata*, preferable futures and collective visioning and future-making is one place to look for possible answers. Speculative design is a reflective, future-oriented and designerly framework for working with exposing, probing and designing for deeper ethics, cultures, assumptions and values in the design and practice of institutions, members and their surrounding ecosystems (Nørgård, forthcoming).

This chapter will introduce collective practices of future-making in the form of speculative design and collective visioning as a conceptual framework for designing for (more) preferable university futures and cultures. Through such an approach, core underpinnings of institutional culture can be revealed, reconfigured and realized to better embody preferable university cultures as well as compassionate and caring institutional futures.

Future-Making: Speculative Design and Alternative Futures

According to Lukens and DiSalvo (2011), speculative design is a particular and specialized design approach that emphasizes speculation, imagination and critical-creative future-making, over usability, probability or solution-making. Speculative design involves practices from, and are entangled with, other fields and disciplines such as design fiction, critical design, discursive design, adversarial design, interrogative design, design for debate, futurescaping and contestational design (Dunne and Raby, 2013). However, it emerged as an independent field and method in the early 00s, as it spun out from the field of critical design (in itself a rather new term first used in Anthony Dunne's book *Hertzian Tales* (1999)). Like critical design, speculative design employs design as provocation and asks uncomfortable questions or as a way of working to integrate dimensions that are often kept separate, such as fact and fiction, science and art, present and future or industry and academia.

Speculative design is a theory-heavy design practice revolving around 'the philosophy of what if' and of 'trying out ideas and ideals' (Dunne and Raby, 2013: 14). In this way, speculative design is a discursive practice, grounded in critical thinking, value tensions, contested but possible futures and inquiring dialogue. But speculative design – *qua* being a design practice – takes criticality and speculation one step further, towards materializing imagination and collective co-construction in *design proposals* for actualizing preferable future scenarios. As such, speculative design strives towards bringing preferable futures into being by highlighting ideals and ethics as well as producing alternative values and orientations in design contexts such as how we might collectively think about the university as cultural place and atmosphere. Its opposite is affirmative design, that is, 'design that reinforces the status quo', colonizing the future by pointing towards how things will be (Dunne and Raby, 2013: 34).

At its core, speculative design can be seen as *informed speculation* that brings into question what is considered to be 'predicted', 'projected', 'probable' and 'plausible' futures (Voros, 2017). Speculative design emphasizes a break with the *colonization of the future* that predicts or forecasts how the future *will be* based on the actuality and reality of the present. Instead, speculative design works towards widening the imagination in order to design for how things *could be* by bringing all possible futures – even preposterous ones – into play as well as how things *ought to be* by focusing on preferable futures that cut across the preposterous, possible and plausible (Dunne and Raby, 2013). The notion of informed speculation implies that speculative design is not just about proposing alternative future but about grounding speculation in prior knowledge, emerging tendencies, existing contexts and human values within a domain. Through creating imaginative and grounded readings of preferable futures, the predominant reality is put into question and inherent biases, assumptions and premises are revealed. What we think the future *will be* is not the same as what the future *could be*.

The aim of speculative design, then, is to create designerly discourse around how *the present is futuring* and how collective speculative design practices can become a catalyst for social dreaming (Dunne and Raby, 2013). By offering tools, methods and processes for exploring, experimenting and experiencing alternative futures and posing 'what-if' questions, speculative design offers a framework for confronting the future of university culture head-on (Nørgård, forthcoming). Through this, 'Universities and art schools could become platforms for experimentation, speculation, and the reimagining of everyday life' (Dunne and Raby, 2013: 31). By widening the scope of what is considered *probable futures* and by advancing design proposals, not only alternative more preferable futures but also the present institutional world are opened up and put into question. In this way, collectives engaged in speculative design act to widen cultural participation in both present and future institutional life through becoming active anticipators and shapers of (more) preferable futures. The different examples provided in the introduction could each constitute a design scenario for speculating, proposing and actualizing preferable university cultures.

To achieve this, speculative design draws inspiration from fields that practises imagination such as poetry, music, science fiction, visual arts, architecture and similar artistic and avant-garde practices to widen the future (Dunne and Raby, 2013). Such fields are integrated into speculative design practice to challenge assumptions and conceptions about reality, the future and what is plausible. As well as to share critical-creative perspectives or inspire debate while increasing awareness of ethical, cultural and social issues. In this way, speculative design

> is critical thought translated into materiality. It is about thinking through design rather than through words and using the language and structure of design to engage people [...] All good critical design offers an alternative to how things are. (Dunne and Raby, 2013: 35)

The ambition of such speculative design work is to provoke or incite new cultures for thinking about what is possible and what the future might be – to move imagination and collective action from predicted, projected, probable and plausible futures towards possible, preposterous and even preferable futures (Voros, 2017). Working with speculative design in relation to preferable future cultures of the university aims to provoke shifts in perspective, understanding and institutional practice that opens up new spaces and vistas for 'as-of-yet unthought-of possibilities' (Dunne and Raby, 2013: 43). For this to succeed, the university must integrate such speculative practices as part of their institutional culture as well as offer design spaces that aim at nurturing cultural thinking and practice beyond the expected and ordinary.

One case that exemplifies what such a switch could bring about is the *Near Future Teaching* project (Bayne and Gallagher, 2021). In their article, Bayne and Gallagher present in detail an institution-wide project spanning multiple years that is carried out as a speculative design-oriented co-creative participatory project with students, staff and leaders: 'The Near Future Teaching project was political in its attempt to envision "better ways of doing things", and in its attempt to see digital higher education futures as community-based, open and articulated through a set of shared values' (Bayne and Gallagher, 2021: 623). The institutional project's starting point was 'that universities need to get better at crafting their own, compelling counter-narratives concerning the future of technology in teaching' (Bayne and Gallagher, 2021: 607). To achieve this, the project employed speculative design and anticipation studies to develop a methodology for participative futures work within universities. Their paper reports on the outcomes of this institution-wide culturing and future-making project and argues that university communities can work to define their own futures through an emphasis on collectivity, participation and hope.

With its decidedly anti-commercial, non-affirmative and contesting approach and its focus on critiquing widely held social, cultural, and 'rational' beliefs, speculative design is a unique approach for actually changing the future to something more preferable by the members of the involved communities or institutions. As such, the framework and methods of speculative design create spaces for critical-creative reflection and practice to conceptualize scenarios and futures intended to highlight social, cultural or political valued alternatives. Overall, speculative design can, as in the case with the *Near Future Teaching* project, be a way forward for the university to facilitate and foster cultural debates that result in speculative design proposals, the opening up of the future of the university as well as design-oriented culturing interactions and dialogues around possible and preferable futures that were invisible, impossible or missing before.

Building on Erik Olin Wright's (2010) description of emancipatory social science, speculative design offers concrete ways forward towards the generation of alternative and preferable cultures. First, diagnosing and critiquing the reality and actuality of the present culture in the university, which will tell us what is unpreferable, and why we would want to change, transform or overturn the actuality and culture of the present university. Second, opening up the university for all possible futures – including preposterous ones – to imagine the future-preferred cultures (compared to the present) and what future(s) the university needs to bring into being in order for that to happen. Third, by employing speculative design as a transformative future-making practice for arriving at such preferable future cultures and for moving the university from its unpreferable present culture to its preferable future culture (Dunne and Raby, 2013; Wright, 2010).

Through engaging the future culture of the university by way of speculative design, the debate is transposed beyond lamenting the culture of the past or criticizing the culture of the present, and into the actualization of alternative and preferable university cultures of the future. By means of such culturing design processes, speculative design aims to materialize collective imaginaries about preferable futures as well as to suspend disbelief about the opportunities for transformational change.

Importantly, speculative design refrains from *predicting* or *forecasting* the future based on how the reality of the present acts on us. Instead, it invites people to consider the future as open and unknown so as to explore futures that are concurrently utopian and ordinary and incorporate new values, practices and cultures. Through such a summoning of a multiverse of alternative worlds and futures, a space for cultural discussion and debate is created to be acted on through speculative design practices. Such possibility spaces along with their ethical, social, experiential and political implications can then be explored, experimented with and debated before they are implemented into the cultural being of the university.

But for such processes of culturing through speculative design to happen, compassionate academic culture, not forecasted systemic reality, needs to be at the forefront of institutional practice and culture. Through using speculative ethics as 'a tool for exploring notions of future good and future bad' (Dunne and Raby, 2013: 64), institutions can step back, zoom out and look ahead to consider what it means to have a university of and for culture. Envisioning such universities for tomorrow requires tangible exploration and concrete manifestations of future university cultures through employing methods such as future workshops, ideation cards, design fictions, critical fabulations, prototypes or other such methods for speculation (Rosner, 2018; Tharp and Tharp, 2018). Each of these speculative design methods can be used to open up the future and widening the imagination of what is possible as they invoke a wide space of possibility between the probable and the preposterous (Voros, 2017). The question, then, is: What cultures should be brought into existence through such collective design intention, imagination and innovation?

Collective Visioning: Designing for Preferable Cultures

'The way this is done is by making design judgments. What we desire to come into existence is a matter of judgment – based on design *will* (volition) and *intention* (aim)' (Nelson and Stolterman, 2012: 32). Here, 'the ideal, as a focus of inquiry into what is desirable, is essential the ultimate design goal of creating the not-yet-existing' (Nelson and Stolterman, 2012: 35). In the seminal work of Nelson and Stolterman (Nelson and Stolterman, 2012), speculative design is framed as concerning *the ideal* in design. And being placed in the ideal is not so much about changing the *existing* culture, as it is about bringing a preferable (or ideal) culture into existence. Speculative design is, then, not concerned with *that-which-is* or *that-which-needs-to-be* but with *that-which-is-desired-to-be* and *that-which-ought-to-be* (Nelson and Stolterman, 2012: 38–9).

If institutions are interested in bringing about more preferable cultures, 'we will need to turn to speculative culture and what Lubomir Dolezel has called an experimental laboratory of the world-constructing enterprise' (Dunne and Raby, 2013: 69). This implies growing cultures of collective visioning, world-building and future-making. Here, the practice of speculative culturing implies an integrated institutional employment of tools and methods for imagining other cultures and worlds as well as cultural atmospheres based on imagination. In other words, institutions need to develop the ability to think *ideally* and *otherwise* in relation to future, possibilities and outcomes, and then make them 'translated into material expressions, embodied in material culture, becoming little bits of another world' (Dunne and Raby, 2013: 70).

Through the design lens, future university cultures are ethically inspired designs for a humane world unconstrained by realistic considerations and probabilistic feasibility (Wright, 2010). Here, the notion of collective visioning uses the idea of utopia as a stimulus to keep values, idealism and ethics alive and well in the future. The ethical vision or ideal idea is the engine in collective visioning, by which possible, preposterous and preferable cultures unfold through deliberate interactions, collisions and fusions within the collective culture of the university. Speculative design proposals are put forward by the collective, constructed from ideals, ideas and *desiderata* – the valued and preferred within the plane of the ideal. 'Desiderata are about what we intend the world to be' (Nelson and Stolterman, 2012: 107). Desiderata function as a telescope for focusing on futures near and far. Consequently, working from the ideal through the use of desiderate acts as 'the destabilising trigger for transformational change, which facilitates the emergence of new possibilities and realization of human "being"' (Nelson and Stolterman, 2012: 110). Desiderata are design triggers that arise out of the desire for situations, systems or institutions to be and do better. As such, desiderata are the design intentions or focal points that steer a collective or institution towards what is longed for (desires) and what this future world should be (ethics). Overall, desiderata come forth through processes of collective visioning and are the grounds on which design judgements should be made:

> The capacities that become important to the designer, when desiderata are the focus and starting point of design, are those abilities that allow a designer to compose, imagine, and make good professional judgments. Engaging with desiderata as that-which-is-not-yet demands creativity and innovation. It requires attention, imagination, and communication in order to manifest a world not yet seen. (Nelson and Stolterman, 2012: 117)

To achieve this, the university needs to distance itself from *the real* and *the actual* and instead ask of itself and its members to focus on and strive for *the ideal* (Nelson and Stolterman, 2012).

The present culture of the university is so preoccupied with the real and the actual, and so habitual in its forecasting and implementation of predicted, projected and probable futures, that it is almost impossible to dream open future-oriented own dreams, let alone ideal or cultural ones (Nørgård, forthcoming). However, the university needs to (re)gain a 'dream-materializing ability' (Dunne and Raby, 2013: 88). Here, 'Design speculation can act as a catalyst for collective redefining our relationship to reality' (Dunne and Raby, 2013: 2). Such redefinition of the culturing work of universities requires widening the visioning capability of the university itself to envision and engage in seemingly preposterous futures, and to take ownership of them through integrated design proposals for viable and feasible preferable futures – however utopian these might seem at the outset. The purpose of such a more speculative university is to foster cultures of collective imagining and visioning that might be at odds with how things 'really are' inside the narrow scope of predicted and forecasted futures. This might entail a refurbishing of both institutional culture, place and atmosphere to invite its members to become actualizers of preferable worlds and carry out such collective imaginaries. It entails, in effect, the integration of an institutional speculative practice for unreality and non-actuality through pushing the limits of what is deemed plausible while keeping within what is possible.

Opening up such a space for collective visioning and speculative culturing implies the creation of places that resemble cabinet of curiosities (*Wunderkammer*) through exhibiting universities of otherness, estrangement and rupture that invites members to explore and experiment with the future university and its culture. These future-making sites for preferable cultures could take the form of experimental laboratories, arts-based exhibition spaces, junk playgrounds, speculative exploratoriums or design collaboratoriums – sometimes kept inside the university itself and sometimes opened up for engagement and dialogue with broader publics. Such *Wunderkammer* places for engaging the future university would invite participants to step out of the future as closed and colonized to engage with a variety of what-if questions and preferable futures in the form of tangible design proposals. Together such diverse speculative design sites create the opportunity for what Dunne and Raby (2013) call imaginary and imaginative institutions. Such futuring sites – or spirited tomorrow places – advocate imaginary cultural worlds that signal their unreality, non-actuality and preposterousness so that ideas and ideals, not products or solutions, take the centre stage.

Overall, institutional cultures of collective visioning 'strives to overcome the invisible wall separating dreams and imagination from everyday life, blurring distinctions between the "real" real and the "unreal" real' (Dunne and Raby, 2013: 160). Such cultures carry with them the promise of ending the colonization of the future (in the singular) to invite seven billion different futures (in the plural). Such a multiverse can then give rise to the actualization of on–off micro-utopias rising from the desiderata and design proposals of an institution, a department, a discipline, a research centre, an interdisciplinary research project or even a single person: 'seven billion little utopias emerging from the bottom up, facilitated by, not determined by, design' (Dunne and Raby, 2013: 164).

Conclusions: The Preferable University and Its Preferable Cultures

Speculative design renders social and cultural dreaming possible for universities. A way for universities to reclaim the right and need of dreaming that today is taken up by corporate strategies, neoliberal paradigms, colonized futures or governmental forecasts. Weighed down by the gravity of reality, the university cannot look ahead beyond practical solutions, future survival and the justification of its socio-economic value. To invite for speculative cultures of collective visioning is to insist on the possibility of impractical, improbable or inconvenient futures and allow for the institutional exploration of alternative ideological systems, micro-utopias and social imaginaries:

> As we rapidly move toward a monoculture that makes imagining genuine alternatives almost impossible, we need to experiment with ways of developing new and distinctive worldviews that include different beliefs, values, ideals, hopes, and fears from today's. If our belief systems and ideas don't change, then reality won't change either. (Dunne and Raby, 2013: 189)

To achieve this, institutions and their members must engage in what culture in the university could and should be through actualizing the university's desiderata and realizing its nascent preferable worlds. A first step is for universities actually to engage in critiquing the reality and actuality of their present institutional culture and facilitating the opening up of the university for all possible futures, also preposterous ones. But, even more importantly, institutions and their members need to take steps towards actually employing speculative design (or similar perspectives) as transformative future-making practice for bringing about more preferable future cultures. This is needed more than ever as ideas and culture of the university are hopelessly impoverished:

> 'Impoverished' because they are unduly confined to a small range of possible conceptions of the university; and 'hopelessly' because they are too often without hope, taking the form of either hand-wringing over the current state of the university or merely offering a defence of the emerging nature of 'the entrepreneurial university.' [...] This then is the problem before us: the problem of the place of imagination in developing the idea – and the institutional form of the university. (Barnett, 2013: 1)

To move beyond an impoverished and hopeless university future, we need to craft imagination-driven telescopes, such as speculative design practices, so that we might look beyond the immediate and forecasted future, to the starlit sky where seven billion possible futures and one-off micro-utopias sparkle. One such co-creative agenda for bringing preferred universities into being is speculative design, future-making and collective visioning, an agenda where members – leaders, researchers, staff, teachers and student alike – become envisioning future-makers of the university. If seven billion possible futures are lying in wait beyond the colonizing headlights of tomorrow, the university must take a leap of faith into the space of all possible futures to discover and claim preferable ones. The next chapter will present examples of what such *futurescaping* practices might bring about.

8

Futurescaping Alternative Universities

Introduction

Universities find themselves in a reorienting and reconfiguring state as they try to envision what comes after the neoliberal, managerial and accelerated reality they find themselves caught up in, which has characterized the discourse surrounding higher education for several decades. Through the last three chapters, the concepts of place, atmosphere, genius loci, speculative design and collective visioning have been introduced and described as potential frameworks to establish deeper and alternative understanding of culture and the university. Together, the chapters do not propose a uniform or fixed idea of the university or definition of culture. Rather, the chapters try to offer vibrant, living, heterogeneous and multifarious approaches to culture and the university that are decidedly different from those characterizing the current discourses surrounding the role of culture and the university.

Today, emerging agendas and movements around academic activism, societal engagement, sustainable futures, ecological growth, widening participation, equality, decolonization, digital transition and other major developments will be some of the main drivers of change for the new decade (see e.g. Nørgård and Bengtsen, 2021a; NLEC et al., 2021; Morreira et al., 2021). Amid these pressing agendas and movements, universities are (re)discovering their footing as enduring placeful and atmospheric institutions that have existed for a millennium, expanding the frontiers of knowledge, educating citizens and driving societal change. Rather than merely *being of use* to society, universities (and higher education) are working to establish more dialogic, co-creative and communal frameworks in becoming an equal partner that does not leap for society, but work with and for society and the above emerging agendas and movements (Nørgård and Bengtsen, 2016). Overall, higher education must safeguard, support and promote civic values through active dialogue, engagement and commitment to society and the world.

This requires that universities are able to reconfigure and transform themselves into something *new but old* to fight for and use their academic freedom, contribute to public debates, encourage open discussions, counter misinformation and demonstrate openness, connectivity and *generous thinking* (Fitzpatrick, 2019) as cultured and culturing institutions in the world. Furthermore, universities must take up a leading role in promoting civic engagement, developing participation, respect for diversity and open debates – requiring a switch from thinking of the inhabitants of the university as (future) workforce to thinking of people as critical-creative citizens in society and the world (European University Association, 2021). Universities must, then, establish cultures that push against corporate culture (Giroux, 2002), and where universities can maintain their *moral bases* (Nixon, 2008), be *good universities* (Connell, 2019) and constitute *feasible utopias* (Barnett, 2018), given that 'instrumental reason is tending to colonize the "lifeworld"; that getting things done to fulfil ends comes to be more important than arriving at a deep interpersonal understanding of matters' (Barnett, 2018: 49) – or, in other words, culture.

University culture, as described through the last three chapters, does not sit comfortably with, and nor is it supported by, culturing practices of bureaucracy, commodification and competition or the continuous acceleration of academic life. Instead, it kindles a more earthbound, dwelling, far-seeing, preposterous, co-operative and collective spirit that works to support communal growth, public good and placeful atmospheric cultures. They are all frameworks occupied with creating the right settings for a culture worth living in. While the dominant tendency regarding the role of the university has been to progress ideas of excellence, world-classness, employability and certain forms of academic capitalism (Englund and Bergh, 2020; Rider et al., 2020), there is now a need to provide alternatives more occupied with universities as *spaces of life* (Arndt et al., 2020), *networked and networking communities* (Nørgård et al., 2019), *value-sensitive and ethical institutions* (Nørgård et al., 2020), *place-based spaces* (Carvalho et al., 2017) or entire new breeds of *hybrid higher education* (Nørgård, 2021).

To nurture collective societal engagement, social responsibility and cultural cohesion in the university and the world, we need cultures that are deeply dialogic, democratic, inclusive, diverse, inquiring and sensitive (Kandlbinder, 2007; Englund and Bergh, 2020). This has been the case historically, and is still the case moving forward. Evident in such university cultures is the prominence of value conflicts, heterogeneous visions, opposing viewpoints, disputed positions and contested academic cultures as the inescapable starting point for collective deliberation, communication and co-operation. Through this, *collective will-*

formation can be reached, leading to mutual understandings, visions, positions and cultures (Englund and Bergh, 2020).

Pulling the above works together, the university becomes a networking public sphere, a hybrid place with open walls for deliberate dialogue, critique and opposition with an atmosphere of diversity, inclusion and difference functioning as a site for spirited thinking, collective visioning and future-making towards preferable (sometimes even preposterous) worlds. Moving forward, university culture must stress the public character of the university in the sense that universities are potential public places with a preference for a pluralism of views and where authoritarian views may be challenged (Englund and Bergh, 2020). University culture for the public good has the task of connecting people and worlds and liberating the individual from her or his private world into a public collective (but heterogeneous) world (Englund and Bergh, 2020).

Given the right culture, place, atmosphere and collective visions, universities can play a central role in such a democratizing project constitutive of deliberation where different values, visions and opinions can be set against each other, judged and begin to work together:

> The deliberative academic developer will be involved in a discussion of the processes of collaboration and thus, at the very least, will need skills that are relevant to the complexities of community [and culture] building: negotiation, mediation, facilitation, and consensus building. (Kandlbinder, 2007: 57)

This, according to Englund and Bergh (2020), necessitates a shift from Kant's solitary moral consciousness to Habermas's idea of community of moral subjects developing a shared ethical consciousness through dialogue and deliberation. All of this might seem quite vague, abstract and, perhaps, even preposterous. Consequently, the following sections will give two such examples of university *futurescaping* with a focus on placefulness, atmosphere, collective visioning and academic values: a networking university culture and a hybrid university culture. This is done to glimpse wider and deeper futures for the university – as well as to point towards alternative and possible more preferable cultures for the university.

The two frameworks sketch out a design-driven speculative agenda for creating alternative infrastructures for university cultures. Such alternative future-oriented speculative design agendas for the university and its possible and preferable cultures – as networking university cultures or hybrid university cultures – might be considered a form of 'futurescaping' (Jain et al., 2011), a designerly look ahead towards universities and their multiple trajectories into the more or less unknown preposterous but plausible futures. Such frameworks, integrated on larger institutional scales or smaller classroom scales, open up alternative future pathways where new realities become feasible and noticeable in the corner of our eyes as we look beyond the present landscape that we are currently caught up in.

A Networking University Culture

The first futurescape is the networking university described in the chapter 'Networked learning in, for, and with the world' by Nørgård et al. (2019). With the concept of the ecological university (Barnett, 2017) and mode 3 universities as an underlying basis, the chapter considers how traditional formats for institutions and higher education can be rethought, reconfigured and redesigned in order to facilitate cultures of networked learning in, for and with the world. The possible future of a networking university culture takes on a more tangible form through integrating concrete organizational guidelines, pedagogical formats and educational patterns for bringing this about. The main contribution of the chapter is to develop the notion of the networking university – as place, atmosphere and preferable world – along with its implicated institutional formats and practice.

As such, the networking university implies a future institution where institution, society, teachers, researchers, students, professionals and societal citizens enter into closer dialogues and equal partnerships:

> The aim is to create future knowledge and societal value together that go beyond immediate use-value, present demand, or measurable output – thus substituting the economic and instrumental university-figuration of the mode 2 university with a configuration of the mode 3 university focusing more on human societal value and citizenship. (Nørgård et al., 2019: 74)

To achieve this, university and society need to integrated and embedded into each other to such an extent that they acknowledge each other as part of the same ecological system, world or culture. This has at least two sets of implications for the networking university:

> The first is that enrolling students in networked learning practices should help them build the capabilities they need to participate in searching for and constructing better ways of living. The second is that enrolling more teachers in networked learning practices should help transform the character of our educational institutions [. . . through] strengthening connections between institutions and communities. (NLEC, 2021: 318)

The networking university culture implies that the university as place and atmosphere is open to society and that it (re)configures itself as an open network entangled in and connecting with other networks. Here, citizens, professionals, workers, researchers, teachers, students and whoever is interested and engaged in the university as network can think, do and be together. In this way, it is a *university without walls* (European University Association, 2021). To achieve this requires a culture of mutual commitment, care, respect and integration of networks to co-create a shared world (Barnett, 2011; Nørgård et al., 2019), what we have elsewhere termed *participatory academic communities* (Aaen and Nørgård, 2015), *academic citizenship* (Nørgård and Bengtsen, 2016) or *universities of the future* (Canals et al., 2018). In such a networked and networking university culture, people inside and outside the classroom, cubicle or campus get intertwined in joint dialogues, co-operation and communality. Hierarchies are transformed into networks in order to invite for other kinds of academic knowing, doing and being. Overall, the perspective of networked higher education brings with it four understandings that emphasize different sets of connections:

(1) Between people and how they develop, maintain and learn from networks of others.
(2) Between situations or contexts – how people make connections between such situations, transforming or reconstructing knowledge for use in different situations.
(3) The ICT infrastructure and how it enables connections across time and space, including connections between situations (as in No. 2), boundary crossing, mobility and so on.
(4) Between (human and non-human) actants – understanding learning situations as entanglements of people and things (NLEC, 2021: 316).

More concretely, in the context of the networking university (Nørgård et al., 2019), these sets of connections are engaged through the timeless guidelines for co-operatives (the Rochdale Principles), future-oriented pedagogical frameworks and concrete educational formats in order to create a culture of networking in, for and with the world.

The co-operative guidelines, or Rochdale principles, are one set of guidelines by which a non-hierarchical networking university culture can be constituted. In Nørgård et al. (2019), the Rochdale principles are reworked into seven principles for a university culture that invites more networking and networked institutions:

- The university is open to all through voluntary and democratic membership.
- Higher education takes place through democratic organizations controlled by their members, who actively influence and decide their policies and practice.
- Members contribute to, and democratically control, the mandate of their university.
- Higher education takes place in autonomous networks controlled by their members.
- University teaching provides education and professional development for their members so they can contribute efficiently to the development of their university and society.
- Universities serve their members most efficiently and strengthen the Networking University by working together in hybrid networks through local, regional, national and international structures.
- Higher education aims for sustainable development of its members' communities through policies approved by their members (Nørgård et al., 2019: 77–8).

Such general guidelines, in the form of co-operative principles, enable the macro-formation of the networking university as place, atmosphere and culture. Networked higher education cultures are characterized by 'processes of collaborative, co-operative and collective inquiry, knowledge-creation and knowledgeable action, underpinned by trusting relationships, motivated by a sense of shared challenge and enabled by convivial technologies' (NLEC, 2021: 320). At its core, a networked and networking university promotes a culture of connections between people, places, ideas, practices and across time, space and technologies (NLEC, 2021).

To make the networking university emerge as place, atmosphere and culture, it needs to be carried out in concrete academic practices. Aaen and Nørgård (2015) provide a concrete case of an entire higher education course organized as a networked and networking community, while Nørgård et al. (2019) offer a range of different educational formats for practising networked and networking cultures in higher education. Two of these examples are 'Collaborative Open Online Projects' (CO-OP) and 'Global Online Interuniversity Teaching' (GO-IT).

In CO-OP, students, teachers and researchers work together in groups or collectives with people outside the university. CO-OP connects people in flat networks across sites to engage them in shared projects, societal issues or community interventions. The projects can be large-scale Massive Open Online Projects (MOOPS) where multiple communities, courses and companies work together within a concrete context to generate shared value or lasting change. But this also works on a smaller scale. For example, small-scale projects can create shared websites or products connected to a concrete course, local community and specific organizations or companies. Or such networking can take the form of collaborative book projects, on-site festivals or open community conferences.

In GO-IT, teachers work together across universities to co-teach courses through video conferencing, shared documents or online learning spaces. One benefit is that teachers have an opportunity to take advantage of their professional networks to invite research colleagues across the globe into their classroom to think, talk and teach together without having to pay to bring them there physically. It is not just expertise that is added but also a complex network of perspectives and voices across courses, disciplines, student and teacher perspectives; and potentially the formation of global student networks (Nørgård et al., 2019: 82–3).

Through concrete academic practices, the macro-structure of the networking university is brought to life, interweaving different public arenas and actors into an academic network. In this way, academic culture itself becomes a form of societal co-operation and co-commitment taking place in, for and with society. Accordingly, the culture of the networking university becomes a driver for academic citizenship where students, teachers and researchers are positioned explicitly as citizens and members of the society through their networking practices. In this way, networks are formed with other societal, professional, political and private domains. By inviting such mutual processes of being networked and networking, university and society may regain trust in each other (Nørgård et al., 2019).

If a culture of mutual trust is consolidated across academic, professional, institutional and societal domains, the network has the potential of creating an atmosphere of interconnectedness and embeddedness. In this way, the networking university as ecology and culture goes well beyond carrying out research, teaching and learning within the institution, but uses co-operation, openness and connectedness to contribute to wider societal needs and become closer coupled with the world. The networking university might be a potent metaphor for transforming the performance culture of the present-day university into a networking culture where its diverse members participate in, for and with society (Nørgård et al., 2019).

A Hybridizing University Culture

The second futurescape is the hybrid university (Hilli et al., 2019; Nørgård, 2021). Through the concepts of hybridity and hybrid higher education, the two texts identified here consider how hybridization can help bring about new 'breeds' of higher education formats, spaces, environments and institutions.

Some distinctions between the notions of hybrid, hybridity and hybridization might be helpful in considering the composition of hybrid institutions and cultures:

- A hybrid refers to a new species, form or culture that is a fusion or dissolution of already-existing species, forms or cultures. A hybrid such as a mule is neither a donkey-horse nor a horse-donkey, but something *other*, a new form: a mule. A hybrid carries a double value because it reminds us of the distinct forms from which it originates, while simultaneously it is something new and previously unknown.
- Hybridization describes the process of fusing or dissolving species, forms or cultures in order to create a hybrid, that is, the processes undertaken to develop or design for new hybrids. The process of hybridization underlines that what is termed a 'hybrid' is in a state where it is not yet fully established as a mature species, but is, rather, something on its way to becoming.
- 'Hybridity' is a term for the relation between a hybrid and its source material. Hybridity highlights what makes a hybrid as such when compared to other species, forms or cultures. In other words, hybridity is the distinctive or salient characteristics of a new entity coming into being (see Nørgård (2021) for a more thorough description).

A hybrid institution, culture or environment, then, utilizes the concept of hybridity to dissolve or fuse traditional dichotomies between for instance offline/online, digital/analogue, institution/society or formal/informal to create new breeds, or types, of academic spaces, interactions and experiences, multiple dichotomies being fused to create something new:

> In this way a hybrid learning environment exists as an in-between and neither-nor space characterized by constant signification, translation and negotiation where there is neither a beginning nor an end, nor any unity nor purity, and where primordial notions of culture and nation have been replaced by a floating and multiple, indistinguishable and indeterminate existence. Hybridization,

then denotes the process of bringing new species of into existence through cross-fertilization or cross-breeding existing ones. (Nørgård, 2021: 1715)

Hybrid cultures are characterized by being polyphonic, rhizomatic and heterogeneous by nature. Consequently, the hybrid university is not *known* or *determined*, but is always on the move towards something new, never fully formed or determined. Hybrid university cultures are distinct in trying to think *otherwise* about time, space, place and roles, and are not dependent on a location-bound campus, the boundaries between researching, learning, working, playing and living becoming entangled, with a hybridization of the online and offline, on-site and off-site, synchronous and asynchronous, formal and informal, vocational and recreational (Nørgård, 2021): 'people connect and interact through a hybrid network of physical and technology-mediated encounters to co-construct knowledge and . . . [to] engage in positioning practices necessary for their work' (Cook et al., 2016: 125).

Generally, participating in and through hybrid cultures or environments implies uncertainty, risk-taking, experimentation, open-endedness, dialogue and disorder. Work on hybrid higher education (Köppe et al., 2017, 2018; Pedersen et al., 2018, Kohls et al., 2017) highlights a shift in the structure of education towards transformations and transgressions, that asks researchers, teachers, learners and citizens to reflect on the value, purpose and reasons for upholding traditional or taken-for-granted dichotomies. At the heart of the aforementioned works on hybrid higher education is a value framework consisting of six core values with accompanying sub-values that underpins the place, atmosphere and culture of the hybrid university: (1) empathy based on respect, care, commitment and compassion, (2) belonging and being with sensitivity and generosity, (3) playfulness through curiosity and creativity, (4) agency and empowerment through autonomy, resourcefulness, freedom and courage, (5) *bildung* in the form of thoughtfulness, discipline and professionalism and (6) discovery as experimentation and exploration.

On the basis of this value framework, Hilli et al. (2019) formulated four general design principles for developing and practising hybrid spaces in higher education. Adapted to culture and the university, these principles can form the foundation for more hybrid university cultures:

(1) *Rhizomatic places and knowledge forms*: Hybrid universities emerge as new institutional forms through a process of hybridization that creates an open-ended entanglement of places, atmospheres and cultures in ways

that support and invite for rhizomatic, polyphonic and heterogeneous knowledge forms – and even experimental or disorderly acts of research, teaching and learning. A hybrid university emerges as *vibrant matter* (Bennett, 2010) that intentionally hangs in the balance.

(2) *A culture of dissolving dichotomies*: The composition of hybrid universities is simultaneously the decomposition of dichotomies – rather than thinking in an exclusive *or*, hybrid cultures think in an inclusive *and*. A hybrid university culture works towards a continuous and reflective dissolution of traditional or taken-for-granted dichotomies to create new *breeds of otherness*. It is a space of heterogeneous inclusion, not exclusion.

(3) *Creating a dislocated spirited place*: The drawing together of a hybrid university creates a dislocated but placeful ecology given that a hybrid university is not delimited to one campus, configuration, system or platform, but forms through an entanglement of localities, technologies, channels and layers. The hybrid university constitutes a dislocated spirited place, where scholars, teachers, students, citizens, employers, contexts, media, materials and so on connect in intimately integrated ways and uphold an atmospheric culture in the form of a permeable membrane towards the surrounding societal domains.

(4) *Breadth and depth of the collective*: Hybrid universities are made through the pulling together – across localities – of heterogeneous people that breathe, live and learn together. As such, it is a hybrid culture with atmospheric depth and breadth – a culture beyond traditional academic boundaries emerging from mutual empathy, belonging, playfulness, empowerment and *bildung* between individuals, partnerships, teams, groups, collectives and communities. It is people who, like burdocks, hang on to each other and the world by forming a hybrid culture in the form of a hybridized institution. In hybrid university cultures, depth emerges through breadth via the burdocks holding the university together as the inhabitants get together to work across places and platforms. It is an emergence of hybridity through a constant entanglement of being together across spaces, time, technologies, materials, contexts and roles (Hilli et al., 2019: 77–8).

Founded on such explicated values and principles, hybrid university cultures draw people, contexts and places together to form a holistic new hybrid out of disparate locations, diverse tools, distinctive contexts and different people. A university can be considered hybrid if it works towards dissolving dichotomies and facilitating an entanglement along the axes of learner-professional, institution-society, thinking-tinkering, open-closed, informal-formal contexts, on-site-online, acquisition-performance (Hilli et al., 2019). In order for this to happen, it is necessary that the university take on the challenge of becoming hybrid in both thinking and practice transforming itself into a new breed in the process. Overall, a hybrid university culture points towards new forms of entangled and complex cultures and institutions. This implies the development of new hybrid institutional frameworks, environments and spaces.

On a macro-level, Staley's (2019) book, *Alternative universities: Speculative design for innovation in higher education*, offers a range of hybrid university breeds such as the Interface University, the Nomad University and the Microcollege. On a meso-level, a range of hybrid teaching and learning formats can be found in publications on hybrid higher education, such as Kohls et al. (2017) on 'sharing is caring' containing pedagogical patterns such as Interuniversity Teaching, Bidirectional Home Visits and Open Creative Commons sharing and Köppe et al. (2018) on 'hybrid collaboration patterns', the latter pointing to pedagogical patterns such as Hybrid Classroom Discussion, Student Shared Resource Space and Collective Annotation. Finally, on the micro-level and as a concrete case, Hilli et al. (2019) and Nørgård and Hilli (2021) describe and analyse a *hyper-hybrid* course taught across a Danish and Finish university. The first article describes the course from the teachers' perspective as it was designed and intended, while the second article describes the course from the students' perspective as it was conducted and experienced.

Conclusions: University Culture Moving Forward

In the European University Association's (2021) report, *Universities without walls: A vision for 2030*, universities of the future are described as co-operative and networking institutions which take the form of communities with open boundaries that build bridges between countries, cultures and sectors:

> When looking to the future, we envision universities without walls; these are universities that are open and engaged in society while retaining their core values. [. . .] In this decade, universities will build on their capacity to evolve and will become engines of societal change. They will provide an open, transformative space for common knowledge production through research, education, innovation and

culture. Together with other societal stakeholders, they will shape the future of a knowledge-driven society. (European University Association, 2021: 5)

Such entanglement, through hybridizing and networking, positions universities, and their inhabitants become co-operative, networked and networking with and in the world. Universities can use hybridization to build future bridges and create deeper dialogues between different people, societal ecosystems and cultures. Here, hybrid and networking university institutions and cultures are characterized by being *spirited places* that create a cultural atmosphere of being a somewhere for someone. In this way, the hybrid and networking university is not a system or space but a home and a place. This necessitates an opening up of the university – to let itself become both hybridized and hybridizing, networked and networking, through working with the fusion of dimensions and the dissolution of dichotomies to create new networks and hybrids. Such a university sprawls across an array of technologies, systems, spaces and cultures to constitute a networking and networked ecosystem where new hybrid forms of thinking, doing and being emerge.

> Universities . . . will continue to be characterised by being cooperative and networked institutions locally, nationally and internationally. As such, they continue to build bridges between countries, cultures and sectors. On the one hand, universities are places of . . . refuge . . . for lateral thinking and for creating new knowledge that still lies outside of mainstream awareness. On the other hand, knowledge production can benefit from a dialogue with society, actively involving citizens and non-academic partners such as business, non-governmental organisations, public authorities and others that share objectives with the university. Both areas will remain fundamental for the universities' service to society. The nature and structure of universities will be hybrid. (European University Association, 2021: 5)

Within such future universities, there is an academic engagement with known unknowns and even unknown unknowns to drive societal change, create transformational learning environments and open up institutional spaces to form universities without walls and beyond traditional dichotomies. This establishes the future university as a holistic open ecosystem nested within – and in dialogue with – other ecosystems.

Such alternative future-oriented speculative design agendas for the university and its possible and preferable cultures – as the networking university culture or the hybrid university culture – might be considered a form of 'futurescaping' (Jain et al., 2011). Here, future universities beyond our present imagination might be very real and on the brink of coming into being. Futurescaping the university requires careful work on the macro, meso and micro levels – like the work of an imaginative landscaper working with the landscape of the now to call forth a future landscape lying in wait. In this way, landscapers are simultaneously attentive towards the present reality and the future potentiality as they work with both world and future as media. Through attentive futurescaping alternative places, atmospheres and visions emerge that can be tested as potentially preferable worlds thereby broadening and deepening the future of the university. Working on the brink of the possible – and well beyond what the untrained landscaper can imagine – the futurescaper escapes the predicted and colonized future.

Through working with the world (and, here, the university) and futures as material, new hybrid university breeds – that might seem like preposterous ideas or unfeasible utopias – come into being. What might seem preposterous to a landscaper caught up in the reality of the present landscape can be real possibilities for the futurescaper. Preposterous futures – like space tourism, global pandemics or mobs storming the US Capitol Hill – are happening all around us. The future is more open than we think, to both good and bad, and this also goes for the future of the university. Thinking carefully about the long-term effects of the present university and its cultures, what would we then like to get away from? And envisioning the long-term effect of possible future hybrids, where would we then like to go? The answers to these questions will tell us what we need to do, no matter how preposterous it might seem in the reality we find ourselves caught up in. Speculative design practices and alternative university futures remind us that the limits of our designerly imagination – our futurescaping power – are the limits of our reality, in past, present and future.

Part III

Within and beyond Culture

Søren Bengtsen

Higher Education as Cultural Formation

Introduction

With the aim of overcoming the duality of higher education *and* culture, as sometimes encountered in academic and public debate, I advance the understanding of higher education *as* cultural formation. Where higher education is often linked to educational, knowledge and economic achievements and outcomes, I argue for greater awareness of higher education as, first and foremost, a *cultural achievement*. Understood in this way, higher education should be seen not only as an intellectual, albeit critical, commentary and assessment of our societal and cultural situation. Rather, higher education should be seen as a way of taking root and increasing understanding, belonging and critical awareness of our own cultural membership and identities.

I aim to explore the connections between higher education, individual and personal growth, increase of societal and cultural awareness, and a heightened sense of cultural belonging. The autonomy achieved through higher education should never be understood as a negative freedom, where the individual may detach himself from his societal and cultural surroundings – and the values that shape him – but always seek to critically judge his own actions and own privileges in the light of his achieved knowledge, competence and opportunities.

We often find a political and societal interest in the usefulness and impact of the knowledge academics create, but more rarely do we see much awareness of, or interest in, the cultural practices and virtues by which knowledge is created and curated. In some circles, such critical practices that uphold the academic ethos go by names such as scientific criteria, research methodology, research design or simply criticality. However, such 'culture-neutral' terminology is ultimately anchored in deeper cultural values and virtues. Culture understood as the development of the 'ethos' from Aristotle, linking disposition (virtue), thinking and education together, makes us realize that thinking, researching, teaching and learning all rest on the understanding of the academic as having certain duties, which include not lying, telling the truth, being critical, seeking the common and not the individual gain. I draw from Aristotle and more contemporary scholars to show that the foundational communal nature of academic culture can only be upheld and societally recognized and accepted because it aligns with deeper cultural virtues in our society and personal lives.

The early-modern understanding of academic culture has a part to play in this understanding, in René Descartes and even in earlier mediaeval philosophy such as the scepticism of St Augustine and the dialectics of Thomas Aquinas. Truth-seeking is still, not least in a post-truth era, foundational not only to our academic but also to our wider cultural heritage. With Descartes and contemporary scholars, I argue that truth-seeking, as such, makes impossible the acquisition of knowledge for personal or instrumental gain and that the inbuilt scepticism, or criticality, in academic culture forms the basis of a democratic and inclusive society. Examples such as plagiarism, knowledge theft and research forgery happen when the ethical and the epistemological in academic culture have been separated – that is, when academic practice is devoid of its cultural ethos.

Virtues and Community

Paradoxically, as universities and higher education become increasingly more widespread and with record-high enrolment numbers globally, the crisis in our academic culture seems to increase too. According to Naidoo (2016, 2018), '[u]niversities world-wide are trapped in a competition fetish' (2016: 1), where transformation and change in universities follow one primary 'master economic imaginary' (2016, 2018). The academic culture has become infected by neoliberal language and speech acts – as when 'excellent' research covers for meanings of economic, and not academic (i.e. scientific), success. Smyth (2018) warns that the *universitas* and fellowship-oriented community of universities slide towards a 'toxic university', where the financially most successful researchers are worshipped as rock stars (star researchers) and cultural leaders. Giroux (2018: 39) argues that the erosion of academic culture has far-reaching societal consequences. Higher education has become an element of corporate power and culture and is being 'denied its value as a democratic public sphere and guardian of public values'. Threats to democracy and criticality in universities and societies more generally are mirrored in each other.

The threat to academic culture is that, on the one hand, the intellectual and the moral ties of academic work are being severed, leaving little room for encouragement of research and higher education being connected to cultural, and not only financial, sustainability. On the other hand, the chord and connection between individual and collective, or communal, efforts are threatened, leaving universities and higher education open and vulnerable to increasing competition, individual rivalry and 'de-collegiality' – and the forgetfulness of the extent knowledge creation and scientific efforts depend on community efforts, both in the present and through building on prior research and experiences and forms of institutional leadership and knowledge stewardship.

As academic culture comes under pressure, it becomes similarly increasingly visible, and part of everyday discussions in universities around the world, that academic culture rests on a foundation of virtues, which make scientific progress and higher learning possible. I use the term 'virtue' here as it connects with the Aristotelian understanding of a social bond and community building – so, linking individual effort and collective achievement. To Aristotle (1976: 99), virtues form the social glue that holds communities (on different levels) together as 'virtues are neither feelings nor faculties (. . .) [but] dispositions'. Virtues favour the collective effort over the individual, and even though the uniqueness and originality of the individual researcher, student or teacher is hugely important, it is 'a greater and more perfect thing to achieve and preserve that of a community' (Aristotle, 1976: 64). There is a deep and strong, and perhaps underrated, foundation in our academic culture that, luckily, does not erode and crumble so easily – that academics come together and work on a common project, which is the advancement of knowledge and the societal and cultural growth of our wider communities.

The importance of academic culture connects strongly to the Humboldtian idea of 'Bildung', sometimes translated into the term 'formation'. As Humboldt (2018: 46) points out, higher learning hinges on the link between 'intellectual and moral culture'. To develop a new understanding of theory and core concepts or to design and conduct field research is only possible through a particular form of *cultural practice* – being at the same time intellectually *and* morally active and agentive. As Humboldt (2018: 47) writes:

> The intellectual exertions of men, however, only prosper through a process of collaboration. This does not mean merely that one individual supplies what another lacks. Collaboration operates through a process in which the successful intellectual achievements of one person arouse the intellectual passions and

enthusiasms of others, and through the fact that what was at first expressed only by one individual becomes a common intellectual possession instead of fading away in isolation. Given this collective character of individual accomplishment, the inner life of these higher intellectual institutions must be such as to call forth and sustain a continuously self-renewing, wholly uncoerced and disinterested collaboration.

In contemporary studies of 'Bildung' and higher education, it is argued that the student of higher education 'is thus able to – while retaining his own individuality – lift himself out of the particular and to place himself in the universal' (Karlsohn, 2018: 108). There is, therefore, no conflict between individual and collective efforts, but their synergy and embeddedness are essential for intellectual as well as moral formation. While the higher education curriculum today has a formal focus on the acquisition of certain knowledge, skills and competence of the individual student, the community aspect of the learning trajectory is surprisingly tacit and may be said to form a hidden curriculum (Elliot et al., 2020).

Academic and scientific practice and higher learning are founded on a peer culture. The practice of peer review and discussion is as old as the university itself. Peer learning and peer culture are embedded within academic culture and any processes of higher learning. Peer culture does not mean assimilation into a shared hegemonic or ideological knowledge regime. Engaged, energetic and critical disputes are essential to higher learning whether it takes place in the classroom in the first year, in the auditorium for the doctoral dissertation defence, or at research conferences around the world. As Barnett (2011: 90) puts it, 'the culture lies in the anarchy: the anarchy *is* the culture', and academic culture cannot be 'separated from anarchy; not counterposed to anarchy, but identified by anarchy. Culture and anarchy as one, together'. The critical imagination, daring and playfulness inherent in peer discussions are constituents of the community building and sustaining higher-order learning processes.

Embracing and engaging intellectual diversity constitutes perhaps the most important of academic virtues, that of magnanimity. Nixon (2008) argues that the virtue of magnanimity underscores the differing views on how research and scholarship should be conducted and why, including variation in disciplinary tribes, clusters and paradigms. Despite the differences within academic world views, important to change and growth, the deeper cultural value is that what 'we are trying to do through our research and scholarship is [to] understand what we do not yet understand', and research and scholarship 'are the supreme emblems of an autonomous self that is seeking to move beyond itself – reaching out in curiosity and a spirit of enquiry. They are inherently magnanimous' (Nixon, 2008: 107). Going back to the Aristotelian sense of virtue as a supra-individual aspect of community building, I would argue, with Szadkowski's (2018) terminology, that the notion of the common is the political ontology of academic culture per se. Being able to gather around a shared, common goal and feeling joint ownership and responsibility lie at the heart of academic culture.

Mutual respect, inclusion, diversity and collective responsibility are not only values that our present societies strive so hard to develop, sustain and integrate, but, already, lie at the heart of the higher education curriculum and the process of formation inherent in higher learning. Scientific achievements and higher learning are impossible without a virtuous community and a shared culture, and these cultural issues mirror wider societal and political challenges for the coming time.

Truth and Integrity

Through history, truth has been one of the most important identity markers of academics, and their sense of scientific, intellectual and cultural contribution rests on it. Gibbs (2004) links truth and trust together and argues that societies trust universities, and academics, because they expect them to speak the truth and uphold the truth; without personal or political gain. Truth-seeking and truth-telling are a form both of service to society and of academic citizenship. Truth is, therefore, connected both to the individual academic and to institutional integrity. However, as Bengtsen and Barnett (2020: 9) point out, in the 'growing climate of "alternative facts", academics find themselves having to defend the very idea of truth (. . .) where the line of demarcation between truth and falsehood is *intentionally* dissolved by some in power who seek to undermine authorities of truth'. As Harsin (2015) and Peters and colleagues (Peters et al., 2018) have argued, academics and their institutions face different political regimes of post-truth, where universities and institutions for higher education are challenged on their own remit of truth-telling and knowledge expertise. Collin (2019) argues that the foundational contract of trust between universities and society is currently under threat and that a new social contract is needed. As both corporate research funding and ministerial interest in the political gains of research bring universities closer to strategic research, the meaning and ethos of academic freedom and integrity is being heatedly debated in universities around the world.

What it means to tell the truth and the proper methods to apply for that purpose have been actively discussed across historical periods, disciplinary paradigms and research traditions. However, there has been a consensus in favour of actually striving for finding and telling the truth – and, thus, not to lie or manipulate – as one of the chief goals of research and higher learning. One of the hallmarks of higher learning and thinking has been to challenge dogma, destabilizing habitual and normative assumptions, and to fearlessly challenge one's own preconceptions and possible mind snares. Descartes (1999: 16–17) is a defining example of the relentless strive for truth and certainty while avoiding manipulation, demagogy and dogma:

> Anything which admits of the slightest doubt I will set aside just as if I had found it to be wholly false; and I will proceed in this way until I recognize something certain, or, if nothing else, until I at least recognize for certain that there is no certainty. (. . .) [S]o what is left at the end may be exactly and only what is certain and unshakeable.

Descartes exemplifies not only the strive for truth, and the integrity of sober and thorough inquiry, but also the inherent optimism and belief that truth-seeking is a possible and meaningful endeavour. As Descartes (1999: 43) announces, he shall 'unquestionably reach the truth, if only I give sufficient attention to all the things which I perfectly understand, and separate these from all the other cases where my apprehension is more confused and obscure'. In his writing and own scientific pursuits, Descartes exemplifies the boldness, sobriety and fearlessness we still today connect with academic integrity and the raison d'être of the university.

Paul Gibbs (2019) and Sharon Rider (2018a) argue that a vital part of academic culture is truth-telling. To sustain a truth-culture in higher education and beyond does not only mean being able to demonstrate how truth may be practised, but it also requires that academics exhibit the courage to *speak* the truth, even or especially when it is not wanted. The notion of a truth-culture here covers not only epistemic but also moral concerns, which becomes visible in current debates on research integrity. Gibbs (2019: 7) explains that truth-telling includes speaking out 'when the consequences may be unfavourable to oneself requires courage and a reconstitution of what higher education has become', which, according to Gibbs, heralds 'a return to an ethos of personal growth that better represents what humanity might become, rather than offering a service of blinkered higher skills training'. To live up to and honour the trust invested by, and the contract entered with, the wider society, academics are obliged to speak up if they feel their academic freedom is being compromised.

The aim of institutional integrity, for universities, is that they maintain their positions as 'institutions of truth', which Rider (2018: 26) defines as 'human constructions devised to uncover, unfold and preserve the common world'. In times where universities become pressed by governments, corporations and industry, who all claim their particular say in the matter of the higher education curriculum, it is vital to 'establish and maintain institutions, "safe zones", (. . .) where the presence of personal interest and conviction have limited coercive force' (Rider, 2018: 28). Institutions of truth aim to give voice and stage (also) to unpleasant national trauma (e.g. colonialism and imperialism) and to marginalized social groups otherwise not being recognized and heard except for in research projects or in a curriculum of integrity. Institutions of truth must speak *to* the cultural centre and *for* and *from* the cultural (and historical) peripheries by giving voice to the silent and the silenced who may no longer have the voice to speak, or have disappeared in prison camps, secret jails or fallen on battlefields in forgotten wars.

In a similar vein, Nixon (2008: 129) argues that universities should constitute a 'buffer zone between the crude forces of personal self-interest and the impersonal interests of the state'. With almost unnerving prophetic precision, Nixon continues, more than a decade ago, stating that when 'nation states fall apart in the aftermath of war, economic disaster, or the ravages of pan-epidemics, then the regeneration of institutional life has a major and pressing priority' (2008). If science and higher education fall prey to political populism and nationalism, the notions of truth and integrity can be very difficult to restore, together with the trust between universities and wider society. Universities endure *because* they have not (yet) been devoured by ferocious and corrupt regimes, and because the subtle bond, which makes out the social contract between higher education institutions and civic society, has not been broken – albeit it has been shaken by scandals of scientific fraud and the tampering of data by external partners. Despite current challenges and pressures, universities remain concrete examples of the possibility of truth-seeking and moral integrity. Still.

Criticality and Activism

Universities today are often funded either by the state according to their student throughput (graduation number) or in private institutions through student fees. Political (and sometimes leadership) focus is on student enrolment numbers, completion time and enhanced efficiency and quality of student programmes (measured by performance indicators). In the midst of maintaining the machinery of higher education, Gildersleeve (2016) reminds us not to forget the knowledge imperative inherent in academic culture. The knowledge imperative reminds us to move the gaze beyond the walls of academia and to engage with the surrounding societal contexts. There is a criticality embedded in the knowledge imperative. Criticality is not, first and foremostly, about the truth value of research and higher learning – but the ability to leave room for other perspectives in one's own striving for knowledge and meaning.

There is an ethical vein in the awareness of other and different viewpoints, world views and belief systems – and even, I will argue, an imaginative and activist ore in the critical striving to make changes for a better world. As Barnett (2013: 45) states, only the 'imagination can offer transport to a new world' and thereby 'freeing the university from its entrapment within dominant discourses and working towards social emancipation'. Being critical is a form of epistemic-moral action and agency, complementing and enhancing (and amending when necessary) one's own perspective and understanding for a greater social and cultural goal. Criticality is a form of cultural dialectics.

Criticality has formed the identity of universities and academics from the earliest times, from the Platonic dialogues to the teaching and discussion format in the mediaeval university. In the work of St Thomas Aquinas (2008), the critical stance is particularly visible – first, in the precise distinction between the text presented and the author's own interpretation, and, second, in the succession of presenting views and counterviews until a higher (more critical) understanding has been reached. The deep ethical vein of criticality is visible in the work of Emmanuel Levinas (2003) and in resistance to turning one's understanding of the world into suppression and assimilation, which leads inevitably to 'imperialist dominion, [and] to tyranny' (Levinas, 2003: 47). Levinas (2003: 43) defines ethics as 'the calling into question of my spontaneity by the presence of the Other'. In work on critical pedagogy by Paulo Freire (2013) and Henry Giroux (2011), the calling into question of one's own understanding is being taken to a societal and a cultural level. Here, criticality moves beyond academic reasoning and enters the scene of societal involvement and cultural action.

In the literature on higher education, critical thought is described as a blend of intellectual scepticism, moral vigilance and societal action (Bengtsen and Barnett, 2018; Davies and Barnett, 2015). In Barnett's work, criticality is seen as being embodied in the student as a 'critical being' (Barnett, 1997: 63ff), which would include the three dimensions of critical reason (knowledge), critical self-reflection (self) and critical action (society) – the latter of which I shall focus on the latter. As Barnett argues, if critical action is to achieve 'its full potential of encouraging the student to come forward with imaginary and emancipatory possibilities, it must reach out to the received definitions of the world and engage with them' (Barnett, 1997: 89). The notion of critical action connects intellectual, moral and societal pursuits of academic culture with the inherent imperative that compels the academic to *act*. Critical action may take many forms such as speaking out critically in newspapers, radio or television programmes, keeping an active and critical internet presence on social media and public blogs, or becoming a member of non-governmental organizations. Being critical, however, and to maintain criticality, requires academics not to fall victim to current ideologies. In engaging critically and constructively with the world, the critical action itself 'has to maintain some critical distance from the world' (Barnett, 1997).

Critical action creates a social and cultural leeway where institutional and social critics may air and discuss their viewpoints undaunted. The ability to create and manoeuvre within a cultural leeway, Arndt and Mika (2018) terms 'dissidence'. As Arndt and Mika (2018: 51) argue, dissidence allows for a subversion and dismantling of dominant common thought 'with more likelihood of arriving at fresh, critical insights, of diverse thought and ways of being beyond the status quo'. In academic dissidence, there is an inherent 'willingness to open oneself up to unanswered puzzles, connections and contradictions through critical analysis of what may be, or first appear to be, irresolvable, internal and logical disjunctions' (2018). Dissidence, as a form of criticality, never allows the critical party to avoid critical evaluation himself. Thus, dissidence does not separate but *connect* diverse social, ethnic or political groups. Through dissidence one becomes vulnerable and exposes one's own limitations and uncertainties.

There is a connect between criticality and social welfare. Shumar and Robinson (2020) argue that it is the responsibility of academics to 'identify disharmonies' in the societies they are a part of, such as climate issues, marginalization of ethnic groups or gender inequality. As most people are willing to accept disharmonies, or prone to think they cannot do anything to change the situation, academics should 'engage with others in a process of attempting to imagine what a world might be if we could transcend the disharmony' (Shumar and Robinson, 2020: 163). With the notion of criticality, we see a direct line and connection between critical discussions in the higher education classroom, student assignment, research paper, conference debate, public debate, societal engagement and different forms of 'academic activism' (Nørgård and Bengtsen, 2021).

Where academic virtues enable and aid cultural cohesion and solidarity, and where truth enables personal and social integrity, criticality enables social and cultural change *and* at the same time safeguards this changemaking from the clutches of ideology and regimes. Criticality may challenge and provoke, and oftentimes take the form of self-challenging and self-provoking thought and action, but with the underlying aim of making room for difference and otherness. In contrast to some forms of political activism, academic activism is inherently ethical in nature.

Higher Education as Cultural Formation

Not only is political culture and integrity being debated around the world today, but academic culture too. Just as we follow political scandals about fake news, corruption and public neglect, we hear (too regularly) about scientific scandals concerning fraud, knowledge theft, plagiarism, lack of integrity and ethical neglect. One of the vital challenges for the university in the years to come is to maintain trust with, and enter into new and approved relationships with, the public and political spheres of societies. This challenge is reflected both in the culture within universities themselves, including leadership and the curriculum, and the ways universities and higher education connect to the wider culture(s) in the surrounding societal arenas and contexts. University leaders, research programme directors, student presidents and other academic representatives must face this challenge of academic culture head-on in order for the institution to endure and thrive. There is no hiding. There are no shortcuts.

Luckily, our academic culture has, still, a very strong ethical foundation without which knowledge creation, critical discussion, research and higher learning would be impossible. Not just in their present forms, but in any form. Relying on the work of colleagues, where one has not taken part, requires mutual trust and respect – and assumes honesty and sobriety. Sharing work in progress and admitting to errors and dead ends require courage and the ability to show vulnerability. Moving beyond collegial rivalry (at least on the best of days) and working together towards a common goal, and being willing to hand the result of one's hard labour (often several months and sometimes years in the making), require community feeling, generosity and magnanimity. It is important to make students, and the wider society, more aware of the inherent virtues and cultural values of higher education. Where the focus recent years has been on the scientific expertise, skills and competences, perhaps the focus for the coming years should be on the ethical and cultural foundation that makes such other academic endeavours and results possible at all.

While academic culture may be described in terms of collegiality and community within universities, one of the main terms that applies in wider societal contexts is 'citizenship' (Macfarlane, 2007; Nørgård and Bengtsen, 2016). Importantly, students of higher education bring these virtues and this culture with them when taking up jobs, positions and responsibilities in contexts outside academia. As Arvanitakis and Hornsby (2018: 95) point out, academics within society 'aim to live an ethical and fulfilled life, continue in the pursuit of knowledge, and are prepared to question the status quo, and engage with community', and they continue to 'treat information and knowledge critically and aim to improve society'. Stakeholders within and beyond the university need to focus not only on societal contributions in terms of knowledge expertise, skills and competences, but the virtues within the higher education curriculum too.

Perhaps the even deeper foundation of academic culture, which may be hard even for academics to articulate, is respect (or 'esteem' as the German word 'Achtung' is sometimes translated into). Respect does not 'just' refer to decency, or the desire for knowledge, but has a deeper ethical root. In Kant's understanding, 'respect (. . .) is hardly an analogue of the feeling of pleasure, although in relation to the faculty of desire it does the same thing but from different sources', and actions are not done 'merely in conformity with duty (. . .) but from duty, which must be the true end of all moral cultivation' (Kant, 2001a: 98). Integrity arises from respect and from the ethical notion of duty.

Respect is activated due to the realization, through study and learning, of the dignity and absolute worth of the matter studied. Despite the current winds of funding regimes, worth should not be understood in economic terms, as what 'has a price can be replaced by something else as its equivalent' – but 'what on the other hand is raised above all price and therefore admits of no equivalent has a dignity' (Kant, 2001b: 42). Through higher learning, we witness and experience that events, foreign cultures and peoples, animal species, system of cells or star dust particles have 'dignity, that is, an unconditional, incomparable worth' and 'the word respect alone provides a becoming expression for the estimate of it' (Kant, 2001b: 43). Scientific research and critical academic discussion are responses and ways of trying to react with respect towards the richness, subtlety and dignity of the world around us.

Conclusion

The American philosopher Alphonso Lingis (1998) points out that when we allow for deep study of creatures, events and cultures, we become invaded by them and are forced to treat them with respect. Science starts with the fascination of what is strange and other to ourselves. Research is the response to being touched by the wonder and potency of the world around us. We consider how 'the lonely circles the condor flies in the wake of the storm touch us', and we experience how 'the humble endurance of the fossil mollusk absorbs us!' (Lingis, 1998: 121). As Lingis argues, every scholar 'knows how the mental force to forge consistent concepts is weak without the force of this awe' (Lingis, 1998: 122). The possibility of academic inquiry rests ultimately on this awe – the respect for difference, diversity, otherness and strangeness.

From this foundational respect and recognition of the dignity and absolute worth of the world around us – past, present and future – the drive for research and study is ignited, and the motivation for higher learning is kindled. From this deep respect, academic culture and its scientific and curricular practices are structured. Due to this respect, higher education is a central part of the cultural formation of current and future generations. Thus, higher education is not separated from culture, or distant to or removed from culture. Higher education is, always, a form of cultural formation as higher learning and research resting on values of communality, generosity, respect, honesty and acknowledgement of autonomy. These values are underlying and make possible our academic practices of research, teaching and learning.

10

Cultural Leadership

Introduction: Leadership Challenged

Where is the university going? Who is the university for? The lines between universities, external professional contexts and wider political, societal and cultural contexts have been increasingly blurred and permeable over the last decades. On a positive note, universities have moved to centre stage with all that it brings of political and societal spotlight and interest. However, being in the spotlight requires a certain form of leadership (and not only management). A leadership that may create stronger cohesion across the levels of the expanding institutions (many easily count 50,000+ students and 15,000+ staff), building more robust communities within and outside the institutions themselves, connecting strategy and policy with research and teaching and learning practices in a meaningful way, and to inspire hope that will energize the members of the university (and not drain them).

Despite the success story of increasing enrolments numbers, many universities are pressed on resources and have to constantly stretch their funds and do more with less. Macfarlane (2012: 25) frames the picture comprehensively when he writes that universities today 'must try to offer mass, or perhaps universal, access to higher education with a lower unit cost' but 'at the same time they must respond to a broader social mission'. Being visible to many different contexts creates a variety of expectations and demands. Governments 'expect universities to meet the needs of multiple stakeholders: students, parents, professional bodies, taxpayers, business and industry and their own social and economic objectives. They must be all things to all people' (2012). Researchers feel the stretching when being met by expectations about their research coming not only from their peers and research environments but also from the company Board, or political organ, funding the research. Consequently, research integrity and research ethics are also, at times, being stretched. Teachers and students feel the institutional stretching when employable skills and competence are called for by accreditations systems, bending the course work and types of assignments towards a more generic education.

Critical voices within the literature argue that the loss of a clear purpose, goals and direction are visible in the very institutional 'bone-structure' (Smyth, 2018) of the university. It has even been suggested that life has gone out of university leadership and resulted in a 'zombification' (Smyth, 2018) of the university. Smyth argues that the role of the university as places of sustained social critique and debate has been 'superseded and supplanted with the notion of them being places that are responsive to the "knowledge economy" and the ideas of transparency and accountability that bring with them a fetish for "recordation" – meaning bookkeeping and the official recording of evidence' (Smyth, 2018: 78). The cohesion is crumbling within neoliberal institutions that pitch leaders and staff against each other and make colleagues compete vehemently for the same funding. To other critics, if we do not take care, we even face the death of the public university as we know it (Wright and Shore, 2018).

Less aggressive discussions of university leadership agree, in substance, with this picture. Ellis and Goodyear (2019: 98) point out that disturbances to 'established "ecologies of learning" are brought about by new demands, new pedagogies, new learning resources, and new course designs and credential structures'. A common issue for universities is the difficulty of connecting 'the learning challenges identified in courses (the micro) to the goals expressed in strategy for the whole institution (the macro)' (2019). In a similar fashion, Neumann (2020) argues that more focus and attention should be given to the 'institutional-faculty and the faculty-departmental nexus' (Neumann 2020: 205), as the opportunity for building stronger formal structures around, *and* informal communities within, universities lies at the heart of such across-level connection and cohesion. The challenges, with the lack of coherence and common focus and understanding of their role and purpose that universities face, seem to mirror a horizontal trajectory (universities and stakeholders outside the institution) in a vertical trajectory (across institutional levels within universities). This could be called the leadership-challenge-nexus in universities today, where the within-outside fragmentation requires leadership not only at the top of the pyramid but distributed and integrated into the research and teaching milieus themselves. After decades where the academic leadership has been pushed upwards and centralized, new forms of leadership are needed that are both vertically *and* horizontally embedded in the institution.

In the following, I will argue that the issue of leadership cannot be dealt with through yet another series of institutional or curricular reorganization and adding of extra funds (from yet another stakeholder who wishes for a piece of the cake). The issue of leadership (both institutional and societal) hinges on mainly two issues: first, leadership presence and community building within universities, and, second a renewal of the social contract with external partners and contexts. As I will show in the last section of the chapter, both forms of leadership should aim at creating a cohesive force, allowing for diversity and difference and yet still being able to gather all members of the institution around a shared common goal. The fragmentation and individualization of universities has reached its end, and it is time that universities come together around a shared culture of leadership, where leadership is communal and acknowledged and, at the same time, may speak with a common voice when collaborating with external contexts and stakeholders. This is a double leadership challenge facing the stretched university.

Institutional Leadership: Being *There*

The gap between university leadership and the research, work, educational activities and people they are leading has become too wide. In our vast departments and schools, leaders are not seen on a daily, or even weekly, basis. Their voices are heard mainly through occasional newsletters or echoed in circulated strategy papers or as cautions in times of a pandemic. I am not arguing that the academics (students, teachers and researchers) should be herded like sheep or steered through the same few mechanical channels of communication or work outlets. On the contrary, I am arguing, and in line with Macfarlane (2012: 91) that when leading academic work, there are responsibilities and duties, and it perhaps even 'necessitates a selfless disposition and skills that will enable others to develop. It is about full participation in, and making a contribution to, building intellectual communities often associated with the discipline.' It is crucial that leaders are visible, accessible and present within the research, educational or other academic and institutional environments that they lead. Not present in the way that they participate or even directly influence such work – but present in the sense that their support and backing is noticed and felt.

The experience of togetherness and a shared (but *not* uniform and hierarchically aligned) academic culture is central to academic work and identity formation. As argued by Elliot and her research team (2020: 139), it is only possible to create the feeling of a cohesive and collective academic environment 'if the person or people leading it are easy to approach, both structurally but also very much in person'. When the person(s) in charge become visible, the '*life* of the leadership becomes tangible and receives credibility and legitimacy' (2020). Cultural cohesion and growth are dependent on an open, free and critical dialogue, and within institutions. The dialogue has to be engaged, lively and inspirational. The goal is not for one leader (of a huge organization) to engage one-to-one with everyone constantly – but to form a shared culture, a 'University of We' (Nørgård et al., 2020), where leadership becomes less associated with policy and strategy (though it will often include this) and more strongly associated with an ethical awareness both within and outside institutions and community building practices.

With inspiration from Heidegger, I argue that, in leading, the leader(s) have to be *there*, and to *be* there. Not just through emailing, or staff meeting information speeches, or the friendly (and often well-meant) smile when passing in the corridor busily heading for the next strategy meeting. Leadership hinges on its ontological 'there', which Heidegger describes as the facticity of the Dasein. As Heidegger writes, '[w]henever Dasein is, it is a Fact; and the facticity of such a Fact is what we shall call Dasein's "*facticity*"' (Heidegger, 2000: 82). The 'there' is inextricably and unavoidably a constituent of the being-there of leadership. As Heidegger further writes, 'Dasein brings its "there" along with it. If it lacks its "there", it is not factically the entity which is essentially Dasein; indeed it is not this entity at all' (Heidegger, 2000: 171). In a related manner, I argue that the challenge of leadership in many universities is that it is *not there* – that is, where the student and staff facticity is taking place. The facticity of university leadership has been dislocated from the majority of the members of the institution. University leadership has to (re)gain its institutional and academic facticity – leadership has to be *there* and has to *be* there!

Despite the vastness of the organizational complexity in universities today, it is absolutely central that leaders, teachers, students and external partners work together. Not only in the meaning of being on the same page and aligning expectations and agendas, but actually *working* together. Of course, it is a challenge to get deans working on specific projects with students and teachers, and getting deans to teach, just as enabling students to lead, seems like blue-eyed-pie-in-the-sky fantasies. However, this is just what is required in order to regrow the community and cohesive direction and goal-setting that universities lack in our societies today. An important study funded by the Carnegie Foundation (Walker et al., 2008) showed that in order to form long-lasting intellectual communities at universities, it is just as important to get students on decision-making boards and committees as it is to have leaders contributing with their knowledge and expertise specifically by being in the classrooms and teaching, discussing and socializing with students and teachers. Such a project hinges on leaders being acknowledged as proper academics with strong intellectual and disciplinary expertise (and not just written off as professional managers) – and that students are acknowledged as mature adults capable of taking on complex and difficult leadership tasks (and not just written off as incapable and peripheral in-constant-need-of-support-academics).

To gain a sustainable leadership culture, and also to promote cultural leadership beyond institutional boundaries, we need to be able to understand higher education and research as academic *work*, where all have to work together. I am not using the term 'work' here in the sense of the machinery of large industries (even though the term 'factory' has been applied to universities before; e.g. see Goldman and Massy, 2001), but in the sense of transformative processes of learning and growth attributed to the term by John Locke (1999). As Locke writes, when a person has 'mixed his *Labour* with, and joined to it something of his own, and thereby makes it his *Property*' (Locke, 1999: 288). I am not talking about intellectual property and cognitive capitalism, or any form of economic liberalism. On the contrary, Locke has a point in that something new and transformative happens when work is being undertaken – it generates a facticity that anchors the person to the place and the purpose and goals she is striving towards. Work generates a *there* and a *being-there*.

Also, in Hegel (1977), work is related to the emancipatory movement away from bondage and towards self-realization and emancipation, as it is '[t]hrough *work*' that the 'bondsman becomes conscious of what he truly is' (Hegel, 1977: 118 – SB's italics). To Hegel, work is the transformative power that connects the individual consciousness with others and with the social-material, and political, lifeworld. It is 'work [that] forms and shapes' our projects, and the 'consciousness *qua* worker, comes to see in the independent being [of the object] its *own* independence' (Hegel, 1977). Work constitutes a dialectical movement, potentially cutting across hierarchies and different socio-intellectual and socio-material levels of reality. It is through working together that students and teachers understand, acknowledge and respect each other (as shown in so many studies on the power of collaborative learning), and it is through learning and *leading together* that students, teachers and leaders would be able to find common ground and build a community too.

In Nørgård and Bengtsen (2018), academic work is related to the work of the craftsman, and the institution is being compared to that of the community of the guild. Academic practices (including leadership) may be compared to craftsmanship, or work, and 'the university is also something generated by our hands, our being, our movements, and our ability to dwell and build in the world' (Nørgård and Bengtsen, 2018: 177). Gathering students, teachers, researchers and leaders in the same physical (or virtual) settings is a challenging task in many universities as the different academic groups work in entirely separate buildings, or different parts of the campus even, only occasionally crossing each other's path in the classroom, cantina, at staff meetings or funding meetings around upcoming research grants. Academics are rarely actually *working* together across institutional levels, on course plans, educational or research designs, outreach projects or around engagement in the wider society. They work separately, in separate physical sections, on different floors where they will not casually meet and enter into informal conversation.

Reducing the leadership of huge organizations, as many universities are, to simply working together across institutional levels would be a gross simplification and would lack the respect for what leadership in universities today also requires. However, we seem to have lost the ability to work together in our institutions across levels, and I suggest that at least some of the potential for sustainable leadership lies hidden in that fact. While many universities have a strong focus on cross-disciplinary (or interdisciplinary) collaboration, there is much less focus on cross-generational and cross-level collaboration within universities. A central part of leadership is being able to work closely together on the same projects and tasks, and to share the responsibility (albeit in different ways). Perhaps the distribution of leadership has gone too far, allowing certain leaders to entirely avoid engaging with students and teachers. We need to hear the voice of the dean in the classrooms more often, and the voices of students in committee meetings in decision-making over the design and financial balances in educational programmes, in order for both parties (and all in between) to make the university their own.

Societal Leadership: Forging the Social Contract Anew

By societal leadership is meant that universities have to make themselves manifest on the societal scene with ideas and forms of social engagement concerning human purposefulness – and especially in a politically and healthwise conflicted world. As Nixon writes, human purposefulness 'is a public good because it contributes to a society of active citizens rather than passive subjects' (Nixon, 2012: 115). There are no easy answers here, and theorizing alone cannot build the bridge required. The university has to fully recognize that 'the public is not an abstraction – but a presence' (Nixon, 2012). To repeat my aforementioned point about leadership, universities and academics have to be *there* societally, and they have to *be* there! Multiple questions arise, and are being tackled around the world in different ways, around what it means for universities and academics to be publicly present, or present publicly. There are no final, or easy, answers, and it is often a highly contextual matter depending on the political and social scene in a country, and the institutional and curricular type and profile.

According to Gibbs (2004) and Collin (2019), the contract, and trust, between universities and society is threatened by recent scandals concerning fraud, theft of intellectual property and issues around failed research ethics and integrity. Further, the shift towards corporate influence and industrially oriented research threatens to undermine basic research and academic freedom. Consequently, Collin (2019) calls for a new contract where academic freedom and public trust goes hand in hand. Who should form this new social contract and by what means? How may a university, and its members, not only show institutional leadership but societal leadership as well?

A new social contract or 'social pact' (Rousseau, 1968: 60) between universities and the wider society is needed. Perhaps even a social pact between universities, the government, the industry, the professional domains and civil society is needed – the term 'society' broadly stated seems to be of little help in this matter. Rousseau (1968: 59–61) reminds us of the importance of the social pact stating that 'by uniting [the] separate powers in a combination (. . .) uniting them so that their powers are directed by a single motive and act in concert', whereby 'every member [becomes] an indivisible part of the whole'. What can universities do to regain the trust of society – and to, perhaps as well, regain its own trust in government and corporate stakeholders? Rousseau (1968: 150) reminds us too of the foundational crisis that may threaten the social contract, when the society (Rousseau wrote 'state'), 'on the brink of ruin, can maintain itself only in an empty and illusory form, when the social bond is broken in every heart, when the meanest interest impudently flaunts the sacred name of the public good, then the general will is silenced'. There is an inherent democratic and pluralist premise on which the possibility of mutual trust and respect hinges. To form trust and gain respect requires a being-together and working-together. The social pact hinges on joint facticity.

As Bengtsen (2018) argues, the main premise of the contract between universities and society, over the last century, has consisted mainly in providing higher education and in increasing the enrolment numbers across the broad population. As higher education has increasingly been tied down to socio-economic drivers and short-ranged professional outcomes, so have the universities. However, we do see other ways of renewing, or establishing, social contracts and pacts. As Schildermans and colleagues have shown (Schildermans, 2019; Schildermans et al., 2020), the university can become a central part of a social and cultural reconstruction and regrowth, exemplified by the emergence and sustaining of civic society in Palestine refugee camps. Here, the university is not connected to state-governed programmes of higher education but to a fragile and vulnerable rebuilding, and rethinking, of a cultural identity and social structure and community.

The members of the university in this case are not students of higher education but participants in a social in-between-place who, through the university, 'have created a place for ongoing study of and discussion about the future of the camp' (Schildermans et al., 2020: 40). In this context, the university becomes a social and cultural intervention, but 'intervention is not a resolution (...) [and it] does not take away the question by giving an easy response. Nor does it allow to take refuge in the imaginations of Edenic pasts or salvific futures. It is rather (...) a way of *staying with the trouble*' (Schildermans et al., 2020). The university, as institution and idea, does not willy-nilly have to identify itself through higher education. The university may find its societal identity and legitimacy through social community building and forming an ethical foundation for the wider development and cultural growth of a social group or community.

The societal leadership of universities is narrowing when only concerning itself with the broadcasting of higher education. As Sørensen (2019) argues, the social mission of the future university may not lie in the global or societal centre, but in the periphery and the margins. Sørensen wishes to turn the tables and argues that 'marginality has epistemological value *per se*' and being 'marginal adds to the epistemic sensitivity, especially when it comes to perceiving injustice, inequality, reification, alienation, difference, etc' (Sørensen, 2019: 109). The social pact between universities and society may be formed *from* the social and cultural peripheries rather than from the centre.

In Sørensen's words, 'marginality is a privileged standpoint for grasping the significance of crucial political, social, and cultural distinctions that imply hierarchy and inequality', for example 'man vs. woman, center vs. periphery, white vs. black, North vs. South, the First vs. the Third world', and this idea can be extended to 'epistemology analyzing and criticizing distinctions such as knowledge vs. opinion, science vs. religion, necessity vs. contingency, reality vs. appearance, etc' (Sørensen, 2019: 110). Universities may have over-focused on, and overestimated, the importance of higher education compared to social engagement through its knowledge practices. The future of universities may not even include higher education programmes at all, and higher education may be a bridge towards other, and more sustainable, academic practices (Bengtsen, 2018).

Societal leadership may consist in assuming roles and responsibilities that lie beyond the mandate of being the provider of higher education in a given society. Without question, higher education programmes should still be one of the main priorities of universities as it ties together important stakeholders and forms an important knowledge ecology. However, I encourage universities (and their leaders, students, teachers, researchers) to see academic work as forms of engagement that may extend beyond higher education programmes. The keyword, again, is *work* and through the social and cultural work, academic practices may assume forms and open up possibilities we are yet to understand and imagine.

While higher education programmes usually act as a mediator, or broker, between academic work and societal activities and domains, I would hope to see academic involvement, also with an institutional mandate and legitimacy, which is not part of any educational programme. This does not mean that such engagement could not be educational or relevant to include in educational programmes. It does mean, however, that curricular learning should not always be the top priority of academic involvement. Sometimes building and sustaining social realities could be more directly performed without the mediator of state-accredited higher education programmes. The university has many roles to play societally, and many ways of working together with social and cultural communities beyond its own institutional domain. Higher education is only one of them.

A New Ontological Contract

A new social contract between universities and the surrounding world would entail academic engagement in societal, global and geopolitical issues around climate, ethnicity, gender, social marginalization and stigma, equity and equality, and social and epistemic (in)justice. However, there is also a new 'ontological contract', which needs to be engaged in before the true meaning of cultural leadership can be enacted. The contract between universities and their surroundings is not 'just' about the institutional and social contracts. The university has to form an *ontological contract* and to link that back, or even embed it, within the social and institutional contracts. As Barnett (2018: 75) argues, the ecological contract of the university is built on an 'Earth philosophy' and is for the 'whole Earth'. Through such an ecological contract, the university should strive to 'create new understandings of the world and reveal the world in strange ways. It may even glimpse new possibilities for and in the world' (2018: 174).

Through the ontological contract, universities may grant dignity, value and worth not only to people and institutions but to the things, animals, historical events and cultural and natural places and environments that sustain and uphold us. The university has to pursue such an 'ontological sustainability'. As has recently been argued by Gildersleeve and Kleinhesselink (2019), discussions around the Anthropocene reveals to us the unfathomable scope of life forms and ecosystems that uphold us as human beings, and the work by Bennett (2010) discloses a similar range of material diversity that create the social and societal backdrop of our social and cultural value systems. To enact cultural leadership means to be able to understand how knowledge and learning at universities and within higher education is being influenced by other, and diverse, ecosystems.

The ontological contract rests on universities' ability and power to evoke the *sincerity* of the world and everything in it. As Harman (2002: 43) writes, life expresses itself through sincerity and by taking everything 'seriously'. Not just ourselves, or different human cultures, but the various phenomena that uphold us and our activities such as moon rays, puppets, numbers, empty parking lots, birthday kisses, broken promises, lady bugs, straw, lemons and flat tyres. Our knowledge pursuits are pluralistic, but perhaps not pluralistic enough. Just as we are fascinated by famous wars or influential people, other things absorb our attention too, though they are not always deemed relevant or important enough for academic attention and are being left to writers, artists and interest groups. More mundane entities such as 'violins, olives, ink, the pointless chant of hooligans in the street' also 'take a stance within the world and command our attention, [and] lure us into taking them seriously even if only to ridicule them' (Harman, 2002: 241). Not until universities shed their ontological elitism can they unleash a truly inclusive and pluralistic form of cultural leadership embracing not only certain social, ethnic or political cultures, but the cultures of things, animals, events and serendipitous moments that few may acknowledge as worthy of academic pursuit, or where no human beings take part or even become aware of their existence.

Engaging in the ontological contract means that universities would have to refrain from spiralling down a possible trajectory of epistemic narcissism, where we become intoxicated by the apparent splendour of our own conceptual and semantic complexity of our own academic work. On the contrary, Harman (2005: 110) points out, the 'infinite depth of candles, stars, and moons is far more interesting than the supposed infinite complexity of multiple meanings', and the 'charm of objects is their innocent absorption in being just what they are, which in each case is something we can never be' (2005: 137). In a provocative, but also strangely inspiring way, Harman underlines that no one really wants to be 'a Cartesian subject, but everyone would love to be some version of Isis, Odysseus, Aquaman, Legolas, or Cordelia' (2005: 140). This point always inspires me with much hope as it reveals an inner drive in our knowledge pursuits not to more thoroughly and deeply to understand ourselves, and not even to understand better people or societies resembling us – but that we have an often-unacknowledged drive to understand what we are *not*, and may never be.

The cultural leadership of universities includes the ability to bring one's own culture to its value peripheries and margins and explore value systems, life forms and forms of being that may seem either strange, unsettling or irrelevant and worthless to ourselves and our habitual knowledge pursuits. The university has to probe the depth of sustainability, which may not be about our own well-being and survival as human beings, but the survival and importance of obscure insects, apparently useless materials and random events never before acknowledged as a part of a given cultural narrative. The ontological contract not only 'present us with new solutions and synergies, but also with riddles and forms of education that are alien and unsettling' (Bengtsen and Barnett, 2019: 19). How may we educate when not knowing what we are educating *for*? When we cannot foresee the end result economically, socially or culturally?

We have to ask the question: Are there 'missing pieces that we simply cannot detect, and a murmur we simply cannot hear, in the ecologies we characteristically perceive today?' (Bengtsen and Barnett, 2019: 140). Through the ontological contract, the university has responsibilities 'towards all of the ecosystems with which it is inter-connected, tasks now made more complex when the hiddenness of so much of its environment is revealed – or reveals itself' (Bengtsen and Barnett, 2019: 35). The notion of the ontological contract adds a further dimension to the call for universities' awareness of peripheries and action in the margins. With the notion of the ontological contract, the meaning of peripheries and margins are taken to a radical point beyond the social and cultural realm.

Conclusion: Realms of Leadership

Leadership, in this chapter, shows itself to include the following meanings: (a) to connect across levels or domains not automatically or traditionally connected, (b) to be present within all levels and contexts where leadership applies and (c) to reach beyond one's own (institutional and societal) culture and, with a real and sincere interest and care, to acknowledge the depths of sustainability, which may rest on life forms, social and historical events, and cultural values and belief systems that may have formed us, or are forming us, even though we do not care to realize it, or are not able to.

How, then, to form cohesion across such different and various realms? The university cannot, and should not, take on this leadership task on its own but has to engage in and form pacts across several levels within and across the different realms. Within the institutional leadership realm, institutional contracts must be formed between leaders, researchers, teachers, students, administrators, maintenance staff and many others who everyday enact and sustain the university as an institution. Within the societal leadership realm, social contracts must be formed between universities, municipalities, other institutions and organizations, companies, civil society and the state. Within the cultural leadership realm, ontological contracts must be formed between human beings and cultures and the cultures of various animals, plants, things, natural phenomena and Earth phenomena.

What the leadership responsibility hinges on, across the different forms of leadership mentioned in this chapter, is to embrace and be a part of social, curricular, institutional, societal and cultural peripheries. Not to assimilate all into a new academic hegemony or to, falsely, imagine that all can mutually understand and embrace one another. We do not respect our leaders because they can unite and streamline difference and variation into neat institutional strategies encompassing and aligning all. We respect our leaders because they understand the importance of being *there* – and *being* there – also in the peripheries and margins, where leadership should also belong.

The Indivisible

Introduction

In discussions today, we sometimes find the perspectives that universities and the wider social and cultural domains are separate poles: from outside universities, policymakers, professionals, companies and even the public desire for universities to contribute more to society and culture; and from within universities, academics sometimes express their frustration with the demands from actors and stakeholders who are not part of the academic communities and knowledge interests. I argue that a paradox can be detected here – that universities and their cultural and societal environments for some reason should belong to separate worlds and world views.

Even though universities and their wider societal and cultural surroundings and stakeholders may have different interests *in* society and culture (practical level), and may even differ in their understandings and viewpoints *of* society and culture (epistemic level), they all share the condition of emerging and speaking *from* society and culture (ontological level). The point is that we need a layered, or deep, concept and understanding of culture, and usually the debates about the cultural role and purpose of universities merely take place on the practical and epistemic levels. I continue this discussion, where universities and culture reveal themselves as not being separate entities but rooted within a shared realm of being.

In my analysis and discussion, I draw from philosophies of openness, otherness and mystery, especially those of Martin Heidegger, Graham Harman, Gabriel Marcel, Simone Weil and Emmanuel Levinas. Instead of seeing culture as a mere domain separate from universities, I show that, ontologically (and even into the realm of mystery), culture may be seen as the foundational glue, or cohesion, which holds universities and societies together – and that one cannot grow and develop without the other. Where universities, in current debates, are sometimes understood as floating around in a cultural vacuum, I argue that universities and their societal contexts are always rooted within, and moored to, their cultural foundations. Culture, here, should not be understood in the fluctuating sociopolitical sense of a social constructivism or social pragmatism, but in the Heideggerian sense, where culture is the very expression of humanity, and perhaps even the beyond within which humanity dwells.

I argue that the implications of a more organic understanding of the relation between universities and culture make possible a new sense of cultural belonging and societal cohesion for academics and their institutions. The universities form a communal, institutional space and being within societies (as scientific, educational *and* spiritual institutions), and they belong, first and foremost, to their cultural depths.

Opening Up Humanity

In recent years, the role of the universities not only as cultural custodians but also as sites for cultural action has been accentuated. If the university is only understood as a curiosity shop displaying fascinating ideas of freedom, democracy, astrophysics, forgotten sagas and so on, the target of higher education is being missed. Universities are the sites *in* our culture and *as* cultural actions that ongoingly and critically engage and challenge our ideas of who we are, where we come from and what our place is in the wider spiritual, biological and cosmic ecology. As Heidegger (2008: 147) notes in his famous 'Letter on Humanism', our thinking 'acts insofar as it thinks'. Research and higher education are not merely a commentary on the world and our societies, but academic 'thinking is the *engagement* of Being' (Heidegger, 2008: 148 – SB's italics). The university is a cultural pulse that pushes on the sides of our cultural horizon, our cultural cells and heartstrings, and effecting our cultural muscle and consciousness to expand and grow in awareness and endurance. If you wish to know the level of cultural openness of a country, look to the universities and the openness and criticality of the specific research programmes and higher education curricula.

Universities are institutions, where the limits of culturally accepted knowledge and belief systems are reached, challenged and, sometimes, transcended. The knowledge pursued, and forms of learning encouraged, engage with matters and issues central to our societies, cultural values and belief systems. The cultural view of the university has to be far-reaching in order to focus not only on the here and now concerns but also on concerns and questions only glimpsed and sensed in the far periphery of our awareness. For Heidegger (2008), cultural growth may only take place if we 'learn to exist in the nameless' (Heidegger, 2008: 151), and in the 'clearing of Being' (Heidegger, 2008: 155), where we face the unknown and the aspects of our cultural history, heritage, but also future, which have no names and no cultural reality – yet. Universities are windows looking into a culture emerging – into possible cultural futures.

Any form of *higher* learning moves beyond the well-known problems and answers belonging to the status quo whereby it turns into an epistemic and curricular 'adventure' and 'a search and an inquiry into the unthought' (Heidegger, 2008: 180). Not that academics themselves decide what can be thought and not thought, or believed and not believed, but they lend their work, voice and knowledge to wider cultural discussions and beliefs and thereby enlarge and explore them. In the classroom and auditoriums, students and teachers do not seek to own their knowledge explorations – they lend, or give, their thoughts, voices and curricular work to the common quest. Per definition, academic pursuits belong to the 'communitas', the community and not the individual. Academic achievements become possible through gift-giving and the formation of a common, or joint, (ad)venture.

Across all disciplines and research and learning approaches, creative and imaginative engagement is central, and often unique, to universities. Also drawing from Heidegger, Paul Gibbs (2021) argues that learning to think is conceived as mystery and wonder, which opens up new realities and news truth. Higher education calls for an ontological pedagogy, where not only standard discourses and descriptions of the world are reproduced, but new worlds and social and cultural imaginaries are being disclosed and enable cultural integration and growth. Higher education functions as a cultural scouting, or cultural vanguard, testing and challenging, but also harnessing and conserving, understandings of ourselves, our societies and the natural world.

Inherent in creativity and imaginative thinking, within all disciplines, there is an inbuilt ontological and cultural optimism. Researchers, teachers and students believe not only that new knowledge about the present world may be obtained but also that new knowledge may lead to the discovery of new world views associated with cultural maturation and growth. Barnett and Bengtsen (2017: 8) point out that such an 'optimistic university thinks from the world as we know it and it thinks from what the not-yet-ness of the world'. It is difficult to imagine higher education without an inherent optimism. Students and teachers believe that learning new things and acquiring new knowledge is possible – the optimism is the foundational driver of higher learning. Higher education rests on the idea that formation and growth are possible and are worthwhile pursuits. There is an emancipatory core in the higher education curriculum.

Knowledge creation and higher learning, in the sense mentioned here, should not be understood as an epistemic trick where academics conjure up new worlds matching particular sociopolitical or institutional agendas of the day under the slogans of innovation and entrepreneurship often tying universities to sociocultural surface layers. Cultural growth happens in the humble receiving of access to new dimensions of the world, otherwise kept apart from a given cultural realm. Again, drawing from Heidegger (2004) and his understanding of thinking as a form of thanking, I argue that universities are forms of a deep cultural thanksgiving. Giving of one's own time, resources and energies in order to try to advance one's own, or one's culture's, understanding of a given matter links 'supreme thanks' with thinking and 'profoundest thanklessness [with] thoughtlessness', which leads Heidegger to conclude that 'all thanking belongs first and last in the essential realm of thinking' (Heidegger, 2004: 143). Thinking and higher learning in universities harness our cultural sensitivity to what lies beyond our own horizon of knowledge and meaning and extend our capacity for containing and enabling cultural diversity, variation and multiplicity.

Universities aid personal and cultural growth through the development of the capacity to care (Barnacle, 2018; Dall'Alba, 2012). As Barnacle (2018: 81) points out, the 'conception of care is distinctive and important for learning' because it 'involves a genuine openness' to other people, cultures, species and the natural world around us. To really know and achieve an in-depth understanding of a particular aspect of the world (a certain species of frog, bacteria and geological stratum, or certain wars, diseases or political rhetoric inherent in renaissance sculpture) demands careful attention, openness to new ideas and the ability to try to see beyond one's own sociocultural value paradigm and scientific world view. Besides an intense interest in a given subject matter studied, higher learning requires a profound respect and reverence for the complexity and subtlety of the often very specific phenomena studied – be it a bone structure in the knee, roman coin production and trade, loading techniques of sixteenth-century muskets, the concept of freedom in Kantian thought, the distinguishing painting technique of Jackson Pollock or the anatomy of whales.

Care has 'relevance not just for what we think *about* but also *how* we think', and includes the 'intrinsic attraction of ideas, and other beings and entities' that allow them to 'draw us in and hold us enthralled' (Barnacle, 2018: 83). Universities are the windows of culture, perhaps even the eyes and ears too at times. Through universities, a culture may see and listen into other cultures, contemporary and past (and perhaps even future), and into itself. Not with a cold and uninvolved stare, but with interest, heart and care. Also, with the aim of improving and bettering our societies and sociopolitical situation. We do not send our young adults to the university in hope of seeing them returning with similar knowledge as ourselves. We send the next generation to the university with the hope that they may see further, learn more and return as culturally grown – and to have outgrown ourselves culturally and intellectually. The university is the site not only for cultural growth but, and perhaps even more importantly, for cultural hope!

Culture beyond Humanity

Universities and higher education do not only connect us to other human cultures, but to extra-human, or alien, cultures as well – as they appear in the realms of plants, trees, animals, stars, rock formations and electrical waves. The great potential of higher learning is not to reach a complete understanding of, and pass judgement over, our biological, geological or physical surroundings, but to try to become entangled *with* them. In higher learning, knowledge is not understood as a way of becoming remote or distant to the things studied and researched, but to delve into the heart of things (Bengtsen, 2014). In higher learning and research, academics are not trying to grasp 'the carpentry of things in their appearances nor subjectively fabricating images of them' but on the contrary to become 'caught up in their images, their shadows, their reflections, halos, the harmonics of their colors, the rhythm of their forms' (Lingis, 1998: 101). Higher learning is about engagement and participation – not only learning about the matters studied but learning *from* them.

The deeper a study takes a student or a researcher, the life forms, gaseous clouds, or geological strata 'do not outline something of practical interest, but involve us in themselves', and we 'find ourselves among them and carried on by them' (Lingis, 1998). Through knowledge pursuits and higher learning and study, universities enable cultural understandings and connections not only within our own species but also cross-species, cross-material and cross-planetary understandings and cultural connections (Bengtsen and Barnett, 2017). To be sure, we do not become bees, or forms or volcanic activity, ourselves merely by studying them, but we experience them on a deeper level through study, which enable us to develop respect and appreciation. Such kinds of cross-species, or cross-material, understanding and appreciation, I would argue, forms a cultural bond.

Through research and higher learning, forces are unleashed, which takes us ever deeper into the strangeness of living beings and inanimate objects different, and sometimes even bizarre, to human nature and existence. Deep study and learning about other species or star systems do not immediately focus on the practical use or economic benefit here and now (though it may in many cases do so later on). I would argue that in-depth study of particular subspecies of frogs in the Amazon jungle or various types of snow or electrical frequencies happens because we become enthralled by their beauty, weirdness or incredible powers. As Harman (2005: 137) states, perhaps there is 'no better technical term than *charm*' to describe this cross–life form connection. As Harman writes, this word should be 'heard with overtones of witchcraft rather than those of social skills', and what is at issue 'is not some sort of people-pleasing faculty in things, but a sort of magic charm or elixir that we sense in each thing, as when warriors devour tiger hearts or druids cautiously approach forbidden trees' (2005). Research and higher learning are ways of gaining access to the beauty and drama of the world. As the world opens up, we realize its complexities and depths, leaving behind our self-interests and egos. Through investment and sacrifice of our own time, energy and resources, we receive a rare and unique entry into a perhaps otherwise overlooked or ignored aspect of the world.

Through research and higher learning, we discover (or perhaps remember) that 'the world resembles the hideout of a sorceress, with its numerous medicines, poisons, vegetables, (. . .) and omens', and in 'our most memorable moments, the world is certainly no less interesting than such a witch's hut would be' (2005). The university does not shut its gates on the world, but is arguably the institution that to the largest extent encourages understanding and knowledge of, and engagement with, life forms, bio-systems, electrical and chemical fields, and interplanetary and interstellar powers, which reach beyond our own cultural borders.

My argument here is that the relevance of culture and cultural connections does not only relate to interhuman cultures, which would typically include most of the humanities and social sciences. I argue that culture should be understood to span across all disciplines as to define the human–non-human encounters and connections in the widest sense possible. In present-day experiences of climate change and pandemics, the human–non-human connection becomes more important than ever, and the notion of culture cannot be expected to sit only within the human realm alone.

The cultural dimension of the university must certainly be understood in an ecological sense in which the university is not only responding to but is influenced by and engaged with various social, political, economic, societal and cultural contexts and lifeworlds (Barnett, 2018). However, I argue that there is a further depth-ecological dimension, which needs to be included – that of the alien. As Bengtsen and Barnett (2019: 31) point out, higher education ecologies are 'not only about understanding the socio-cultural and socio-political role of universities in contemporary societies' but also about 'letting higher education be formed and shaped by alien horizons and forms of thinking that we cannot yet account for'. Through its knowledge pursuits and disciplinary practices, universities and higher education are part of 'alien ecologies' (Bengtsen and Barnett, 2019) through which human societies and cultures become aware of their wider natural, geological and biological entanglements. Such cultural connections, on the extra-human level, disturb current dominating, short-sighted job market narratives. Such connections even disturb our traditional interhuman cultural narrative about the university as mainly a site for human development and societal growth.

An 'alien ecology challenges the cohesion of the present state of things', and it questions the traditionally understood 'fundamental role and purpose of the university and higher education in contemporary society' (Bengtsen and Barnett, 2019: 32). Universities do not only form windows through which we may look into other cultural belief systems, political systems and historical periods. The fascination and engagement with life forms, events and phenomena beyond the human realm make universities unique cultural portal and connections between our own human lifeworld and other species, forgotten time eons, electrical pulses and forces in deep space.

The meaning of culture here does not refer to what we already know and wish to harness or develop in our societies, but what is utterly strange and may worry or even haunt our human culture. Such extra-human cultural links are forged in the 'alien university' (Bengtsen, 2018), and the 'alien university holds within itself emancipatory possibilities from ontological layers not yet activated by present state discourses' (Bengtsen, 2018: 1541). Research agendas and the higher education curriculum increasingly address the post-human situation and the Anthropocene (Gildersleeve and Kleinhesselink, 2019; Lysgaard et al., 2019), where '[d]ichotomies such as human-nature and human-Earth, no longer work or fit' (Gildersleeve and Kleinhesselink, 2019: 5). This way seen, the university and higher education may become more *biopolitically* powerful and important than it ever was. Not in order to turn into ideology or become party political, but to reclaim its biocultural mandate and responsibility.

Mystery and Culture

To be able to explore, shape and transform one's own culture in depth, the cultural horizons, both socially and politically, cannot be too narrow and tight. The cultural values and belief systems we live by should not be too exactly defined as it would leave no room for further interpretation and maturation. This is equally so with the attitude and awareness with which we meet other cultures, both other human cultures and the cultures of other species, life forms, organism and forms of vibrant matter (Bennett, 2010). If one's cultural mindset and awareness is too tightly structured and defined, it easily slips into ideology and exclusiveness. This way, culture risks becoming a totality trapped in the 'imperialism of the same' (Levinas, 2003: 39), where every difference, diversity, strangeness and otherness become assimilated into the already-culturally dominant discourses.

As Barnett (2011) argues, to thrive culturally, and to be able to dialogically meet and engage with other cultures, there has to be an element of mystery within one's own cultural framework. This sense of mystery in our universities and higher education curriculum is being challenged. As Barnett (2011: 15) states, we live in 'an age of explicitness', where all matters from research funding and leadership strategies to educational programmes have to be 'susceptible of measurement, of precise descriptions, and of rules, performance against which can be ascertained with objectivity'. In many places, the idea is today that if you cannot explicitly explain the exact outcome of your research, the course you follow or the leadership approach you take, the whole endeavour is unviable.

Universities are no longer permitted to be 'places of mystery, of uncertainty, of the unknown', and the loss of mystery has that further consequence that the 'university is itself diminished' including '[h]ow it is, what it is, how it understands itself and its responsibilities in the world' (2011). One could ask, if the openness for strangeness and surprise is not permitted in universities and higher education programmes, what cultural sites would otherwise ensure it? As Hansen (2020: 66) argues, universities should be places for 'deep wonder', which 'flourishes and becomes visible in the acknowledgement of the Other, the Otherness or Thou of the phenomenon'. Deep wonder sustains the aspect of mystery not only in our universities and higher education but in our societies more generally. Mystery, in turn, sustains the possibility for cultural growth and transformation.

According to the French philosopher Gabriel Marcel (2000), we need to distinguish between cultural issues as problems and as mystery. Cultural issues in our societies, such as integration, social and national identities, societal values, and political culture and subculture, may on the one hand be seen in terms of problems to be solved. As Marcel (2000: 211) notes, a 'problem is something which I meet, which I find complete before me, but which I can therefore lay siege to and reduce'. In other terms, a problem can fully grasped, clearly defined and objectively agreed on. On the other hand, a 'mystery is something in which I myself am involved, and it can therefore only be thought of as a sphere where the distinction between what is in me and what is before me loses its meaning and its initial validity' (2011). When a cultural issue is allowed the form of a mystery, it cannot be easily solved or rejected, as the involvement of myself and others becomes pivotal in its meaning and scope. When the individual person, group or society starts to explore the depths, entanglements, nuances and complexities of a cultural issue, the dimension of mystery opens up to them.

Cultural transformation and growth are only possible through the experience and engagement with the mystery. Problem-solving may be instrumentally useful, but contains no real potential for growth or change. When the mystery of the issue studied or researched makes 'itself felt, it can refresh my inner being; it reveals me to myself, it makes me more fully myself than I should be if I were not exposed to its impact' (Marcel, 2000: 205). To engage with the mystery, we have to invite it into our own horizons of meaning and belief systems even though it does not belong there or can be fully integrated (immediately so). Marcel (2011: 217) calls this 'a metaphysics of hospitality', where we regard the other person, culture or even the strangeness of a (physical, chemical, mathematical or social) matter researched or studied, as 'the guest' to be 'regarded as all the more sacred'. A similar approach characterizes research and higher learning, where the aim is not immediately to reduce, explain and solve a strange and intriguing occurrence in our experiments or studies, but to, with respect and openness, invite in what is strange, bizarre and alien.

Another French philosopher, Simone Weil (2002) argues that the challenge in our own personal lives, societies and world views we belong to is not for us to fit in and become further assimilated. The real, or deep, challenge is to escape the social, political and cultural bonds that hold us in mindsets and belief systems ongoingly. Contrary to what might be expected, Weil argues that only when we are on the verge of lapsing into utter confusion, bewilderment and cultural trembling are we approaching personal and cultural growth. We have to 'take that feeling of being at home into exile', and the most important challenge is becoming uprooted – as by 'uprooting oneself one seeks greater reality' (Weil, 2002: 39). In line with Marcel, Weil encourages a stronger focus on the mystery, and she states that the 'reason should be employed only to bring us to the true mysteries, the true undemonstrables, which are reality' (Weil, 2002: 132). Higher education provides opportunities to experience, endure, reflect on and let oneself become transformed by the mystery. In higher learning, the mystery is the realization that our understanding of a given matter will never be complete or exhausted and that study of the same questions may continue across decades, perhaps even centuries or longer. This does not mean that scientific or educational progress is not possible or should not be encouraged. On the contrary, it means that research and higher learning progresses even though it takes place in a void – without final and absolute limits and boundaries.

However, as Weil states, a person 'only escapes from the laws of this world in lightning flashes', which are experienced as '[i]nstants when everything stands still, instants of contemplation, of pure intuition, of mental void, of acceptance of the moral void'. Weil continues to say that enduring the moment of the void 'is a terrible risk, but one that must be run – even during the instant when hope fails' (Weil, 2002: 11). Higher learning and research should not be taken on lightly, as the insights achieved, or the self-realization acquired, may leave us more uncertain or unsettled than before embarking on the learning quest.

Gaining knowledge of one's own country's shadowy colonial past may be unpleasant and existentially unsettling. Realizing that the climate change happens with greater speed and wider biosocial consequences that hitherto documented may be politically unnerving. In the study of dark matter and black holes, discovering strange signs that our known theories and common understandings of the universe are on the threat of collapse may be discomforting. In higher education, there are no guarantees, and striving for cultural growth demands strong institutions and highly skilled researchers, students and teachers who have the cultural and existential fortitude, in lightning flashes, to escape the world as we know it.

The Indivisible

Subtle and important arguments have been made to show that the role of universities and higher education is pivotal in facilitating societal growth and in rebuilding social solidarity and mobility in fractured societies around the world. Here, the university and culture are indivisible elements in the forming of the *common* good, as Marginson (2016) terms it. In a similar way, Nixon (2012) argues for the role of universities in furthering the *public* good by connecting social, civic and political sectors, and institutional, national and global contexts, in order to create cosmopolitan spaces for learning and development. My argument is also that the notion of the *good* is the aspect through which we may realize that the university and culture are indivisible entities. However, I would argue that the link between the university and culture is formed around a different notion of the good.

In my view, it is not enough to agree on certain forms of knowledge, skills or competences are good for society – which they probably are. I would also argue that universities do not just further understandings, practices, public spaces and political cultures that we *already* know are good in order to sustain the societies we *already* know and value. As current climate and health crises have shown, the world and societies we know may very quickly change drastically, and global concerns like mobility and higher education itself may become gridlocked. The notion of the good that I am trying to highlight here is a deeper good. It is the good that invites reflection on what the various good*s* (plural) in our societies are for, and suggests that knowledge, research, education and personal growth are not pursuits valued in themselves but are bound to an even deeper form of respect, dignity and love. In our current societies, we start to realize that life itself is at stake, and not merely human life but life in general. Universities and culture are indivisible in the sense that they both are interlinked forms of life, but, and even more important, they respond to life itself (Barnett and Bengtsen, 2019).

The university and culture are indivisible in their joint (emergent) awareness of the good by reference to which just things and all the rest become useful and beneficial (Plato, 2002: 740). Plato's notion of the good does not relate to particular goods, nor to economic, political, personal or societal. All such goods are 'offspring[s] of the good', where 'the idea of good (. . .) [is] the cause of knowledge, and of truth', and it is more 'fair as they both are, knowledge and truth' (Plato, 2002: 743 and 744). Following this line of thought, culture does not, ultimately, rest on a specific set of moral ideals, educational goals and political agendas. Culture and universities allow for the value of acknowledging a great variety and multiplicity of life forms, social codes and forms of morality – and not only human.

As Plato (2002: 744) notes, 'the objects of knowledge not only receive from the presence of the good their being known, but their very existence and essence is derived to them from it', and that 'the good itself is not essence but still transcends essence in dignity and surpassing power'. The good is what allows knowledges and values to emerge, not the knowledges and values themselves. As Levinas remarks, the good is 'beyond the logos, beyond being and non-being, beyond essence, beyond the true and non-true', as it is 'the utopia of the human' (Levinas, 2000: 45). Even though goodness 'will indeed show itself in ontology metamorphosed into essence, (. . .) essence cannot contain it' (Levinas, 2000: 137). Followingly, one could argue that culture is beyond cultures (plural), in a shared human endeavour to bring various specific notions of goodness, beauty, truth and community into the world. Today, Levinas's call for the 'utopia of the human' seems more important than ever – that universities, through their knowledge pursuits, advocate for the acknowledgement and dignity of the cultures *not* easy to understand, welcome or embrace. Such cultures are rooted in the same pre-ontological goodness as our own culture.

Culture rests on goodness, and as Levinas (2003: 305) states, 'goodness is produced as pluralism'. Pluralism makes way for a 'pluralist society' in which the 'unity of plurality is peace, and not the coherence of the elements that constitute plurality' (2003: 306). The university and culture are indivisible due to their co-formation of pluralism. The utopia of the human lies in the ability to escape one's specific culture and respect and embrace other cultures. The mystery and wonder embedded in research and higher learning are signs of such utopian pursuits. The ways that the presence of otherness refreshes my own being, as Marcel argued, is a form of actualized pluralism and the resonance of goodness. The university is perhaps the most important link (that we know of) to nameless (Heidegger) and alien (Levinas) cultures, human and non-human alike. The university does not stand besides, above or below culture – but is a cultural stretching and openness not only towards the goods but also to the good.

12

Beyond Culture

Losing Culture: Regaining the University

Over the last decades, the quality of the relationship between the university and culture has been passionately debated. Readings (1997) asks if universities are breaking away entirely from the cultural project, comments that the university 'no longer participates in the historical project for humanity that was the legacy of the Enlightenment' and asked if we were entering the 'twilight' of the university (Readings, 1997: 5). More recently, Collini (2012: 86–7) insistently discusses what could be said to form the 'spiritual legacy' of the university, and holds fast in the idea that the university must 'incarnate a set of "aspirations and ideals" that go beyond any form of economic return'. However, the faith in Western culture as the leading light has been shaken, and with it the faith in universities as an institution of enlightenment, emancipation and truth-seeking.

Further, we see critical discussions not only of the primacy of Western culture but of the primacy and meaningfulness of human culture altogether (Gildersleeve and Kleinhesselink, 2019) and a fundamental challenge to ideals of enlightenment, rationality and reason. Counterpoints to rationalism include how denial, insanity and death (Lysgaard et al., 2019: 47) form human culture, sparked from glimpses of a dawning realization that the future may hold a 'world-without-us'. As Lysgaard and his colleagues argue (Lysgaard et al., 2019: 106), the Anthropocene paradox 'showcases the manifold ways in which human beings are deeply "enmeshed" in and "haunted" by non-human aspects of Earth's planetary reality'. In contrast to its historical roots in enlightenment and a positive understanding of culture, the university and the culture it belongs to, perhaps the very concept of culture, as such, is today ridden with ambiguity, uncertainty and pessimism.

In the world of today, we are not looking into a progressive and optimistic future but one of ecological destabilization 'in the wake of accelerating loss of biodiversity, rising water levels of the oceans in the wake of the de-icing of polar ice caps and growing emissions of greenhouse gases in the wake of the Arctic Tundra's melting permafrost' (Lysgaard et al., 2019: 107). After a millennium, where the university has been seen as a hallmark of human culture and one of the highest forms of cultural achievement, we witness how 'nonhuman forces break in and disturb our self-centred, speciesistic and imperialistically invasive behavior' of our cultural institutions and societies (Lysgaard et al., 2019). One of the most pressing challenges to universities today is not to navigate in a context, where the meaning of culture is being critically debated and negotiated politically and economically, but to navigate in a context where the meaning of culture as such is being challenged and doubted – and where universities are challenged and doubted too.

However, according to Barnett (2011), the situation should not stupefy the university as an institution more generally, although it may challenge the modern version of it and its enchantment with humanity and human culture as the meaning of culture as such. As Barnett (2011: 17) points out, earlier institutional iterations of the university 'recognized that it [the university] was not only linked to God, the universe and human being in fundamental senses but that it has responsibilities towards them'. The meaning of culture in pre-modern universities 'represented encounters with a meta-reality', and it is only recently that such a 'sense of other-worldliness has disappeared' and that universities 'have abandoned their metaphysical background' (2011). Perhaps the biggest challenge is to accept that universities are not only for the benefit of human beings, and that knowledge, learning and formation do not have our own societies, children and cultures as their only aim. We begin to realize that universities play a much greater role than hitherto acknowledged. Universities pave the way for futures of the cultures and beings that may come after us – after humanity. *That* is the true metaphysical anchoring of the university.

In Nietzsche (2010), we find a similar view of the role and purpose of universities. To Nietzsche, the university should not so much be seen as the endeavour of harnessing a particular culture and value system. The university links human beings with what was before and will be after humanity. To Nietzsche, the universities are failing when they focus only inwardly on what can be meaningful and useful to a human culture. Nietzsche (2010: 214) states that our 'institutions are not good any more' but 'this is *our* fault, not the fault of the institutions'. To Nietzsche, we have lost the foundational 'instincts that give rise to institutions', and 'we lose the institutions themselves because *we* are not suited to them anymore'. The university is *for* humanity, and *of* humanity – but should also have a deeper aim, that of moving on the fringes of humanity and even reaching beyond.

Other Humanisms

Perhaps leaving humanity is not the correct phrasing, but leaving one form of humanism and exploring other humanisms. According to Braidotti (2019: 19), the so-called post-human condition is 'an opportunity to empower the pursuit of alternative schemes of thought, knowledge and self-representation', and the 'posthuman condition urges us to think critically and creatively about who and what we are actually in the process of becoming'. In a post-human view, humanity is not the centre of the cultural field. Culture extends beyond humanity and merges with nature and technology. A clear definition of culture, even, starts to erode and become superfluous. Where culture before was used as a line of demarcation in relation to nature and cosmic powers, culture, in a post-human view, is inextricably embedded within nature and the wider cosmos. Life itself has become our new cultural arena and life 'expresses itself by actualizing flows of energies, through codes of vital information across complex somatic, cultural and technologically networked systems' (Braidotti, 2019: 190). In the same way, the university is caught up in a hybrid circuit of powers and forms of entanglement that are not entering the stage in order to enlighten or educate humanity – even though a higher education may be inspired and formed around them.

The university is, ultimately, not a project of humanism, and academic endeavours are, ultimately, not directed primarily towards human flourishing – but the flourishing of life. With inspiration from Haraway (2016: 58), I would argue that the university is not a world-making institution but a 'worlding-with' institution – a vein connecting us with other beings and life forms, where some will, eventually, outlive us. The post-human university challenges the idea of the walled and fenced in campus area with its own autonomous micro-cosmos. The cultural future of the university lies in the interconnection and embracing of life forms that will

> interpenetrate one another, loop around and through one another, eat each another, get indigestion, and partially digest and partially assimilate one another, and thereby establish sympoietic arrangements that are otherwise known as cells, organisms, and ecological assemblages. (2016)

The post-human university has the mandate and power to bridge to meta-realities when current societal and political understandings may not be able to. Higher education is usually appreciated in its endeavours to make us more, and not less, human. I am not arguing that it should make us less human, but perhaps aim to make us more, or other, *than* human. Interestingly, the meta-reality emerging does not distance the perspective of higher learning from our material, emotional and animal aspects but links up with them ever more strongly.

Will the university be able to aid interconnections not only between institutions and societal realms, and between national and cultural contexts, but between species? Lingis (2000) advocates for a stronger 'bestiality' inherent in our knowledge pursuits. While the tradition for academic becoming connects strongly with reason and rationality, Lingis argues that 'besides reason, we must acknowledge that the substance of our bodies (. . .) are coral reefs full of polyps, sponges, gorgonians, and free-swimming macrophages continually stirred by monsoon climates of moist air, blood, and biles' (Lingis, 2000: 28). What is fascinating is 'the multiplicity in us – the human form and the non-human, vertebrate and invertebrate, animal and vegetable, the conscious and unconscious movements and intensities in us' (Lingis, 2000). Our universities rest not only on a cultural heritage but also on the materiality of our bodies, our hunger, lust, passions and feelings that make us human or more than human and which connects us with other species and life forms.

The university is stretching and moving beyond the anthropocentric paradigm, where its cultural ethos consists in sustaining and developing the human anchoring and platform in the world, including awareness of, and attention to, formation (*Bildung*), citizenship, diversity and social justice. In interesting ways, the university is linking back to its concerns for a meta-human reality in the mediaeval university and certain strands of enlightenment thinking. However, the meta-human dimension, now, is not directed at a certain religious or spiritual curriculum, but a trans-species and life (or 'bios')-oriented cultural ethos. In this sense, the cultural investment and nestedness of universities has perhaps never been more important, as the universities take on their share of the responsibility of providing hope and a sustainable future for life beyond just humanity – but, hopefully at the same time, including humanity. Already, we see specific practice-based pedagogical and curricular concepts, models and designs being worked out by researchers within higher education studies (Barnett and Jackson, 2020) and even within researcher education and formation as well (Barnacle and Cuthbert, 2021). In these works, we begin to see a new cultural ethos, one which includes the extra-human (the beyond-human) dimension as a natural element of the higher education ecology and curriculum. The university and culture are one in their attempt to leave the anthropocentric and 'speciecistic' curriculum behind and to embrace a future that belongs not to humanity first and foremost, but hopefully *also* to humanity.

The Genealogy of the University

Having the university balance on the edge of culture and challenging traditional understandings of humanity and humanism have sparked a new wave of awareness of, and interest in, the historical trajectories of universities and higher education (Karlsohn, 2018; Peters and Barnett, 2019; Rider, 2018). It seems that in order to understand what lies beyond our current cultural borders, it is required to better comprehend what history and heritage lie within. To be able to see into what lies ahead, one has to understand what goes before. The historical aspect of the university is important as it connects our own institutional and cultural realities with 'the memories, stories, and lives of our ancestors and *their* thoughts, *their* societal engagement and visions for a higher education' (Barnett and Bengtsen, 2018: 4). However, and as Karlsohn (2018: 104) underlines that if 'we are to draw from historical lessons of enduring contemporary importance, they must be securely anchored in the multi-faceted realities of the past'. There is not just one historical reality; there are several – and our history, like our future, keeps changing in relation to the societal and cultural realities that are emerging.

As Nietzsche argues, culture is in a state of perpetual becoming, and every time the boundaries for cultural values and belief systems are being pushed, it requires a tremendous amount of institutional, political and societal energy and power. Nietzsche (2014: 65) asks, have we ever 'asked [ourselves] properly how costly the setting up of every ideal on earth has been?' and 'how many lies had to be sanctified, how much conscience had to be troubled, how much "god" had to be sacrificed every time?' It will be costly indeed to set up new ideals not only favouring a more sustainable humanity and human culture, but realizing that the purpose of the culture we are building now is to realize ideals for a culture not yet existing. The responsibility lies with our highest education to ask such complex and demanding questions and to thoroughly and critically discuss possible ways forward.

The university is perhaps the most central institution when it comes to asking questions about a cultural future not featuring humanity as the leading actor on the scene. Staring into an epistemic and cultural unknown, we will be needing 'the use of a rare and singular measuring-rod, (. . .) [and] a divining of values for which scales have not yet been invented' (Nietzsche, 2006: 49–50). Paul Standish calls for a university of the day after tomorrow, which will 'demonstrate its essential public place in the democracy to come' (Standish, 2011: 164) and to be able to release itself from its 'most comfortable thoughts, unloosen [their] fixed assurances, [and] be ready to live in a new way' (Standish, 2011: 163). Through research projects with external partners and stakeholders, and through a 'connected curriculum' (Fung, 2017) – not only connecting across societal domains and cultural realms but also connecting across species and biocultures – universities and higher education are the opening *within* our culture to move *beyond* culture.

The university has a responsibility to explore the meta-human dimensions of our cultural understandings and practices. We need not only the metaphysical university (focusing on our spiritual dimension of the higher education curriculum) but also the meta-human university (focusing on the extra-human or post-human futures). The need for a meta-human focus does not substitute for other dimensions of our cultural practices, which are interhuman or intercultural – they are equally important. However, the meta-human university takes the discussion about preferential cultural understandings and practices to discussions of the meaning and value of (human) culture as such. It provides the opportunity to reflect not only our past, present and future state of a certain culture, but as a species. The meaning of culture, here, is being stretched to include the meta-human dimension. This way, disciplinary boundaries and silos may be transcended to form interdisciplinary, and even transdisciplinary, joint ventures. Because cultural values cannot be equal to human values – but include other beings and life forms – the notion of culture should be stretched beyond its linkage with humanity.

In Nietzsche's genealogy of morality, there is a light at the end of the tunnel. Our culture is not lost; it is 'just' transforming itself, which may be perfectly natural but not necessarily easy or pleasant. Nietzsche holds that the 'man of the future will redeem us, not just from the ideal held up till now, but also from those things *which had to arise from it*, (. . .) which gives earth its purpose and man his hope again' (Nietzsche, 2014: 67). However, we may not understand the human being, or being, we are to become – and looked at from our current cultural stance, such a being may even 'seem *terrible* . . . in his kindness', and if we could glimpse such a being, we might 'flee from the sunburn of wisdom in which the overman joyfully bathes his nakedness!' (Nietzsche, 2014b: 114). As I have argued elsewhere (Bengtsen, 2020), crossing a cultural threshold may seem terrible and strange, and this existential dimension of our entire species (and not just existential in relation to the individual) is what we need to tackle in the coming years. Who are we? What is our purpose? What is the meaning of our *human* lives in relation to the wider life on our planet? Interestingly, glimpses into new cultural futures always create a double-pull – it directs the existential gaze on ourselves once more. Again, universities are *within* culture and *beyond* culture.

Cultural Death and Transformation

In the face of the climate changes, and perhaps more recently the Covid-19 health crisis, our habitual cultural concepts and practices are being challenged. We are haunted by the fear of cultural death. Cultural death, perhaps only a generation ago, was closely connected to nuclear annihilation, where humanity might be swept off the earth suddenly and rapidly. Cultural death would here mean an end to culture as such. This form of cultural death is described in Lingis's early work (Lingis, 1989: 177) as the 'death of all the future generations, of all the unborn ones', which is a death 'inapprehendable, unimaginable, [and] beyond the powers of any feeling'. In this form of death, the individual and cultural fear of a sudden and violent death are mirrored in each other.

To Heidegger, death is not only a peripheral quality lurking in the penumbra of life. Death is a nested existential quality within our very being. Death is the foundation of being, and the 'existential Interpretation of death takes precedence over any biology and ontology of life' (Heidegger, 2000: 291). We *are* death, or, as Heidegger puts it, 'Dasein is dying as long as it exists' (Heidegger, 2000: 295). Being enshrouded in a 'deathbound' (Lingis, 1989) existence does not leave our lives void of meaning or disintegrating into despair or apathy. Experiencing the flow of life through us, but also from our very existence, leaves us with a sensitivity to care. As Heidegger (Lingis, 1989: 296) notes, with regard to '*its ontological possibility, dying is grounded in care*', and care defines our very existence as a 'Being-towards-death' (Lingis, 1989: 378). To Heidegger (Lingis, 1989: 381), living/dying is not a withering-away but a spending and transforming of our life energy into something else that may live on after we have gone. In 'utilizing itself', Dasein 'uses itself up', and in using itself up, 'Dasein uses itself... [and] its time'. The death of an individual or a culture does not mean its ending or extinction, but a transformation where the individual and cultural life is a necessary part of the process of transformation from one state or form of being to another. There is a generosity in dying, a giving of oneself through the medium of time, which translates itself into an existential care.

There is a strong life force in the cultural transformation process. As we are searching for a new humanism reaching beyond humanity, certain values must be left behind for new values to emerge and consolidate. Aiding the process of cultural transformation is difficult, and oftentimes it seems easier and more secure to stay in the cultural known – even if it is a form of cultural pessimism. As Nietzsche (2014b: 165–6) writes, we are hesitant to board the cultural 'death skiff' and may prefer clutching to our feeling of being '*world-weary*' and 'still lusting for the earth, still in love with [our] own earthly weariness!' Culture is a part of the cycle of life, and the cultural skin needs to be shed and replaced from time to time. Just as cultural values change, so does the humanism (or humanisms) we found the culture(s) on.

For the university and higher education, there is work to do! Now is the time to co-define the meaning anew of humanism and cultural values for a world with, but also after, humanity as we know it. It must be a humanism directing its attention, awareness and care beyond itself. As Barnett (2008: 22) states, '[a] brave new world beckons for the university; it is not one for the faint-hearted'. In our present time, it may be difficult to see that the university may have 'no clear legitimizing purpose, no definite role, no obvious responsibilities and no secure values' (2008). To Barnett, this may be just the remedy to the cultural and institutional fatigue that is creeping up in the universities. New paths must be explored and new opportunities sought out, and we must do so until the university reveals from its cultural nestedness a humanism for the future. Together with Barnett, we must join in the cheer: 'The university is dead; long live the university' (2008).

The university rising from the ashes will be able to conceptualize and enact a new humanism that not only connects institutions with their societal context but also connects different and diverse national contexts, cultures and species. The new humanism is not defined by the meaning of culture as in opposition to, and more advanced than, nature. Further, it moves beyond the sheer dichotomy between culture and nature, and beyond humanity and world. The new humanism, as we have seen indicators of in the works by Braidotti and Haraway, and with a prevailing Nietzschean undercurrent, focuses not on the global but on the world – and not on humanity but on the earth.

World Entanglement

Forging understandings and practices for a new humanism and new cultural practices seems like a tremendous and daunting task. How do we move forward from here? Where do we start? What values and norms do we build on and which do we leave behind? What role does the university play in all this? How do we design a higher education curriculum around emerging humanisms? The university is leading the way not only into the epistemically but also into a *cultural unknown*.

As a portent of today's cultural challenges, we recall Lyotard's critical analysis of the postmodern condition and the, already at the time, 'pessimistic impression of this splintering [of cohesive cultural narratives]' (Lyotard, 1984: 41). Even though Lyotard was not apprehensive of the vast geopolitical and biopolitical conflicts emerging in the wake of his report, which was itself directed towards the emerging knowledge economy of the 1970s and 1980s, the destabilizing of the cultural ethos and integrity seems to haunt our societies and universities still. As Lyotard (1984: 60) notoriously pointed out, we can no longer, culturally or individually, rely on 'the grand narratives – we can resort neither to the dialectic of Spirit nor even to the emancipation of humanity as a validation for postmodern scientific discourse'. Lyotard mercilessly disclosed the impossibility of any universal and global narratives about humanity, culture and the common good. The condition of cultural diversity and epistemic and curricular supercomplexity (Barnett, 2008) requires to be met by 'a politics that would respect both the desire for justice and the desire for the unknown' (Barnett, 2008: 67), a politics not only for the cultural centres but also for the cultural margins. And a politics that goes beyond culture – a politics for the species of the earth.

A stepping stone to the formulation of such a new cultural politics is found in Connolly's (2017) concept of a 'politics of swarming'. Connolly's understanding of politics does not start with the definition of an underlying political programme or vision statement, but finds momentum in the synergies of specific cultural practices. As Connolly (2017: 125) argues, the 'politics of swarming, then, is composed of multiple constituencies, regions, levels, processes of communication, and modes of action, each carrying some potential to augment and intensify the others with which it becomes associated'. Culturally, as well as institutionally, we have to rebuild our common and shared values from the bottom-up. The advice from Connolly (2017: 128) is 'to pursue micropractices of creative experimentations, as you invite potential allies in multiple subject positions to do so with you', whereby you might become 'part of a rhizomatic complex with considerable growth potential' – a '*pluralist* assemblage of multiple actions' that 'foster a spirituality of freedom through experimentation'. In a politics of swarming, diverse cultural realities and belief systems come together (for a time) to form a shared cultural contract and to solve certain issues transcending each individual cultural realm. Not in order to form a permanent, universal cultural union but to join hands around urgent political matters. Such political swarming can take place on the level of nation states, between stakeholders within a single nation state, between and within institutions, groups and individuals. The scale may differ but the idea of swarming stays the same.

An important point is that institutions, groups and individuals within a culture are not only entangled. The entanglement goes beyond the cultural realm, which means it may transcend what we understand as meaningful, logical and sensible. We live in the entanglement of cultures – and even more radically, the entanglement of species. Connolly (2017: 168ff) terms this an 'entangled humanism' and states that the humanist dimension in entangled humanism means that 'we become more aware of other modes of experience . . . we both extend the net of species appreciation more widely and learn that we must cast our lot with some species more than others' (2017: 172). Elsewhere (Bengtsen, 2021), I argue that research and higher education play a central role in aiding such positive forms of 'world-entanglement'. Universities may become a biocultural and biopolitical broker when connecting 'stakeholders, communities, and even worldviews through the diverse forms of knowledge creation and knowledge work'. Universities may aid the formation of the future of a cultural politics. Not as a new construction of ideology or a hierarchical institution but as *the* cultural institution for helping individuals, organizations and nations navigate and take part in the entanglement of cultures and species. We glimpse a higher education curriculum of entanglement that, besides its epistemic and educational core, has a strong ethical vein. When boundaries between stakeholders become permeable, ethical dimensions of trust, care and respect are brought to the fore.

The University beyond Culture

In our societies, and in cultures throughout the world, the centres of power and privilege continue to grow, while, as a consequence, the size of the margins and cultural peripheries grow too. The gaps between political and social legitimate spaces are widening. Refugee camps are growing in size and multiplying in numbers. Families live for several months, even years, in such cultural in-between spaces, where they do not really belong anywhere and are being tossed from one authority to the next. Stripped of identity, rights and a future, they occupy the cultural grey zones, while their voices are being muffled by the border police and policies of exclusion. As Heidegger (2004: 49) ominously reminds us, 'the wasteland grows' – within us as individuals, and within our cultures. There is a loud cultural 'scream' (2004) that haunts our cultural pursuits of inclusion, integration, respect and dignity. In some countries, academics are even politically harassed for strengthening the research focus on marginalized social groups, ethnicities and gender identities. A higher education curriculum for entanglement, and not cultural cleansing, is needed, which also critically discusses curricular margins and 'wastelands'. As universities rely increasingly on strategic funding, even epistemic and intellectual margins and peripheries are created and widened too. Both in our societies and in our universities do we need to see an inclusion of the margins and the embracing of peripheries.

Species become extinct in still growing numbers. Plants, fish and insects we have never even heard of, never experienced, never understood. Forests are cut down, energy reservoirs emptied, oceans polluted and the air carbonized. It starts to dawn on us that the actual challenge for universities and higher education goes beyond-human culture. After two centuries where the main challenge for universities was how to develop, enhance and sustain our human culture and societies, the university has to change gear – has to transform itself from within. The challenge is even greater than that. Not only do we need a new institutional awareness; we also need a new *cultural ethos*. Where the disciplines have been separated and in conflict since the early nineteenth century, they must come together again and form a new epistemic and curricular contract. Culture is a joint responsibility; it does not belong within some disciplines or faculties, and it does not include some objects or contexts of study and not others. A new cultural ethos requires the disciplines to join forces and jointly contribute to the dissolvement of margins and the epistemic, curricular and institutional embracing of otherness and strangeness.

It is not the earth we are destroying but ourselves. Humanity exists at the mercy of the earth, not the other way around. Humanity is, essentially, without power. The world abides by its own laws and its own will – it is 'a monster of energy, without beginning, without end' that does not 'expend itself not only transforms itself' (Nietzsche, 1968: 550). Humanity is utterly caught up in its 'play of forces and waves of forces, at the same time one and many, increasing here and at the same time decreasing there; a sea of forces flowing and rushing together, eternally changing, eternally flooding back, with tremendous years of recurrence' (Nietzsche, 1968).

The prophecy of Nietzsche (2014b: 158) starts to become very vivid and imposing, that 'human being is a bridge and not an end' and that 'everything *now* [is] *in flux*' – have 'all railings and footbridges not fallen into the water?' (Nietzsche, 2014b: 161). Will universities fall into the water too? Or are they the very cultural railings keeping us above water? The fundamental meaning of culture is 'coming together'. It is essential that the coming together does not stop on an institutional or a national level. The coming together has to be across organization and nations. The coming together has even to include disciplines coming together and undoing the technocratic silos of knowledge. Finally, the coming together has to happen with an interest beyond our own species and human culture. The concept of culture needs to be stretched beyond its traditional borders.

Truth, knowledge, science, legitimacy and validity: all are central to higher education and research. However, the foundational question is one of culture, not culture understood as ideology, habitus, social norms, customs and sociocultural belief systems. But an ontological understanding of culture, shaping not only our citizens, institutions and societies but also our species, our very human *being*. And shaping our efforts to reach beyond ourselves, beyond humanism and beyond culture. We need an institutional swarming. We need entangled universities. Where will the university be in 50 or 100 years? Where will we all be? We have to live up to our institutions – we have to live up to the university. Living up to the university means to anchor the university strongly both *within* and *beyond* culture. Seeking what we do not understand and being critical of our own judgement, right and privilege have always constituted the culture of universities – what academics came together for. Embracing the strange, celebrating the unknown and welcoming voices from the peripheries are, still, foundational to the cultural ethos of universities.

Part IV

Dialogical Imaginings

13

University Culture as Force, Coexistence, Endeavour and Entanglement

Rikke Nørgård

Introduction

This chapter attempts to pull together all three parts and twelve chapters of the book. These chapters are written by three individual authors each presenting their own vision and set of ideas when it comes to culture and the university. All in all, it amounts to a lot of words. Actually, well over 60,000 words on culture and the university. So, what more is there to be said? What new sentences and ideas can be put forward? The three authors of the book have, in their individual chapters, been in deep conversation with the world, with the concept of culture and with the reader – but not with each other. Not until now. So, what would these individual chapters have to say to each other? When combined, how would they think and talk about culture and the university? Could there be something more than a conversation with pleasantries?

As I hold the two authors in high esteem, I am convinced it would indeed be a highly stimulating and pleasant conversation. But, for something more – something *other* – to happen, this chapter will not be a reading *of* the parts or be talking *to* the authors' chapters. Nor will it be about what those eight chapters tell me about my own four chapters. Rather, I want to speak with them, or perhaps more accurately, *through* them. But, then, the next questions immediately arise: How can I absorb the chapters and become absorbed by them to such a degree that we speak through each other? How can I entangle the chapters to a point where the in-betweenness of the chapters begin to run free? And how can I invite for this *other*, that is not me or the authors, to make itself heard and speak from this in-betweenness?

To achieve this, something slightly fortuitous might be needed. To make something other speak from the in-betweenness of the chapters, we need a way to be surprised – a method of randomization or serendipity. A way to realize the authoring and authoritative grip and gently shuffle the twelve chapters. A reading across the three parts, rather than a reading of the parts. A lateral thinking and reading that is on the prowl for nuggets of wisdom, poetic gems, evocative sentences, vibrant matter and random acts of inspiration. But as any design thinker knows, to invite for serendipitous randomness you need a clear structure. A method to the madness, in order to figure out what ideas, imaginaries, *Wunderkammers* or *thinkscapes* that might light up when we rub the chapters against each other. And that, in turn, might shed a new light on culture and the university.

We can draw inspiration from methods for randomness and creative thinking within design and ideation. Methods like 'Random entry technique', 'Random word stimulation', 'Random input' or 'Random combination'. All these techniques aim to unlock the mind, if thinking has become caught in its own headlights so to speak. These methods can here be employed as a way of listening to the whole book beyond the individual chapters and the authors' control. A listening to both things said and things lurking in the cracks between the three parts. A method that opens the door for strange creatures, new hybrids and unexpected linkages that might take thinking somewhere else through intentionally tripping this author up – just a little.

The method of 'Random input' was created by psychologist Edward de Bono in 1968 and published in his book *Serious Creativity* (1992) as a thinking strategy for getting fresh ideas and new perspectives. Random input, and all of the other methods for randomness mentioned above, uses lateral thinking techniques to inspire new ways of thinking. Random input is a method for using random words, pictures, texts or similar to assist the mind with thinking in new directions. The intention is for thoughts to move not only in a linear way, but in new and fresh directions outside of the analytical way of thinking. The essence of methods for lateral thinking and random input is to invite for thinking in nonconventional ways and see new connections. To link other thinking patterns into the ones we are already using. For instance, where would random combinations such as the word 'keyboard-skyscraper' take us when writing a book about the future university? Or what would the combination of theories on game worlds and martial arts have to offer a PhD student working on a dissertation on embodied gameplay? Or how could the notion of 'spaces of life' bring us to think about world-class universities?

The objective is to create associations that connect the meaning of each input or combination to a subject at hand, here culture and the university. In this way, methods for random acts of thinking build on Aristotle's three laws of association: (1) *Contiguity*: A law explaining how associations work by the stimulation of contact or nearness. A saddle may remind you of a horse, a foot of a shoe and so on. (2) *Similarity*: A law explaining how similar things produce associations. A cat could remind you of a tiger, the human eye is similar to a camera and a stair is similar to a lift. (3) *Contrast*: A law explaining how we associate things that contrast one another. Day is a contrast to night, a sad face to a happy face, tall to short and fresh to stale.

Drawing on these methods and laws of association, the first, second, third and fourth chapters of each part were bundled together, creating four new lateral parts: Chapters 1-1-1, Chapters 2-2-2, Chapters 3-3-3 and Chapters 4-4-4. These four slightly reshuffled parts were then read. In total, the chapters comprised 12 times (approximately) 5,000 words, that is, more than 60,000 words. Or, 15,000 words per part. Through the reading, each part was condensed from 15,000 to 4,000 words by extracting (without too much thinking) inspiring, thought-provoking, strange or otherwise striking sentences. After the read-through, the body of text then ended up being a total of 4 times 4,000 words, or 16,000 words. Still an abundance of things the book wanted to say, but also a rumbling randomness nearing something particular to tell me. The next step was cutting the three chapters in each part into pieces and putting them into closer contact with each other in order for them to begin to speak about something new together. This reduced the twelve chapters to four new sections. The last decision of randomness was to cull the 4 parts from 4,000 words to 1,000 words by merging and transmuting the authors' voices in their individual parts of the book into a new kind of voice speaking from *somewhere else* – from outside the three parts but in a language originating from them. This hybrid beast and what other things it had to say can be found in the following four sections.

1-1-1 A Constructive Force: The University as Cultural Place, Pharmakon and Formation

This section speaks with a voice emerging from the chapters 'The Cultural Crisis of the University' (Barnett), 'Placeful Cultures and Cultural Places' (Nørgård) and 'Higher Education as Cultural Formation' (Bengtsen).

Fusing the three chapters, we find ourselves with a university at odds with culture and at a loss regarding its role as an institution of and for culture. Today, the tight coupling of higher education and culture has all but disappeared and the university has become culture-free, culture-less or exposed to culture wars. No matter if it is an abundance of cultures at war or in opposition to each other or the lack of culture, we find today a university characterized by *cultural neglect* and in a *cultural crisis*. Today, the university might be overflowing with a multiplicity of cultures but not daring to speak the name of 'Culture'. Given this situation, is it, then, in any way possible for the university to help in advancing culture in the wider world? And are there ways forward for a university of and for culture?

Perhaps one way forward is simultaneously to turn away from the loudness and intensity of current culture wars and the silencing and disappearance of the university as a beacon of culture. How can the university in subtler or gentler ways become a place for and of culture(s)? A cultural and culturing *terrain of power* (Gieryn, 2000) that is neither warzone nor elitist ivory tower? What could happen if the university through place-making could envision and reconfigure itself into a place of 'big-C' culture and for 'little-c' cultures? In the book, we find a strong calling for the university to become something *other*, a culturing place creating cultural belonging as well as a site for academic cultures that work together both inside and outside of the university.

The university lacks *remarkable* places for *remarkable* culture(s) that can give form and expressive force to the idea and experience of a cultural and culturing university. That is, a hybridized culturing site for merging big-C and little-c culture(s) through concurrently being a formative unifying place of culture and an inclusive heterogeneous place for cultures – a multilayered university of culture and for cultures. The current disappearance of Culture and emergence of culture wars at the university have devastating implications for both academic individuals, collectives and institutions in relation to their identity, agency and sense of belonging. The challenge for higher education and university, then, is to develop practices of (re)generating place and (re)invigorating culture to manifest itself as a terrain of cultural and culturing power.

But the university cannot concurrently be a cultural and culturing actor in the world and remain exempt from cultural entanglements. Such cultural entanglements go both outwards and inwards. Inwardly, a culturing practice of place-making at the university interlinks academic cultures with each other and with the university as a cultural site. Outwardly, a culturing practice of the university implies that it takes place but also gives place to culture(s) in and for the world. This implies that such a multilayered university as big-C cultural institution and institution for little-c cultures will, on the one hand, *space out* in the world and, in the course of its own *espacement*, make place for cultures to take place (Casey, 1997). On the other hand, such a university is an open invitation to people to *space out* in its cultural and culturing environment, and, in so doing, let the event of culture take place and find form within them.

Through the culturing place-making of universities, higher education, then, becomes a place for cultural dwelling, growth and awareness, which in turn creates a sense of both big-C and little-c cultural belonging. The university as both a formative *culturing* institution and a place for little-c *culturing* practices transforms it into a web of places of and for culture. Through these shared cultural places and culturing events, the possibility of a communal university culture emerges. By working together to develop a university with a critical awareness of how to carefully *produce place* (Lefebvre, 1991) in order to *have* culture, the university might stand a better chance of evading the 'toxic university' culture that Smythe (2018) warns about.

By working to join forces rather than choose sides, the university can, through gentle but virtuous place-making, work towards positioning higher education as a central contributor to the cultural formation of current and future generations. Connecting cultural and culturing places and big-C and little-c culture with the formation of virtuous academic culture, we can see how academic practice and higher education are separated neither from place nor culture, but rest on cultural values of placeful belonging and communality, place-making diversity and generosity as well as the entanglement of big-C and little-c culture(s) to invoke cultural respect, honesty and solidarity.

Today's toxic university culture of increasing academic competition, individual rivalry and de-collegiality, as well as growing threats to academic culture and freedom, might be understood as emerging from the hegemony of *striated institutional space* – that is, a system's exercise of managerial power over the idea of the university and its members which grows from the instrumentalization, homogenization, compartmentalization and functional systematization of the university. Such striated space abolishes both placeful cultures and cultural formation within higher education and the university and weighs down on academic life and culture. The result is a flattening of the academic sphere that leaves the university and higher education culture open and vulnerable to becoming a drained culture-less institution or overthrown by externally induced culture wars.

Cultural places and culturing place-making may provide a strategy for universities to establish big-C and little-c cultural safe havens in the form of academic spheres for dwelling, growth and belonging that encourages all its members to come forward with imaginary and emancipatory possibilities. In this way, the university as cultural place-making agent might indeed be a *pharmakon* offering a route to cultural (re)enchantment in and of both world and university.

2-2-2 Towards Empathic Coexistence: Cultural Atmosphere, Wars and Leadership

This section conjures a voice from the chapters 'Culture Wars: Multiplication and (Possible) Re-unification' (Barnett), 'The Atmospheric University and Cultural Atmospheres' (Nørgård) and 'Cultural Leadership' (Bengtsen).

In the second-placed chapters, we get an analysis of culture and the university in relation to the concepts of atmosphere, culture wars and leadership. All chapters point towards how the university (dis)connects with culture through its atmospheric design, felt leadership or cultural coexistence. In the culture-less university, leadership has experienced a disconnect from the everyday practices of academic culture and been somewhat swallowed up by the task of managing expanding institutions and implementing higher education strategies and policies. Today, leadership of universities has been transfigured into something reminiscent of managing big corporations causing university leadership to disappear from the 'floor' of the institution and become invisible in the communal practice of academic culture. Leaders are not *felt* in the practice of the classroom, their *voice* is not heard in the hallways and their *spirit* is not present in the everyday cultural of the university.

With the disappearance of cultural leadership, there is a growing danger that culture evaporates from the university, creating an atmosphere not unlike the one we find in the *dead spaces* of city areas being devoured by corporations, in effect, transforming cities from cultural spheres and community lifeworlds to instrumental sites for business branding and architectural show-off. There is no life to be found outside of worklife in these areas, and as such, they are devouring dead spaces and slowly taking over the cultural atmosphere of the inner city. Similar cultural dead spaces might be seen to encroach on the university and take over its cultural atmosphere as universities are transformed from cultural communities to corporate institutions. Here, leaders and leadership have a major role to play in whether such a transformation happens or not.

Of course, leaders are busy and cannot be everywhere all the time. But here the notions of atmosphere, genius loci and atmospheric design might help leaders to create *atmospheric* and *spirited* leadership that preserve and emanate cultural leadership in their absence. Shifting the focus, from cultural leadership as physical presence to felt (atmospheric) presence, enables leaders to be leaders of culture and culturing leaders through the atmosphere they create. Approaching cultural leadership through the lens of atmospheric design points towards leaders working closely together with all the members of the university to foster a spirited cultural atmosphere that is the *speaking face* and *breathing body* (Böhme, 1995) of both university and academic community. Thinking in atmospheric design helps leaders in promoting an existential terrain that enables members of the university to perceive it as a lifeworld (rather than a workplace) and manifest cultural leadership as atmospheric culture.

However, the need for cultural leadership and atmospheric culture is needed not only when it comes to the inner life of the university but also when it comes to the relation between university and society as well as the role of the university in the world. Today, we see polarizing culture wars embedded within the notions of free speech, academic freedom, ethnicity, colonialism, gender, religion and many other important agendas. Here, leaders are called upon to lead the university and its members through these conflicts and create an atmosphere where such wars are transformed into an atmosphere of academic debate, inclusivity, respect and equity. This, in turn, requires leaders to be culturally present and felt, and to engage all members of the university in order to stage polyphonic and heterotopic atmospheres of cultural cohesion that overcome such polarizing and conflict-ridden discourses. That is, leaders need to work as attentive atmospheric designers both internally and externally to create a community not of 'warring cultures' but of 'empathic cultures'.

To create deep and powerful cultural atmospheres requires that leaders embody the university and participate as members of the university on an equal footing with all other members. The *staging* of powerful atmospheric cultures, which account for strong cultural leadership, requires that leaders move out of their own closed culture of university managers and immerse themselves in the everyday cultural practice of the university. To keep the university culturally alive, leaders must *practise* the university as cultural lifeworld and academic community and then carefully work together with all members to *stage* an atmosphere that radiates culture even when leaders are not physically present. To avoid corporatized dead spaces and culture wars, (all manner of) university leaders must radiate cultural leadership rather than institutional management. Cultural leadership in the form of atmospheric design has a potential of circumventing the 'zombification' of the university through providing the university with a culturally tinctured atmosphere that gently guides members of the university in relation to both big-C and little-c culture(s).

Overall, such *atmospheric leadership* requires (a) acts of empathic listening to, being with and living through the spirit and culture of the university; (b) acts of redesigning and amplifying the cultural atmosphere of the university in ways that respectfully emphasize the spirit and culture of the place and all its members; and (c) acts of bridge-building between university culture, members' culture and communal culture and existence (Volgger, 2020). Speaking across all three chapters, university leaders need to become cultural leaders and engage in atmospheric leadership. This is important both when it comes to countering the danger of encroaching culture-less dead spaces and the emergence of internal and external culture wars. For one thing, this involves the task of working together with all members of the university in order to stage cultural atmospheres of collegial solidarity, cultural cohesion and heterogeneous cultures, which in turn can embrace academic disagreements and culture clashes in academically respectful, empathetic, dialogic and co-operative ways.

To dissolve dominant internal toxic cultures of funding rivalry, individual superiority and disciplinary supremacy, and instead to promote the staging of university-wide communal coexistence and solidarity, requires cultural leaders that are heard and felt in the inner lifeworld of the university; which again points towards some rather radical shifts in the inner cultural life and mechanisms of the university. This might, for example, indicate a fundamental shift in the inherent value and role of the university from a corporate logic of productivity, professionalization, prestige and socio-economic growth towards a culture of human growth, common good and cultural formation. Such a shift would require a transformation of university, leadership and culture.

3-3-3 A Collective Endeavour: Common, Indivisible and Speculative Cultures

This section speaks with a voice fused together from the chapters 'A Common Culture: No and Maybe' (Barnett), 'Cultures for Collective Visioning and Future-Making' (Nørgård) and 'The Indivisible' (Bengtsen).

In the third chapters of the book, the focus is on the common, collective and indivisible character of university culture. Even though the university, at best, presently is a site of many little-c cultures, it is also a site of cultural exclusion and exclusivity. This might point us towards a rather grim outlook at present-day university culture, where the university does not speak of culture, engage in formative culturing or work to create cultural cohesion among its many warring mini cultures. This, in turn, opens the university up to takeover by dominant cultures both inside and outside the university. To counter such *grimdark* tendencies calls for collective cultural practices of envisioning more preferable cultural futures for the university as cohesive cultural sphere.

There is a need for the university to focus on the (re)construction of shared visions across the disciplines, that in turn can constitute a communal ecology – not as a homogenizing strategy – but as a generative meshwork of interconnected ideas, values, meanings and disciplinary practices working together. There is a need, too, for a shift towards university-wide co-creation, co-operation and communality so that the members of the university over time experience a sense of belonging to each other and the university. This might, for example, entail a heightened focus on internal cross-disciplinary meetings, projects, residencies and co-operation instead of the present firm focus on internationalization. Before working with others, the members of the university need to be able to work together.

Today, many academics have a sense of belonging with departments and colleagues around the world within their discipline that is stronger than that with their colleagues next door outside their discipline. There is no sense of solidarity and communality across the university and its disciplines – departments do not shield each other, cover each other's losses or co-operatively share resources – but, rather, they compete and fight each other for resources, funding, positions and recognition. Such internal wars and divisions and conquer strategies, dispel culture and make cultural cohesion and solidarity impossible.

Culture presupposes, in essence, a set of enduring collective meanings that bind a community or university together in solidarity to such a degree that members feel that they are part of the same lifeworld and come to recognize themselves in the other and vice versa. If a university fails in creating a cohesive culture wherein the profoundly different disciplines, epistemologies, meanings, cognitive cultures and academic practices of the university come together, then the collective endeavour, spirit and culture of the university will dissolve and disappear. What will be left is functional office spaces (dead space), competing disciplinary enclaves striving for excellence and individual academics fencing for themselves to survive. The university might be successful in attracting students, external funding and star researchers, but will fail in creating university-wide solidarity and care and a sense of communal belonging.

This implies a cultural approach of *collective visioning* and *total interconnectedness* by way of a battery of associated concepts such as complexity, indeterminacy, open-endedness, fluidity, emergence, contingency, entanglement, inequality, relationality and unpredictability. Within communal culture, there can be no Robinson Crusoe cultures or island collectives. The university is not an adaptation of the reality TV show *Survivor* where the last academic (or discipline) standing as the lone survivor takes home a million dollars. If anything, it is more reminiscent of the shows where a group of very different people (with different cultures, world views and skill-sets) join forces to build or achieve something extraordinary which can only be accomplished because they work together and take advantage of these differences.

However, a cohesive *and* heterogeneous culture carries with it an innate exclusion. A cohesive university with institution-wide collegiality and communality draws a boundary around that community and culture, thereby excluding all those standing outside it. But such exclusion needs only be the case if this is the only – rather than the first – step the university takes. Like a handful of stones thrown into the sea to create ripple effects that come into contact and criss-cross with each other, so can universities around the globe concurrently possess a strong cultural cohesion and open up in ever-widening circles.

Such a shared realm of being, both internally (as stone) and externally (as criss-crossing ripples in the sea) points towards the potential of a cultural and culturing university. The formation of such ever-widening collegial culture(s) – inwardly across the university and outwardly across the world – creates opportunities for expanded imagination, deepened practice and cultural growth. This entails a willingness to move beyond one's own academic identity and little-c cultures and embrace the strangeness and wonder of other cultures both inside and outside the university. However, coming in contact with what is obscure, alien or unknowable to us might be deeply unsettling to our disciplinary identity, methods and knowledge cultures. To expose oneself to this requires both caring and compelling cultural leadership.

Should the university succeed in such radical practices of cultural formation and cohesion, it carries with it the hope of disciplines that come together to partake in *informed academic speculation* that opens up new vistas and futures through bringing into question what we consider to be 'predicted', 'projected', 'probable' and 'plausible' (Voros, 2017). Reading across the three chapters, in different ways, they all emphasize a break with the *colonization of the future* and points towards a widening of the cultural practices of the university in order to envision how things *could be* or even *ought to be*. Conversely, if the cultural mindset and awareness of the university (and its different disciplinary cultures) is too tightly structured and defined, there is a real risk of becoming a *totality* trapped in the 'imperialism of the same' (Levinas, 2003: 39), where every difference, diversity, strangeness and otherness become assimilated into the already known within the dominant discourses.

What brings hope here is the fact that inherent in the university, and all its disciplines, is an inbuilt academic enthusiasm and cultural openness towards new forms of thinking, new methods, new discourses, new voices, new pursuits and new encounters, however strange, unintelligible, provocative or even repulsive they may seem when we first run into them. Such cohesive heterogeneity is precisely what creates cultural growth within and between the disciplines and what negates the colonization of the future ruled by the totality of projected, probable and predictable knowledge. In this way, a university of and for culture is a university open to the infinity of all possible (imaginable), preferable (good) and even preposterous (unknowable) knowledge forms.

4-4-4 A Culture of Entanglements: Of Earth, Worldings and Hybrids

This last section emerges from the hybrid voice of the chapters 'For the University and the World: A Culture of the Earth' (Barnett), 'Futurescaping Alternative Universities' (Nørgård) and 'Beyond Culture' (Bengtsen).

In the fourth and final chapters of those parts of this book, the focus is on more expansive notions of culture and the university as something for the whole Earth, as a worlding-with and as hybridization and network. Through the image of the Moebius strip and its inherent and unending entanglement – or hybridization – we come to see how big-C Culture and little-c cultures are simultaneously incommensurable and intertwined. Culture is universal and context specific, one and many, unifying and diversifying depending on where you are travelling on the Moebius strip of culture(s). As a coin revealing a picture when it is spun fast, so the image of the Moebius strip reveals a potential new hybrid being of university culture(s). Travelling the Moebius strip, the university is concurrently a landscape barren of and replete with cultures, a landscape wherein disciplinary and academic cultures are expanding as they are moving apart, making it ever more difficult to (re)spawn a cohesive and communal university culture. Such a culture is made even more difficult as this landscape sprawling with cultures is simultaneously a *culture-less* dead space of instrumentalism, economicism, managerialism and corporatism.

So, it seems, that what stands before us are the options of internal and external societal culture wars, technical and organizational culture-less systems as well as disciplinary culture silos in destructive competition with each other. The university has, on the one hand, turned away from its inherent cultural and culturing purpose and towards a disillusioned space of instrumental reason and, on the other hand, been flooded with internal and external culture wars propelling it into a state of *entropy* and *anti-culture*.

However, there is a spark of hope on the horizon of the grimdark landscape of present-day university culture(s), namely the deeper unifying potential of an ecological university culture. Such an ecological culture constitutes a new hybrid being and becoming of the university that connects university and its members to the Earth; a culture of Earthly spirit and care; a university and culture that is not caught up in the grimdark hegemony of projected, probable and plausible future, but is catching fire through an entanglement with the major ecosystems of the Earth.

As an ecological firestarter and reinvigorating firestorm, the university can bring with it new hybrid culture(s) and life forms. Like the Phoenix, the university must reawaken with fiery wings to fight for the whole Earth as a world worth inhabiting. Such a hybrid beast kindles an Earthlier culture characterized by kindness, imaginative speculation, preposterous hopefulness, co-operative endeavours and a collective spirit. The Phoenix rises as a true and extra-cultural hybrid, simultaneously new *and* old, past *and* future, male *and* female, animal *and* element, nature *and* culture, biological *and* magical. It symbolizes rebirth, renewal, hope, progress and the end of oppression. It is a reinvigorating firestorm that allows us to glimpse in the flames wider and deeper futures for the university and the world, as well as pointing towards an unending abundance of possible new beginnings.

The Phoenix is a fitting – and hopeful – metaphor both for the cultural futures of the university *and* in highlighting the Earthly care and soaring imagination required to bring about such a hybrid ecological culture. This, however, necessitates the disbandment of dichotomies, boundaries, silos and wars. To be transformed into something *other*. A new cultural – still unknowable – form bursting with hybridity, which might make it appear preposterous, utopian or abominable at first. The Phoenix, simultaneously a bird, a nest, an egg, a worm and a fire, encapsulates such a hybrid entanglement involved in an ecological transformation of both university and culture; a crucial transformation considering the immanent future of both Earth and university culture.

Every day dozens of species are becoming extinct, with as many as 30–50 per cent of all species going extinct by 2050. Species are disappearing from our planet before we have even had the chance to meet them. Oceans soon contain more plastic than fish, and we are quickly on our way to turning the environment against us to such a degree that there is no turning back. We are becoming our own and Earth's undoing. A realization that is also working its way into the university.

The university stands at a crossroad where it is realizing that it is no longer enough to be working for societal growth, the common good of humanity or a culture for human growth and formation. It must be working for the common good of the whole Earth – which might be at odds with societal growth – and be a culture for all species. If the university succeeds in rising like the Phoenix and forming a university-wide culture where all disciplines come together and join forces, there might be a budding hope for a new hybrid university culture that cares for and takes care of the whole Earth.

Looking into the grimdark of the imminent future, the university might indeed be one of the only candidates for accepting the responsibility (we all have) of becoming a planetary caretaker. But this requires the formation of hybrid and hybridizing, networked and networking culture where humanities, social sciences, natural sciences, formal sciences and professional and applied sciences all work together for the common good of the whole Earth. If the university cannot conquer the present colonization of the future, disperse the grimdark, dissolve pervading dichotomies and overcome internal and external culture wars, whereto shall Earth and all of its inhabitants then turn? The university needs to rise as a unifying and cohesive *culturing-with* institution in order to become a *worlding-with* institution that connects us with and creates intricate meshworks between ourselves, other beings, species and still-unknown life forms.

This will be a costly resurrection of the university and its culture, as it requires both a reconfiguration of the university as an organization, a reframing of the contract between society and university as well as a reconceptualization of its epistemic knowledge cultures. Extending the concept of hybridity, a university culture of and for the whole Earth must emerge as (1) a culture of rhizomatic places, vibrant matter and hybrid knowledge forms, (2) a culturing practice of dissolving dichotomies to create new breeds of otherness, (3) a sprawling spirited and placeful ecological culture that sprawls across and draws together all parts and species of the world and (4) a cohesive culture of belonging and solidarity where all disciplinary practices, knowledge forms, ecosystems and worlding-with practices are entangled and hang onto each other like burdocks – or feathers on a Phoenix – to work together as inhabitants of the same Earth.

Conclusions

Taken together, a hybrid university, ecological culture and worlding-with point towards new forms of entangled and complex cultures and institutions. Such hopeful hybridization calls for a *politics of swarming* where diverse cultural realities and belief systems come together to form a shared cultural contract that transcends each individual cultural realm. This *coming together through swarming* is required both inside and outside of the university and has to happen with an interest beyond our own species and human culture.

We, as members of the university, will have to live up to this deeper purpose of the university through joining forces, overcoming differences, engaging in (preposterous) speculation, materializing the unknown and developing hybrid cross-university practices of ecological culturing. This can only happen through an opening up of ourselves, our disciplines and the university – to become both hybridized and hybridizing, networked and networking for the common good of the whole Earth. Through attentive planetary *futurescaping*, more ecological and Earthly futures and cultures emerge that can be materialized and tried out inside and outside of the university, thereby broadening the future and strengthening hope for both university and the Earth.

14

A University of One's Own

Søren Bengtsen

Introduction

We live amid a sea of universities. Not just a sea but a vast ocean. There are now over 25,000 universities in the world, and in some of the largest countries like China, the United States, India, Brazil and Russia, there are thousands of universities alone. The competition between universities grows, and the battle for world-class excellence continues (Hazelkorn, 2015). Through the ranking game, we see a growing number of performance indicators measuring the success of each university and, thus, streamlining the idea of what it means to be a university and what academic achievement and culture should look like in relation to higher education policies and practices.

Mission statements and vision papers from universities often look alike with the same vocabulary of excellence, global outlook, societal outreach, innovation and entrepreneurship. But how can anything be original and excellent if it is all the same and similar? We are facing a mass society of universities potentially drowning the individual institutional voice and singular academic signature. I argue that universities today face an existential challenge in relation to finding their own voice, vision and values. I argue, too, that the challenge, today, is not to become a world-class university with a top ranking on a bland scale of academic anonymity – but to become a *singular* university, a university of one's own.

Rider and her team (Rider et al., 2020) raise a series of critical questions about the notion of world-classness, and the general push for all (or most) universities towards world-class status. The authors point to the risk of crowding out alternative models for higher education, such as increased access and equity. They ask if citizens might not 'be better served by developing locally relevant systems, without concern for their relative merits in a global comparison', and if 'the definition of "world-class" [is] synonymous with "rich", and if so, what are we prepared to invest and what are we prepared to forego in order to finance such efforts?' – and further if 'only research universities [are] world-class?' or if 'other types of HE institutions (polytechnics, community colleges and open universities, for instance) aspire to be among the best of their kind?' (Rider et al., 2020: 4). By serving the same terms and generic vocabularies of world-classness, universities risk creating a homogeneous and hegemonic university standard, which, paradoxically, will arguably not facilitate originality and independence in thought and action but standardize and clone a generic version of excellence in higher education policy and practice.

Ecologies are only sustaining difference and diversity because the individual life forms interacting contribute to each other by providing unique and irreplaceable inputs. As Barnett (2018) makes clear, an ecology is a manifestation of interconnectedness through the sustainment of diversity and difference. To become, then, a singular university – or, as per Nørgård and Bengtsen's (2016) term, a 'placeful' university – the institution, its leadership, policies and practices have to be singular and 'placeful' too. The individual university should aim to create a specific institution and to be able to state why *this* university exists and what *this* university aims to achieve and how. Once again, the question about institutional integrity and academic culture is brought to the fore. The call for the placeful university has, indeed, become more imperative than ever before.

The chapter builds on the inspiration solely from reading my co-authors' contributions to the present volume. I have deliberately tried to flesh out a new, but interlinked, argument that has absorbed Barnett and Nørgård's points and formed a step in, I feel, our joint thinking.

From Barnett's contributions, I have mainly drawn on the arguments around cultural integrity and cultural glue, and the ways universities should strive to build cohesive institutional cultures that are academically, educationally and societally sustainable. Each singular university needs, at the same time, to anchor its educational and social values to the specific institutional context *and* to a meta-level connecting all universities. In Barnett's argument lies a constructive tension between critical (and culture-free – as in 'free of ideology') institutions and institutions submerged (or saturated) in the specific cultural contexts they belong to and speak into. The notion of meta-culture presented and discussed by Barnett never signifies a detached and remote form of belonging to some transcendental realm of being – it represents an institutional and educational dialectics, where each university participates in, and belongs to, to several ontological realms simultaneously. The university and its culture(s) are always ecologically enacted and sustained.

From Nørgård's contributions, I have mainly drawn on the arguments around place and space and the crucial point that university culture is always linked to a specific institutional, curricular and societal context. As Nørgård underlines, university culture hinges on a specific atmosphere created by the students, teachers and institutional leaders of a given academic setting. The culture is, so to speak, a form of institutional and curricular design. But a living, or *lived*, design – and a living university. A living culture, as Nørgård argues, becomes shaped not only by rational thinking but also by affect, emotion, action and activism. A university culture lives and breathes and develops and changes in close connection with the people and societies forming and sustaining them.

Each University Has Its Own Story

Despite individual differences and characteristics, universities, of course, share various academic norms and values, or forms of 'academic charisma' (Clark, 2006), defining higher education teaching and learning practices, examination conventions, management styles, legal rights, forms of political influence and so on, in a given period of time and national context. This point has been argued by Rüegg (2003) and his team of experts within university history, who have been able to integrate institutional and curricular differences with similarities and patterns of policy and practice across Europe up through the last millennium. The university is part of a wide and far-reaching joint history and journey of cultural becoming, and each university always defines itself in relation to that common and shared culture and institutional trajectory.

However, the very meaning of a university, together with the formation of academic culture, only occurs through individual and specific institutional, curricular and personal *choices*. We know that in the mediaeval university in Bologna students formed the governing body, and 'Masters were fined if they did not begin and end their lectures on time, or if they failed to cover the required ground by set dates'. Here, 'students were elected to monitor the masters and to report infringements; to keep masters continuously on their toes' (Wei, 2014: 91). On the other hand, in Paris, in the same historical period, the university 'was run by its masters whose pre-eminence in arts and theology was internationally recognized' (Wei, 2014). In Paris, the masters were in a stronger position to impose themselves on the students 'because many of them held ecclesiastical benefices and did not therefore rely entirely upon fees' (Wei, 2014).

Universities in both Bologna and Paris have been central in the formation of academic culture and integrity, but relied on entirely different institutional blueprints, and their abilities to enact a unique and singular example of the university have had lasting effects several centuries after. Even though greater political and social winds are blowing, and today often with global aspiration, each university has to acknowledge and critically engage with its own history and situation. Each university has to form its *own* future, which only happens through often difficult, choices and decisions that will have wide-reaching consequences both within and beyond the institutional spaces. We should not forget that in a global age, it is just as important as ever to know one's *own* story and one's *own* institutional self in order to contribute to, and engage with, the wider ecology of universities, and societally too, with integrity and authenticity.

Institutional integrity may take many different forms. Sometimes, the challenge is to act within, in order to enlarge from within, spaces for originality in an orthodox system. As Brockliss (2016: 92) relates in his account of the University of Oxford, even the orthodox mediaeval university still relied on originality, and there 'were no restrictions placed on originality, provided a lecturer did not sin egregiously against religious orthodoxy, and most universities supported the odd original mind across the period [late fourteenth century]'. Later on (sixteenth and seventeenth centuries), however, because of the very same orthodoxy, many universities lost their former intellectual dynamism and with the prolonged domination of scholasticism, 'the university largely surrendered their cultural leadership' (Brockliss, 2016: 135), which moved, for a period, outside university walls and found its home in private intellectual clubs, scientific societies and academic communities.

In Lund University, in the closing decades of the nineteenth century, political tensions between conservative and progressivist academic parties became particularly clear as

> The generation of young students of the 1880s who entered the atrium of the university building with its marble floor and columns, or the ornate great hall with its character of an ancient temple, were not all prepared to accept the cultural and educational ideals manifest there. The opposition between the conservative desire to preserve traditions and the radical, youthful need to rebel is a constantly recurring theme in every university town. . . . The phalanx of young, rebellious students of the 1880s produced some of the foremost teachers and researchers Lund has ever seen, with new values, a new impetus, and a view of scholarship born of a new era. (Fehrman et al., 2005: 115)

Even though such tensions were not particular to Lund University at the time, but may have been felt in many universities in Europe, it played out in unique and singular ways, which only the students, teachers and leaders at that particular university would know how to respond to and act on. The tensions could not be solved through generic models or mission statements from other Scandinavian or Northern European universities, but had to be dealt with by *these* students, *these* teachers and *these* leaders in *that* university at *that* time and place. The university takes part of a living society and is also itself a living institution – a *lived* place. It strives for a common culture between other universities, and between the university and society – but it also strives to form a common culture of its own, within a particular institution. I am not arguing that universities should withdraw from alliances or societal interconnections but about knowing oneself as a particular university in order to take responsibility and to contribute to the wider ecology.

On the college level too (and arguably on department level as well), we find micro-ecologies and micro-institutional narratives and (his)stories. At least with some of the older colleges, like, for example, the University College in Oxford, the smaller institution (within an institution) has been said by Darwall-Smith (2008: 528) to be 'analogous to a car which has had every part replaced'. Besides its original architectural remains, the college has changed drastically over the centuries of its existence but still preserved a continuous succession of Fellows, even in such turbulent times as the Civil War or the First World War. Throughout that time, its members have 'responded similarly to the institution, ranging from dislike by way of indifference to affection. Each era has had personalities to dominate the College, and to give it a particular style' (2008) – and as Darwall-Smith concludes (2008), it is 'for the next generations of Fellows, students, and staff of University College to take that inheritance into the next century'.

Of course, if one were to do a proper historical study of the university, this would require an entire book in itself (or several books more likely). I merely use the scattered examples mentioned earlier to argue that in order to understand the wider societal, political and even global, opportunities and trajectories of the university, we have to also understand the specific, and deeply contextual, choices that are made, decisions that are taken and actions that are performed. Accordingly, we have to consider not only how universities become players on the global scene but also how universities find their own singular voice and form an academic culture of their own through which they engage with, and contribute to, the wider contexts they interconnect with.

Becoming an *Individual* University?

For a university to engage with other universities and create a common culture across institutional, national and cultural differences, it requires that such differences are acknowledged and recognized. Some universities are public and receive funding from, and owe services to the state, while others are private institutions relying on funding from companies, organizations and personal endowments (and fees from students). Some universities focus more on teaching than research, and some develop their curriculum in closer collaboration with external partners than others. Some universities have a long spiritual tradition and historical anchoring to a certain local community, while others have been founded recently and on entirely different grounds and with entirely different purposes. Some universities have not existed for several decades, or even centuries, while others have not yet come into existence (and perhaps never will). Universities may share in a common idea about, or culture around, the university, but they are not identical institutions and communities, and each university will have to form an institutional culture, and legacy, of its own.

Often it is said that in order to know who we are, we need to know where we come from and how we have journeyed to get here. As I have argued elsewhere (Bengtsen et al., 2021: 3), the integrity of the university 'does not mean holding fast uncritically to certain institutional or curricular customs or habits, but, on the contrary, to be able to know what we are changing and what is being changed by whom in our institutions and not least why'. To be able to share in the institutional values of others, each university needs to develop its cultural as well as a historical awareness and to continue a critical discussion of what it means to stay true to the core values of a given university and shared by its members and partners. Paradoxically, one could argue that there are so many demands and expectations put on universities today not only from the public and private sectors but also from students and teachers themselves; and from the wider societal contexts, it is perhaps more difficult than ever for the individual university to decide what *its own* values are and what *its own* curricular and academic ethos is. From within such larger ecologies, and economies (perhaps more often), we glimpse an overlooked *existential* challenge on the institutional level.

Paradoxically, and as recently pointed out too by Barnett (2021), the more successful universities have become and the more significant they have become politically and economically in their nations, the more the governments (and large companies) start to take a closer interest. Being politically and culturally visible brings new challenges. As Barnett notes, politically universities are 'objects of suspicion; culturally, they are accused of being unduly liberal; economically, they are felt to be insufficiently supportive of a country's economy; and socially, they are critiqued for being insufficiently open to those from certain socio-economic classes' (Barnett, 2021: 24). As Barnett also notes (Barnett, 2021: 25), the universities could fall prey to becoming instruments in political agendas of the surveillance society as pawns of learning analytics regimes or computerized agents in a fourth industrial revolution. The university is caught in the tension of forming alliances, contracts and bonds with external partners both in order to survive in a complex society and to realize its deeper ecological potential – and at the same time to stand its own institutional, curricular and cultural ground and sustain its own values and maintain its own integrity. The existential challenges are not only for students, teachers and leaders to make – but also the universities themselves, as institutional signatures, have to make existential decisions.

Such existential choices cannot be automatized, and we cannot rely on others to make the choices for us. As Kierkegaard writes (2009: 87), when 'one is disinclined to make the leap (. . .) then the most cunningly contrived jumping device will be of no help at all . . . the leap, being decisive, is qualitatively dialectical and that it allows no approximating transition'. The singular university cannot rely on the state or other external partners to make foundational decisions for them – even when such partners are benevolent and supportive. Neither are there any previous decisions, or mission statements, that will solve the specific challenges the individual university faces today in its particular situation. Choices have to be made, decisions need to be taken – and the individual university has to make up its own mind. Not alone, of course, and not without the aid of others – but still it has to choose its own path.

The political, cultural and ontological reality and power of the individual choice is perhaps especially important to stress at a time where many universities fear simply being run over (and assimilated), or passed by (and made irrelevant), if they resist generic global trends and dare to go their own way. It is through specific *choices* and *decisions* that curricular and institutional trajectories (including individual student and researcher trajectories) are shaped and reshaped – and changed altogether. As Kierkegaard so importantly underlines, it is only when our political and cultural norms and values can come to a 'halt that a beginning can be made', and they 'can be halted only by something else, and this something else is something quite other than the logical, because it is a *decision* ... [wherefrom] the absolute beginning itself breaks through the infinitely continued reflection' (Kierkegaard, 2009: 96 – SB's italics).

Of course, one decision may not change much (we make several each day), and knowing the consequences of one's choices is almost impossible in the vastly entangled institutional and political realities universities find themselves in. However, if universities slip entirely into the mode of political and societal determinism, they stop making any decisions altogether and simply comply and implement. Becoming aware of which decisions are the more important, one relies on an understanding of what the individual university wants to be and become. The ecological university and the existential university are inextricably linked – one cannot exist without the other. Forming long-lasting and sustainable communities and partnerships with other universities and societal and political realms always depends on exactly which universities are forming them and why. There is no institutional view from nowhere – and there is no generic university. The idea of the university is not an empty place-holder concept but always a singular historical and cultural enacted institutional reality.

Greater Anxiety, Please!

As I am writing these lines, a journal special issue on academic activism has just been published (Nørgård and Bengtsen, 2021a). The issue presents and critically discusses a canopy of understandings of activism and activist practices within universities around the world. As the editors write, '[t]here is a note of activism hanging in the air in many universities, a sense that studying, teaching, and researching is not enough' (Nørgård and Bengtsen, 2021b: 507). The university, and academic culture, cannot be reduced to the generic practices of teaching, learning and research. Academic culture 'couples intellectual, political, and ethical efforts ... [and in] the sinews of the activist university also lies the potential of a caring and compassionate university that functions as a refuge or haven for free thinking, vulnerable positions, uncomfortable truths, or unwelcomed research' (Nørgård and Bengtsen, 2021b: 509). As both Barnett and Nørgård so inspiringly accentuate and persistently point out in the present volume, and elsewhere, that change *is real* and *possible* ontologically, epistemologically and practically (in relation to institutional and curricular aspects). Perhaps change could even be understood as part of the 'cultural glue' (Barnett) and 'atmosphere' (Nørgård) of universities.

Often, students and teachers are told that academic spaces are narrowing – but the present volume argues that they are not, for academic spaces are vast and growing continuously. The policy community, and other stakeholders who aim to reduce and control academic spaces and culture, may have political agendas behind such claims, and they may argue that in economic terms some academic possibilities become more limited. However, academic spaces and academic culture, in the ontologically meaning of the term, are not being reduced – they are fast growing. As I have argued elsewhere (Bengtsen, 2018), academic culture and practices cannot simply be reduced to policy instruments and institutional storytelling, and they most certainly cannot be reduced to programmes of higher education and career trajectories. As I have argued in my previous chapters here, academic culture cannot be reduced to cultural or financial capital; rather, it belongs to the common. Academic culture cannot be reduced to educational programmes and a stakeholder-controlled curriculum as education includes not only learning goals and career planning but also a wider cultural outlook (formation) and an ethical foundation.

Pushing the argument towards what some would find hopelessly naïve, I would argue that the challenge today (luckily) is not that universities are unfree to shape their own and related cultures but that there is still freedom left. The deep challenge for universities is their freedom! As Kierkegaard (1980) points out, fear is not our problem, anxiety is. When you are not free, you may experience fear of consequences you can understand, and foresee as, for example, continued financial cuts that make academics fearful of losing their jobs or fearing that their free research opportunities will further diminish; when students may fear the loss of educational quality and accessibility; and where industry may fear limitations in innovation and productivity. Such fears are, of course, perfectly understandable and problematic in their own right, and we should contest and challenge such threats as much as possible. However, challenging universities in an entirely different way is (academic) anxiety. Anxiety is felt because we *are free* and there are no immediate clear pathways to pursue – and we will have to decide on alternative academic futures ourselves! We may fear taking action when we know the consequences – but we may dread (feeling anxiety towards) taking action when we do not know how to act and what the consequences will be.

As Kierkegaard (1980: 61) famously observes, '[a]nxiety may be compared with dizziness', and he 'whose eyes happens to look down into the yawning abyss becomes dizzy' as 'anxiety is the dizziness of freedom'. It is the very possibility of freedom that announces itself in anxiety. While fear often overcomes academics when we know what we do not want to happen (higher student fees, more top-down leadership, increased instrumentalization of the higher education curriculum, increased managerialism and political surveillance of universities, etc.), anxiety may also set in when we struggle to know how to respond to such initiatives and struggle to articulate and enact what we want instead, as '[a]nxiety is freedom's possibility' (Kierkegaard, 1980: 155). Sometimes, the hardest thing is to realize that we, as academics (students, teachers, researchers, leaders), actually *do* have a choice, and that we actually *do* have spaces for manoeuvring autonomously within our curricula and that there is more freedom in our institutions left to claim, or reclaim (Hodgson et al., 2020).

Several practical considerations follow in the wake of anxiety. How do I want to teach if I do not go and stand behind a desk and have students sit in rows facing me as a teacher? How do I create collegiate and trustful researcher communities in an institution that often favours competition between individuals? How do I start taking leadership from where I am personally situated within the university and expand my own agentive peripheries? How do I design for freedom? As Grant (2019: 23) argues, one of the most widespread challenges in our universities today is to 'incite thought about the university outside the fatalistic binary that places the global neoliberal university as the dominating one and the old Western collegial university (say) as its subordinated other'. As Grant stresses, such binaries threaten to trap us 'in an unhappy mix of fury and nostalgia, nostalgia which might be mobilising but is just as likely to be pacifying' (2019). Daring to be free and to make free choices is, paradoxically, sometimes the most difficult thing to do. It is much easier being unfree (or imagining oneself being so) and critiquing decisions you have no immediate control over for being misunderstood and unfair. Expanding your own free academic territory is the hardest part – as you will need to imagine and enact alternative ideas, actions, discourses and practices.

No matter how sophisticated and detailed we form our critical analysis of the limitations of academic culture and growth, no real change will ever occur unless academics themselves move from fear into anxiety, where the true transformative potential lies, that is, the possibility of freedom. As Kierkegaard (1980: 157) writes, the 'individual must . . . have possibility in himself' and 'in order that an individual may thus be educated absolutely and infinitely by the possibility, he must be honest towards possibility and have faith'. The cultural glue, and the foundational academic atmosphere, is the ability to seize the moment and possibility of change in one's own institution – however miniscule it may seem in the larger political picture. Being a leading Rector of a university, or Chair of a large European Association of universities, does not automatically lead to increased academic freedom. If the amount of power and potential rests on an understanding of freedom driven by fear, and not anxiety, the results might be less than a single teacher or student's decision to break with a single element of mechanistic continuity. We should all strive for greater academic anxiety – and not fear – in order to make foundational decisions and choices for alternative academic cultures.

A Margin of Unpredictability

The singular voice of the individual university *does* matter, and the vision and courage to choose an alternative institutional route *is* possible. Education is not only for students (and teachers) but for universities themselves. The role and purpose of institutional education and transformation have often been neglected. The university itself is on the move, and the university itself needs to constantly learn, grow and change. Not only individuals but also academic communities and entire institutions need to make choices and find their own path of what it means, to that particular institution, to be and become a university.

Every form of education implies change and, as Biesta (2006: 25) notes, with education 'there is always a *risk*'. Also, for institutions, there is not only a risk learning what they hope to learn but there is also 'the risk that [they] will learn things [they] couldn't have imagined that [they] would learn or that [they] couldn't have imagined that [they] would have wanted to learn'. (2006) Education only begins 'when the learner is willing to take a risk' (2006). However, as Biesta also notes, taking the risk out of our universities is exactly what leaders, teachers and students are asked to do. It is what 'policy makers, politicians, the popular press, "the public", and organisations such as the Organisation for Economic Co-operation and Development (OECD) and the World Bank increasingly seem to be expecting if not demanding from education' – they all 'want education to be strong, secure, and predictable, and want it to be risk-free at all levels' (Biesta, 2013: 1). Developing universities into risk-free institutions increases the possibility of control, streamlining, planning and educational forecasting, whereby it may also increase the amount of fear to be converted into a tool of governance. However, removing the risk also removes anxiety and, by implication, removes any real freedom and possibility.

Interestingly, today, we see universities forming ever-larger entities of organizations – even cross-country universities stretching across continents are being formed, and digital universities already exist, reaching, literally, across the globe. However, streamlining and increasing the institutional size changes very little, as usual cultural patterns of earlier institutional models may so easily be repeated just on a larger scale. Further, and paradoxically so, the stronger an institution becomes, in the sense of complying with commonplace benchmarking and ranking protocols and unification systems, the less free it becomes. Paraphrasing Biesta (2013: 24), creating sustainable academic cultures does not require strong and self-sufficient but 'weak' and 'existential' institutions searching for their own voice for a future higher education. Just as research develops from original and singular studies, and just as learning is most powerful through forms of independence and originality (which may be searching and uncertain), universities should aim for institutional originality and independence – and not try to clone the survival strategies of their competitors a few steps further up the ranking scale.

To borrow inspiration from Sartre (2001), it is important to stress that there is no privileged institutional position, no safe haven for universities and no final academic endgame. Because institutions are free (the freedom there is left – and it is there!), creating a sustainable academic culture 'is an *open project* and not a closed project' (Sartre, 2001: 507). Paraphrasing Sartre (Sartre, 2001: 550) a bit further, I would argue that there is 'no absolute point of view which one can adopt so as to compare different situations; each [university] realizes only one situation – *[its] own*'. Each and every university is 'condemned to be free' (Sartre: 553) and to carry the weight of its own academic culture on its shoulders being entirely 'responsible for the world and for [itself] as a way of being' (Sartre, 2001). To build a university for the future, we do not need bland and generic corporate buildings with rows of standard classrooms, coffee areas, bookless libraries and empty corridors. What we need are universities students, teachers and leaders who are proud to belong to and enjoy being in their university.

I do take the point from Grant (2019), and am not pining for a romantic idea of a lost Edenic academic past but, on the contrary, call for academic agency to form risky, uncertain and original universities. With inspiration from Sartre (2001: 507), I argue that each university needs a 'margin of unpredictability due to the independence of things precisely because this independence is that in terms of which a freedom is constituted'. We do not need any further long-term academic planning or forecasting into a predictable and uniform future but, as Sartre mentions (2001) – with some tiny paraphrasing of my own – just like 'the Romans reserved in their temple a place for unknown gods, so in [any university] a certain margin of indetermination [needs to be] created "for the unpredictable'". Here, I do not mean unpredictable as in more precarity, another round of organizational restructuring, or yet further study programme reforms and accelerated curricula – but, on the contrary, the vision and courage to design for originality in the sense of institutional creativity, passion, engagement and hope.

Conclusion: A Culture of One's Own

What really matters to the singular university is not to top the league tables or ranking games but to be able to create an authentic and original culture of one's own, where students, teachers and leaders know why *this* university exists, and why *this* academic culture is being sustained (and is itself sustainable). Building and sustaining a culture of one's own means to learn and grow as an institution and academic community. Perhaps not (always) to excel but (more often) to learn from one's mistakes, bad decisions, curricular detours and educational blind alleys. Here, we see the contours of a university that sometimes stumbles and falls – that gets bruised and take hits. An imperfect university that is capable of embracing and including the bruises, mistakes and imperfections of its members too. A solidary university that rather performs worse in the rankings than letting down its students and teachers. Who wants such a university within their ranks? A university that does not cast its magic dust or glory of success but rather chooses to enter the arena soiled and saturated with culture (as Barnett words it). When another generation of golden set alliances of universities are created, who would want to invite in a university of its own – and not a streamlined and buff institution – perhaps even an anxious and weak university? Who would really like to engage with a free university?

15

An Ecological Culture for a Non-Comprehending World

Ronald Barnett

Introduction

Knowing that one can view one's co-authors' offerings only after having written one's own instils the apprehension that one's own efforts turn out to be non-aligned with the others and missing the point of the conversation. Thankfully, I think that that is not the case, and there are surely large areas of complementarity between our three sets of offerings.

Rikke Nørgård not only alerts us to the centrality of practices in culture but also draws our attention to their ineradicable openness. As we are reminded, the cultural practices of universities are a matter of perpetual design, as members of universities bring their creativity to bear in situ with pedagogies, curricula, research topics, clusterings of knowledge and university positioning. Often, this design work goes on tacitly, in the micro-spaces of the university: every happening is a set of imaginative offerings. And, as Nørgård observes, such design work turns the spaces of a university into places, where its members feel at home and forge their identities.

Søren Bengtsen puts all of this into a metaphysical space. Reminding us that this Earth is comprised mainly of non-human entities, both organic and inorganic, we are invited to place our understanding of culture in a 'meta-human reality', where every entity in the world is taken seriously and so take the university 'beyond human culture'.

In this rejoinder chapter, I shall try to draw on some of the central ideas in my friends' contributions and advance a little further my own position.

Placing the University

Rikke Nørgård develops a strong sense of a university as a place, and its culture wrapped up in it as a place. We recall a university with its configuration of buildings and spaces, of open areas, corridors, its presences in a city or on the edge of one, the movements of its members, perhaps the trees in its grounds and the cafes or other seating areas. But, as a place, it goes deeper. Any university contains its own social settings and social relationships, its pattern of interactions, its symbolic events and its epistemic and professional tribes (with even their own modes of dress across its departments). Among all the other 25,000 universities in the world, there is no other university that resembles a university that we may have in mind. For many, one's 'alma mater' – one's university – is a source of lifelong identity, to which student alumni associations testify. It is its own place.

But we might pose the issue as to how place and culture are connected. A seat in a library or a favoured laboratory may be recalled many years later. However, place is not culture as such but embodies culture in its material, affective, social and epistemic aspects. Certainly, the university as a place can help to engender culture. Its buildings, its social relationships, its events, its own pattern of disciplines, the ages, genders and ethnicities of its students all inflect its cultural profile. That favoured seat in the library is surrounded by a particular configuration of learning spaces and books – and perhaps the books are barely to be seen as a culture of the student-as-learner has taken hold. There is a symbiosis between the university as place and as culture: place and culture are two moments of the university and not one.

What kind of place might a university be? That much depends on the culture to be engendered. Is it to prompt serendipitous interactions on campus (Temple, 2021)? Is it to favour efficiency and productivity? Is it to have a concern for the totality of this Earth, seeing humanity as but a small part of it and to have a concern for all the peoples on this planet? Is it to open itself to its locality and to be a new kind of civic university? Is it to attract international students and to effect real understandings among them? A university as a *cultural place* takes on its hues from these positionings.

Place, then, is more than the visible, more even than the immediately felt; and its relationships with culture are subtle. *However, it is culture that brings place alive, not the other way around.* The culture of a university helps to instantiate its place as *its* place. We fall too easily into the trap of inscribing place with life because we recall the life in it; but it is culture that brings vitality to a place. A university's tone, its generosity or its tendency to judge, its aspiration for itself and for the world, its capacity for give and take: all these and more are its life, its culture, its shared meanings. *Place, in itself, is static; culture is alive; it is life.*

The matter of culture and place comes down to this: What is the character of the life in this place, in *this* university? To be (rightly) reminded – by Nørgård – that the university is in danger of becoming placeless is to say that it is in prospect of losing its vitality, which is to say that it is in danger of being culture*less*. *A place of many cultures, the university may still be cultureless.* How can this conundrum be squared? After all, it is implied that the university is in prospect of possessing no *meta-culture* that transcends its many cultures.

Can the university shape its own meta-culture? To some extent, that option is normally open to a university, but not entirely. The meta-culture of the university has to turn on the matter of thought. Fashionable talk in philosophy – following alternatively Sellars, Habermas, McDowell and (in the philosophy of education) Bakhurst – of the university as a space of reason is helpful but it falls at hurdles. 'Reason' is too static; we should rather speak of reason*ing*, so as to capture a sense of lively processes. *There*, at least, is a hint of shared values and virtues in the processes that mark out a university. But there is more before us.

An Atmosphere of Thought

In fashioning a *cultural atmosphere* – to use Nørgård's term – for the university, we can do worse than draw on the work of Theodor Adorno. Adorno was one of the leaders – with Max Horkheimer – of the Frankfurt School of Critical Theory, a central aim of which was to expose gaps between concepts and the way the world is (Adorno, 2014: 5). This gap could be either negative or positive (Adorno, 2008: 7.). Concepts can be ideologically loaded, perhaps even through their manipulation by the mass media (including 'the culture industry' (Adorno, 2019: 72)) and so fall short of their possibilities in the world; but concepts, through this gap, can hold emancipatory promise of a better world.

Thought was therefore critical for Adorno. Only through thought can what is taken for thinking be properly connected with the world. This is no casual thought, but thought intent on exposing and wrestling with the gaps between ideas and the world. The implied weakness of thought is rarely recognized in the university. Heidegger *did* recognize this peculiar phenomenon, that the very institution that should embody thought was becoming devoid of thought, so much so that 'In universities, especially, the danger is still very great that we misunderstand what we hear of thinking' (Heidegger, 2004: 13). The university slides into a thoughtlessness, born of busyness and freneticism that arises out of an ever-tighter audit, governmentality, disciplinary defensiveness, instrumentality and neoliberal competition, all of which lead to a risk averseness and thence to a diminution of thought.

And so – and again to use Nørgård's term – what is required is an *atmosphere* of and *for* thought or, in other words, a culture of thought. It is a culture in which thought matters.

Adorno's (2003) text on *The Jargon of Inauthenticity* is helpful here. The culture of the contemporary university contains tendencies of inauthenticity. The (just-mentioned) risk averseness brings a self-confinement within contemporary conventions, a fastening onto intellectual fads, and to taking on frameworks such that they entrap their users. In this milieu of institutional, state and even global judgement, to scrutinize each idea, each phrasing, and each idiom and to formulate insights that run across the grain is to incur risk even of excommunication (from discipline or institution or in being a citizen of a state). Entering into a culture of (genuine) thought will be fraught with difficulty.

Culture and the university, therefore, can be sensibly joined only at the *risk of risk*. It is not only that any particular position, any particular run-in with the state or any particular affront to a group excited within a culture war that has – from time to time – to be risked. Much more, the university has to be willing to commit to a *state* of risk. This is partly the problem today: that the university shrinks from risk as such. It is *risk averse*. And so it conducts its risk analyses, its administrators drawing up charts of risk assessment, where attempts are made to compute *and* mitigate the risk attaching to any initiative that might be contemplated. But however laudable the procedure may be for any one initiative, the whole operation has to be seen as forlorn. In a world of open entangled ecosystems, risk can neither be entirely mitigated *nor even computed*. Risk analysis is an attempt to grapple with open systems using the techniques applicable to closed systems.

To believe that risk can be calculated with any degree of validity is to repudiate what it is to be a university. It is ultimately to close thought, to hesitate before risk, such that this risk averseness reaches deeply into a university and comes to characterize its culture. The university goes warily through the world, hedging its bets, playing matters safely and avoiding confrontation. And then, ultimately, it closes in on itself, and its imaginative powers weaken. *That which is liable to provoke, in the end, is not even thought*. And so we read that, for all the exponential outpouring of research papers, the level of creativity of universities in toto is falling (Murphy, 2018). This decline of the culture of thought amounts to a dwindling of the university. It becomes a husk of itself.

Conditions of Thought

So, yes, with Nørgård, we must insist on a university of and for culture. However, even though the university abounds with cultures (epistemic, ethnic, social class and professional) we should be prepared – when we speak of culture and the university – to pose the awkward question: 'Which culture?' For many, the worry will be that the question betrays a universalist mode of thinking, a one-size-fits-all stance, and even – whisper it softly – a impositional stance characteristic of the Global North. In studying universities globally, Marginson has recently referred to the 'cultural hegemony' exerted by 'Euro-American globalisation' (Marginson, 2021). In philosophy, a parallel critique has been levelled at Zizek, he being accused of the crime of 'Eurocentricism' (Wood, 2015): the critiquer, par excellence, is critiqued. In repeatedly holding out for universality and even insisting that it is 'unavoidable' (2000: 101), Zizek's position is depicted as self-serving (of European thinking) and even colonial.

Is a university then to be just a mélange of specific cultures, with no cultural tissue, however flimsy, holding them all together? But then we would not be in the company of a university, for that position would certainly lead to discursive hegemony. Those who have the loudest voices, or the largest wallets or – in some parts of the world – compliant legal and prison services will win.

A response has begun to form over these past few paragraphs. Transcending all the cultures of a university is a culture of thought. Some, we may note, speak of the university as characterized by a 'cognitive culture' (Delanty, 2018) but that is a lesser concept, being overly descriptive. To conjure the idea of the university as founded on a culture of thought injects power into proceedings, for it contains *suggestive* connotations.

Derrida (2001) looked to a university without condition. That was always a fantasy. Ever since its mediaeval inception, a university has been an institution of conditions, albeit conditions that is largely determined by and for itself. The university was licenced by the pope and the king to form and impose conditions: it was especially an institution that provided a licence to teach. And today, the suppliers to the university expect some return for their provisions: the university has to meet its bills. But it is also a logical fantasy because there are *bound* to be conceptual conditions attaching to a university. The idea of the university is not yet empty. So the question is not whether conditions attach to the thought of a university but whether its culture is such that *particular* kinds of condition so attach.

The Condition of Compassion

Nørgård speaks of academic culture as suffering and compassion, and these are important ideas. Newman – the author of the mid-nineteenth century essays known as '*The Idea of the University*' (1976) – once talked in his work of the 'bodily pain' that writing caused him. Even if not universal, this is surely understandable. As a student, Newman drove himself near to ill-health in reading the most difficult texts for up to ten hours a day (Faber, 1954). Scholarship was painful for him. For normal mortals, how could it not be? Reading, conducting sensitive and complicated inquiries, thinking, writing, working out one's thoughts and exposing them to a reader: whatever the suffering of the world (Schopenhauer, 2004), there is – for most – bound to be suffering in this very strange mode of life; having the integrity to give oneself utterly to the tasks in hand and abiding by its standards, to mean what one says and to say what one means (two quite different things, one being about sincerity and the other about integrity) and subjecting one's efforts to critical gaze. This is arduous, and no wonder that one gets up from the desk for yet another coffee.

So suffering, yes; but compassion? Compassion for the world, of course; but compassion, too, for one's craft, one's words. One has a 'concern' for the 'ready-to-hand' (Heidegger, 2000). It is a compassion, really. An inward care for a word, a concept, and its contiguous neighbours in a sentence, in a paragraph. For, in a field and an approach that is open, the *careful* combination of words deployed will be unique. We learnt this from Chomsky over fifty years ago (1968), but then he was pointing to the uniqueness of the strings of words that even young children utter. In sight here, however, is a uniqueness that is a concomitant of the form of life and the culture in question. One cares for one's words because one cares for the reader and for the world. If the rhinos, the glaciers, the coral reefs and the rain forests are to be treated with compassion, then so too must the elements of the life that attempts to bring these matters to public attention. It is a care that listens acutely to the world in order more fully to understand the world.

This culture of thought, then, is imbued with both suffering and compassion, and in any discipline. In my suffering, in my feeble efforts to comprehend the world and knowing that any claim on my part is liable to be countermanded by others, I have compassion for *your* comparable efforts. That academics now work mostly in collaboration and even in very large teams does not dent this point. Deep down, as Søren Bengtsen reminds us, academic culture has within it a natural generosity. Unfortunately, this natural generosity has been overlain by interests in competition, acquisitiveness, impact and reward. A culture of forgiveness has been overshadowed by a culture of judgement.

Put into groups, students may weigh the extent to which it is in their interests to engage with 'international' students from distant parts of the world. (Ironically, it is even in their instrumental interests to engage with international students.) A research team may race against another to formulate a protein sequence and subsequently engage in a priority dispute as to which team secured the first publication of the results. Those who look to advance their market position as academic entrepreneurs – setting up income-generating companies – and those who remain within a scholarly culture may look upon each other with mutual disdain. Therefore, in its micro-practices, the naturally empathic culture of the university is remorselessly being overtaken by a strategic culture that positions others as strangers, *even within a single university*.

Note the paradoxical nature of this *deep culture*. It is a culture that – at its best – attempts to undermine the beliefs within it. It is a counterculture, not in the sense of countering the culture(s) of the wider society, but rather of countering the claims made *within* itself. This is an extraordinary culture, its members naturally contending against each other. Such a culture can only hang together within a common trust (Gibbs, 2004) and forgiveness, but that forgiveness is showing signs of withering. In their viva voce examinations, research students come up against examiners who like to make a show of themselves, not least in front of the other examiner. In receiving feedback on a paper, a hapless academic will not untypically be faced with a referee's review that runs to some pages in length, to do justice to which would take the production of two books. An overly judgemental and even condemnatory culture is in danger of emerging.

Dialectics of Culture

Søren Bengtsen helpfully supplies the idea of cultural dialectics, and this is a concept susceptible to multiple depictions. One canard should be despatched: to speak of cultural dialectics cannot be a matter of juxtaposing an (inner) culture of the university against a university in relation to culture (externally) in the wider world: in the twenty-first century, these must dovetail each other. And, in fact, we have multiple dialectics. In this culture of dissent and assent, of critique and replication, of empathy and even hostility, of reason and emotion and (now) of nation and the world, ideas, theories, persons, positions, centres and identities contend with each other. There is not just a cerebral situation but is *embodied* (Loftus and Kinsella, 2021): persons give of themselves. It is a dialectic between embodied thoughts, as one felt position listens and responds to another, within collective structures of meaning and identity.

No less than *five levels* may be discerned within these cultural dialectics of the university: (i) thought, (ii) imagination, (iii) persons, (iv) institutions and (v) entities of the world. *Each level is itself a manifold*, a complex. We cannot distil the elements of the five complexes here but we may note that *thought* may be at once particular, universal, empirical, theoretical, value-laden, iconic and pragmatic; *imagination* may be within a form of thought or may seek to transcend it and even seek to incorporate concerns for the whole Earth; *persons* may collaborate with others or strike out on their own and may infuse their thoughts with their hoped-for futures; *institutions* potentially embrace *all* social institutions; and *entities of the world* are those of nature *and* technology. Against this multilayered sense of the thoughtful culture of the university, we are fully entitled to speak of dialectics for we have here an interplay – often antagonistic and shot through with power – between the world and thought, between ontology and the imagination and between what is actual and what might be possible and might unfold. *Each of the three elements – world, thought, imagination – provokes and may* change *the other two*.

This is a very curious culture, always on the edge of undoing itself, and it tends towards inner fissiparousness: its self-imposed commitment to critique coupled with the competitive ethos now laid upon it promotes its fragmentation and, more seriously still, a separation of academic labour from the Earth. Begun in the Enlightenment, the separation of thought from Nature now only intensifies: disciplines split into subdisciplines and so on; and this work becomes increasingly divorced from the planet as such. Epistemology and ontology have been growing further and further apart.

This culture has given the university enormous powers, and, in the process, it has become, as Bengtsen observes, a culture 'beyond culture'; and here lies its weakness. Not only (i) does it separate itself from itself – this book began from the reflection that the matter of culture has become invisible in the university's self-understanding – *and* (ii) it separates its internal cultures from each other into non-comprehending subcultures, but (iii) it *also* separates itself from the world and, thence, from Nature. It is a culture of division, internally *and* with the world: it has become a culture unable to comprehend itself and has – until recently – become oblivious to its separation from Nature. It has failed to care about its own culture, and has emptied itself of culture. (To that extent, Readings (1997) was right.) In turn, there has emerged a largely uncomprehending world, unable to discern much value in universities.

Sighting a Meta-culture

Bengtsen poses the challenge of 'rethinking' a cultural identity for the university, even of its 'rebuilding'. As noted, we need to go 'beyond culture' (but let's *not* say 'post-culture'). If the world is totally interconnected – and we have surely learnt that through the pandemic even if not over the past fifty years in the ecological crises – then the culture of the university has to transcend humanity and recognize the claims of the Earth. This would be a new culture, a *transhuman* culture. Culture now becomes an *ambiguous* concept: it has to live in the university, and be expressed by its members and live within their practices, but it has to include all the entities of the Earth. What is in sight here – in Bengtsen's terms – is a 'trans-species cultural ethos'.

This means that the university has to 'cross a cultural threshold', to leave itself behind and transcend *and* transform itself. It would morph into a new culture. Bengtsen talks of the university replacing its 'cultural skin': it is a beguiling metaphor but such a change could be merely skin-deep when what is required is a total change in the self-understanding, self-orientation and dominant value set of the university, in its sheer being.

Is this Utopian? By no means. Many universities across the world are rethinking their positioning and are heeding calls to take on concerns for the 'other'. This is an Other that includes indigenous peoples and the residues of colonialism and coloniality; it includes local communities and those who have not enjoyed higher education; it includes the natural environment and its nonhuman entities; it includes rethinking what it is to be a civic university with a concern for the public interest; and it should surely include the humanities and other marginalized disciplines. But this journey holds traps for the unwary.

The first trap – crudely put – is that of instrumentalism. Instrumentalism has become the dominant culture of the world and its epistemologies and, therefore, of the university. It has crept across the university over the last 100 years or so and matters of utility, technology, and, more recently, value for money, impact, innovation and employability have come to form a set of taken-for-granted frames. This *culture of utility* now sits in the university, daring sentimental educationalists to resist it. These newer forms of instrumentalism are testimony to its self-reproducing powers over time, and it has wreaked havoc on the world, with its extractional character.

So to call for a culture of otherness is not the otherness of this instrumentalism, in taking *from* the world. It is an otherness of concern *for* the world. It senses that the world possesses inherent worth and its entities are to be safeguarded. And here we glimpse the most fundamental of the questions in front of us: *Can a culture of instrumentalism and a culture of concern for the world live together in the same university? There* would lie a true ecology *of* culture.

Another trap is to see a culture of otherness as simply one culture alongside the panoply of cultures in the university. A culture of otherness is *central* to the university. To be concerned with truth, serious inquiry, the collective formation of knowledge and understandings, and the education of students is to embrace otherness in taking on concerns for others and for standards of collective inquiry that stand outside of oneself. It is to displace oneself.

However, the university has been drawn into the centre of society, and this plays out in opposed ways. On the one hand, the university presents *decreasing* opportunities for authentic and genuinely creative thought, as the world envelopes with its entreaties. This foggy atmosphere presents a *cultural miasma*. On the other hand, the university becomes more sensitive to those outside the academic firmament and to Nature. This is a *widening* to a *cultural clearing* of infinite proportions. The whole Earth – human and non-human, organic and inorganic – is being recognized as having legitimate claims upon the university.

For the university, this otherness – this 'alterity' – goes deep down but it also widens. It must retain its sense of interpersonal care, the university having a care for each individual within itself, each student and each member of staff, but this alterity has to include the totality of the Earth (Levinas, 2331969), and not just as a matter of interiority (I can feel it, sense it within myself) but as a matter of explicit institutional policy and practice.

Paradoxically then, this deep care, this alterity, is also a form of transcendence (Levinas, 1999): it is to 'ascend' (to use a term from Newman (1976), another Catholic theologian-philosopher) into a world of total otherness. The individual is transcended and so is the relationship of concern. It is held against a value background of care, recognition, particularity and a sense of possibilities, of this person and of this entity as an entity of value in and on Earth. For Levinas (1999: 132–3), 'the affirmation and championing of specific cultures in all corners of the globe' has been especially evident in the European university and owes much to its 'colonial' and 'imperial' past. But the crisis now before us transcends even this large setting and is a crisis of this Earth, this planet. And by the Earth, we now have to include its oceans: to put it formally, our sense of the world has to understand it as in part a set of 'wet ontologies' (Greve and Zappe, 2020).

We can, then, locate a meta-culture for the university in a culture of the Earth, but pivoting on an acute sense of its total interconnectedness. It would be *an ecological culture*.

Living – and Breathing – an Ecological Culture

In the university today, many are seized with an ecological fervour, in its broadest sense. They have a spirit of otherness, in having a concern for the world in its entirety. This spirit finds its way into pedagogical situations, interchanges in the seminars, research topics, the writing of the academic papers, and the university's interactions with its wider environment (both locally and in distant parts) and in the ways that its members – students and staff – engage with each other. Student stalls may be set up in open spaces on campus, drawing attention to the plight of this particular people (perhaps beset by a tsunami) or that aspect of Nature or part of society. Academics work in challenging situations in developing their understandings of this Earth. Some things matter.

If these happenings are to become a culture, they cannot be left to fend for themselves; and here we return to Nørgård's idea of design. The big battalions, focused on capital accumulation, surveillance, control, production (narrowly understood), evident impact, national advancement and sheer neglect of those aspects of the world that do not promise an evident return on effort, remain dominant in the academy. So the insertion of an ecological culture will be running against the grain in many interstices of the university. It follows that there are considerable responsibilities of *cultural design* in front of a university's senior leadership team (and 'leadership' has to be distinguished from 'management' (Barnett, 2022)). Prompting a university to become ecological can be evident in the efforts of a university's members (and its students often assume a leadership role here) but this shift in favour of an ecological culture calls for the active involvement of the senior leadership team.

The bringing of colleagues together across the disciplines (so rendering their disciplinary boundaries 'porous' (Stuart and Shutt, 2019)), the internal allocation of resources, the sponsoring of individual academics, the design of curricula, working with students' unions, reaching out to wider constituencies, engaging with political and civic authorities, working with corporations and drawing up of 'memoranda of understanding', or forming liminal co-operatives on the fringe of a university: these are just indicative of places in which the seeds of an ecological culture can be planted. Admittedly, in each case, the ecological territory will be particular *and* complex.

I suggested earlier that there are *eight major ecosystems* in which the university moves; and an ecological culture would, therefore, span all eight ecosystems. It might be exhibited in a university forming relationships with local schools (ecosystems of persons *and* institutions). It might be a matter of working through the university's impact on the natural environment (Nature as an ecosystem). It might be a matter of its departments effecting some transdisciplinarity in their curricula (knowledge as an ecosystem). It might be a matter of encouraging its economics department stringently to overhaul its curricula and its research activities so as to pay attention to new ideas of economics, so as to orient the discipline towards public service (the economy itself as an ecosystem). It might enlist its academic development unit in promoting new learning patterns in which students are given space to frame their own learning (learning as an ecosystem). It might use its estate to mount exhibitions of art, installations and sculpture by local artists and architects and others (the ecosystem of culture). And it might combine with other universities to advance global perceptions of what it is to be a university in the twenty-first century, exemplified in the (2020) *Magna Charta Universitatum* (the political ecosystem).

Conclusions

An ecological culture may dimly be seen to be emerging in universities. It is not just one culture among many within the university but is a meta-culture *and* a universal culture. Very many – *but not all* – the cultures of the university can shelter under its umbrella. All those cultures – both long-standing and more recent – that evince a concern for the world, for human beings and for other inhabitants of this Earth, are at home here. Moreover, this culture stretches over disciplines *and* universities across the world. It is evident in the bio-engineers who design new kinds of prostheses to assist the disabled, in reaching out to indigenous communities to effect conversations on their terms, in bringing in schoolchildren to elicit their wonder at the knowledge vistas within the university and in the day-to-day interstices of relationships of concern among the inhabitants of universities.

Even though it can form a meta-culture, *this* ecological culture stands in opposition to the cultures of instrumentalism, extraction, exclusion, control, disparagement, competition, hierarchy, manipulation and surveillance, all of which remain as strong forces within research, disciplines and pedagogies, and leadership and management regimes. Those still-present dominant cultures will not and cannot comprehend this new ecological culture for the latter works in a region of its own. The ecological culture, therefore, is an oppositional culture but is a culture that works in the interests of the whole Earth. It is a culture of and for the Earth. It is a culture for the twenty-first-century university.

Endnote

Uniting the University and Even the Earth: The Twin Cultures

Ronald Barnett

A starting point for this book was, in effect, the following question: Is the matter of culture and the university primarily a matter of culture *within* the university *or* is it primarily a matter of the connections between the university and culture in the *wider society*? Across the offerings here, a response to this double question can surely be gleaned: 'yes' and 'yes'. To be seriously concerned with culture and the university is to be concerned with the university as possessing a characteristic culture – or cultures – of its own, *and* it is to be concerned with the ways in which the university may help to promote culture in the wider society. Moreover, in the twenty-first century, there are the makings of links such that these two matters of culture – within the university *and* in its relationships with the world – are entangled with each other. These are twin cultures.

The entanglement of these two facets of culture and the university lies – so the suggestion emerges here – in the university as an institution that listens to the world and converses with the world. Largely, these acts amount to the same thing: one cannot properly converse with another unless one listens to that other. We have learnt that from Levinas, among others.

In itself, the university has the task of listening, of possessing a culture such that its members – across the disciplines, across the university (students, academics, administrators) – listen to *each other*. They cannot sensibly speak to each other unless they listen acutely to each other. The local student and the international student, the administrator and the academic, the STEM and the humanities academics, and those of different genders, political parties, social classes and ethnicities: each has to listen to and closely attend to others. But this culture of acute attending extends – in the university's interconnections with the whole world – to the polity in its broadest sense (as Latour has more recently been staking out), to include all the entities of the world, whether human or non-human, organic and non-organic. It is a culture of concern for the Earth.

So, there are not two separate domains of culture for the university, within itself *and* in its relationships with culture in the world. The two domains do not so much dovetail as they merge imperceptibly into each other. That observation – with us throughout this book – raises rafts of issues for social philosophy, and for the imagining and design, of the university and higher education.

A broad *cultural strategy* for the university is called for, to which many voices should contribute. It would work on several levels, the educational experience offered to students in their programmes of study, the engagement of the university with the civic and public spheres and the university's concern for Nature in all of its facets. It would be a culture of total oneness, yet with spaces for new imaginings, critique and dissent. We have noted many signs of universities moving in these directions, at both the policy level across universities and their interconnections with the wider world *and* the more operational level *within* universities.

Our book is, in part, an effort to provide a vocabulary and a grammar for those moves already underway but it can only be a start in those directions. The matter of culture and the university is of profound and pressing importance for the world and yet understanding this relationship and untangling it – to the extent that that is possible – and improving it is a set of tasks of the utmost complexity. We earnestly hope that the matter will be taken up by others – across many disciplines and among institutional leaders and others in the policy field – as a matter of urgency.

Bibliography

Aaen, J. H. and R. T. Nørgård (2015), 'Participatory Academic Communities: A Transdisciplinary Perspective on Participation in Education beyond the Institution', *Conjunctions: Transdisciplinary Journal of Cultural Participation*, 2 (2): 67–98.
Adorno, T. W. ([1951] 1978), 'Cultural Criticism and Society', in P. Connerton (ed.), *Critical Sociology*, 258–76, London: Penguin.
Adorno, T. W. ([1964] 2003), *The Jargon of Authenticity*, London and New York: Routledge.
Adorno, T. W. ([1966] 2008), *Lectures on Negative Dialectics*, Cambridge and Malden: Polity.
Adorno, T. W. ([1966] 2014), *Negative Dialectics*, New York and London: Bloomsbury.
Adorno, T. W. ([1964] 2019), *Philosophical Elements of a Theory of Society*, Cambridge and Medford: Cambridge University.
Adorno, T. and M. Horkheimer ([1944] 1989), *Dialectic of Enlightenment*, London and New York: Verso.
Agnew, J. A. (1987), *Place and Politics: The Geographical Mediation of State and Society*, London: Allen and Unwin.
Alt, P.-A. (2021), 'Universities as Places of Culture', Article on European University Association web-site: https://eua.eu/resources/expert-voices/224:universities-as-places-of-culture.html
Amin, A. and N. Thrift (2002), *Cities: Reimagining the Urban*, Cambridge: Polity Press.
Anderson, B. (2009), 'Affective Atmospheres', *Emotion, Space and Society*, 2 (2): 77–81.
Anderson-Levitt, K. M. (2012), 'Complicating the Concept of Culture', *Comparative Education*, 48 (4): 441–54.
Appadurai, A. (1997), *Modernity at Large*, Minneapolis: University of Minnesota.
Aquinas, T. (2008), *Selected Philosophical Writings*, trans. T. McDermott, Oxford: Oxford University Press.
Aristotle (1976), *Ethics*, London: Penguin Books.
Arndt, S., S. Bengtsen, C. Mika and R. T. Nørgård (2020), 'Spaces of Life: Transgressions in Conceptualising the World Class University', in S. Rider, M. A. Peters, M. Hyvönen and T. Besley (eds), *World Class Universities. Evaluating Education: Normative Systems and Institutional Practices*, 251–67, Singapore: Springer.
Arndt, S. and C. Mika (2018), 'Dissident Thought: A Decolonising Framework for Revolt in the University', in S. Bengtsen and R. Barnett (eds), *The Thinking University. A Philosophical Examination of Thought and Higher Education*, 47–60, Cham: Springer.

Arvanitakis, J. and D. J. Hornsby (2018), Citizenship and the Thinking University: Toward the Citizen Scholar, in S. Bengtsen and R. Barnett (eds), *The Thinking University: A Philosophical Examination of Thought and Higher Education*, 87–102, Dordrecht: Springer.

Augé, M. (1995), *Non-places: Introduction to an Anthropology of Supermodernity*, London: Verso.

Auret, H. (2018), *Christian Norberg-Schulz's Interpretation of Heidegger's Philosophy. Care, Place and Architecture*, London: Routledge.

Ayer, A. J. (1962), *Language, Truth and Logic*, London: Gollancz.

Bakhurst, D. (2011), *The Formation of Reason*, Malden and Chichester: Blackwell.

Barad, K. (2007), *Meeting the Universe Halfway: Quantum Physics and the Entanglement of Matter and Meaning*, Durham and London: Duke University.

Barnacle, R. (2018), 'Research Education and Care: The Care-Full PhD', in S. Bengtsen and R. Barnett (eds), *The Thinking University: A Philosophical Examination of Thought and Higher Education*, 77–86, Cham: Springer.

Barnacle, R. and D. Cuthbert, eds. (2021), *The PhD at the End of the World: Provocations for the Doctorate and a Future Contested*, Cham: Springer.

Barnett, R. (1990), *The Idea of Higher Education*, Buckingham: Open University Press/Society for Research into Higher Education.

Barnett, R. (1997), *Higher Education: A Critical Business*, Buckingham: Open University Press/Society for Research into Higher Education.

Barnett, R. (2003), *Beyond All Reason: Living with Ideology in the University*, Buckingham and Philadelphia: Open University Press.

Barnett, R. (2008), *Realizing the University in an Age of Supercomplexity*, Buckingham: Open University Press.

Barnett, R. (2011), *Being a University*, London and New York: Routledge.

Barnett, R. (2013), *Imagining the University*, London and New York: Routledge.

Barnett, R. (2018) *The Ecological University: A Feasible Utopia*, London and New York: Routledge.

Barnett, R. (2019), 'Re-valuing the University: An Ecological Approach', in P. Gibbs, J. Jameson and A. Elwick (eds), *Values of the University in a Time of Uncertainty*, 47–59, Cham: Springer.

Barnett, R. (2021), 'The Philosophy of Higher Education: Forks, Branches and Openings', in S. Bengtsen, S. Robinson and W. Shumar (eds), *The University Becoming: Perspectives from Philosophy and Social Theory*, 15–28, Cham: Springer.

Barnett, R. (2022), *The Philosophy of Higher Education: A Critical Introduction*, London and New York: Routledge.

Barnett, R. and S. Bengtsen (2017), Universities and Epistemology: From a Dissolution of Knowledge to the Emergence of a new Thinking', *Education Sciences*, 7 (38): 1–12.

Barnett, R. and S. Bengtsen (2018), 'Introduction: Considering the Thinking University', in S. Bengtsen and R. Barnett (eds), *The Thinking University: A Philosophical Examination of Thought and Higher Education*, 1–12, Cham: Springer Publishing.

Barnett, R. and S. Bengtsen (2019), *Knowledge and the University: Reclaiming Life*, London and New York: Routledge.

Barnett, R. and N. Jackson, eds. (2020), *Ecologies for Learning and Practice: Emerging Ideas, Sightings, and Possibilities*, London and New York: Routledge.

Barnett, R and M. A. Peters, eds. (2018), *The Idea of the University, Vol 2: Contemporary Perspectives*, New York: Peter Lang.

Bayne, S. and M. Gallagher (2021), 'Near Future Teaching. Practice, Policy and Digital Education Futures', *Policy Futures in Education*, 19 (5): 607–25.

Becher, T. (1989), *Academic Tribes and Territories: Intellectual Enquiry and the Cultures of Disciplines*, Stony Stratford: Open University Press/ Society for Research into Higher Education.

Becher, T. and P. Trowler (2001), *Academic Tribes and Territories: Intellectual Enquiry and the Culture of Disciplines*, 2nd edn., Buckingham: Open University Press and Society for Research into Higher Education.

Bell, D. ([1960] 2000), *The End of Ideology: On the Exhaustion of Political Ideas in the Fifties*, Cambridge and London: Harvard University.

Bendik-Keymer, J. (2006), *The Ecological Life: Discovering Citizenship and a Sense of Humanity*, Lanham: Rowman and Littlefield.

Bengtsen, S. (2014), 'Into the Heart of Things: Defrosting Educational Theory', in P. Gibbs and R. Barnett (eds), *Thinking about Higher Education*, 175–91, Cham: Springer.

Bengtsen, S. (2018a), 'Moving beyond Education', in M. Peters (ed.), *Encyclopedia of Educational Philosophy and Theory*, 1–6, Singapore: Springer.

Bengtsen, S. (2018b), 'The Alien University', *Educational Philosophy and Theory*, 50 (14): 1554–5.

Bengtsen, S. (2020), 'Nietzsche (1844–1900), The Will to Power and the University', in R. Barnett and A. Fulford (eds), *Philosophers on the University: Reconsidering Higher Education*, 13–26, Cham: Springer.

Bengtsen, S. (2021), 'The PhD Revolution. World-entangled and Hopeful Futures', in R. Barnacle and D. Cuthbert (eds), *The PhD at the End of the World: Provocations for the Doctorate and a Future*, 181–196, Cham: Springer.

Bengtsen, S. and R. Barnett, eds. (2018), *The Thinking University: A Philosophical Examination of Thought and Higher Education*, Cham: Springer.

Bengtsen, S. and R. Barnett (2017), 'Realism and Education: A Philosophical Examination of the "Realness" of the University', in P. Higgs and Y. Waghid (eds), *A Reader in Philosophy of Education*, 121–37, Capetown: JUTA.

Bengtsen, S. and R. Barnett (2019), 'Higher Education and Alien Ecologies: Exploring the Dark Ontology of the University', in R. Gildersleeve and K. Kleinhesselink (eds), *Special Issue on the Anthropocene in the Study of Higher Education, Philosophy and Theory in Higher Education*, 1 (1): 17–40.

Bengtsen, S., S. Robinson and W. Shumar (2021), 'Introduction: The University Becoming', in S. Bengtsen, S. Robinson and W. Shumar (eds), *The University Becoming. Perspectives from Philosophy and Social Theory*, 1–11, Cham: Springer

Benhabib, S. (1994), 'Models of Public Space: Hannah Arendt, the Liberal Tradition, and Jurgen Habermas', in C. Calhoun (ed.), *Habermas and the Public Sphere*, 73–98, Cambridge, MA: MIT Press.

Bennett, J. (2010), *Vibrant Matter: A Political Ecology of Things*, Durham: Duke University.

Bennett, O. (2001), *Cultural Pessimism: Narratives of Decline in the Postmodern World*, Edinburgh: Edinburgh University.

Bennett, T. (2013), *Making Culture, Changing Society*, London and New York: Routledge.

Bergquist, W. H. and K. Pawlak (2008), *Engaging the Six Cultures of the Academy*, San Francisco: Jossey-Bass.

Berry, J. W. (1990), 'Psychology of Acculturation', in J. Berman (ed.), *Cross-Cultural Perspectives: Nebraska Symposium on Motivation*, 457–88, Lincoln: University of Nebraska Press.

Berubé, M. and C. Nelson, eds. (1995), *Higher Education Under Fire: Politics, Economics, and the Crisis of the Humanities*, London and New York: Routledge.

Bhambra, G. K., D. Gebrial and K. Nisancioglu, eds. (2018), *Decolonising the University*, London: Pluto.

Bhaskar, R. (2002), *From Science to Emancipation: Alienation and the Actuality of Enlightenment*, New Delhi: Sage.

Bhaskar, R. ([1975] 2008a), *A Realist Theory of Science*, London and New York: Verso.

Bhaskar, R. (2008b), *Dialectic: The Pulse of Freedom*, London and New York: Routledge.

Bhaskar, R. and M. Hartwig (2010a), *The Formation of Critical Realism: A Personal Perspective*, London and New York: Routledge.

Bhaskar, R. (2010b), 'Contexts of Interdisciplinarity: Interdisciplinarity and Climate Change', in R. Bhaskar, C. Frank, K. G. Hoyer, P. Naess and J. Parker (eds), *Interdisciplinarity and Climate Change: Transforming Knowledge and Practice for our Global Future*, 1–24, London and New York: Routledge.

Bhaskar, R. (2010c), *From East to West: Odyssey of a Soul*, London and New York: Routledge.

Bhaskar, R. ([1979] 2015), *The Possibility of Naturalism: A Philosophical Critique of the Contemporary Human Sciences*, London and New York: Routledge.

Biesta, G. J. J. (2006), *Beyond Learning. Democratic Education for a Human Future*, Boulder and London: Paradigm Publishers.

Biesta, G. J. J. (2013), *The Beautiful Risk of Education*, Boulder and London: Paradigm Publishers.

Bille, M. (2018). 'Review: Gernot Böhme, 2017, The Aesthetics of Atmospheres. Edited by Jean-Paul Thibaud. London, Routledge', *Ambiances*, Reports, 20 February. Available online: http://journals.openedition.org/ambiances/1065 (accessed 17 August 2021).

Bille, M., P. Bjerregaard and T. F. Sørensen (2015), 'Staging Atmospheres: Materiality, Culture and the Texture of the In-between', *Emotion, Space and Society*, 15: 31–8.

Boehnert, J. (2018), *Design, Ecology, Politics: Towards the Ecocene*, London and New York: Bloomsbury.
Bloom, A. (1987), *The Closing of the American Mind: How Higher Education Has Failed Democracy and Impoverished the Souls of Today's Students*, London: Penguin.
Böhme, G. (1993), 'Atmosphere as the Fundamental Concept of a New Aesthetics', *Thesis Eleven*, 36 (1): 113–26.
Böhme, G. (1995), *Atmosphäre: Essays zur neuen Ästhetik*, Frankfurt am Main: suhrkamp.
Böhme, G. (2013), 'The Art of the Stage as a Paradigm for an Aesthetics of Atmospheres', *Ambiances: International Journal of Sensory Environment, Architecture and Urban Space*, 10 February. Available online: http://journals.openedition.org/ambiances/315 (accessed 17 August 2021).
Böhme, G. (2017), *Atmospheric Architectures: The Aesthetics of Felt Spaces*, London: Bloomsbury.
Bourdieu, P. and J.-C. Passeron (1990), *Reproduction in Education, Society and Culture*, London: Sage.
Bourdieu, P. and P. Champagne (2002), 'Outcasts on the Inside', in P. Bourdieu et. al. (eds), *The Weight of the World: Social Suffering in Contemporary Society*, 421–6, Cambridge: Polity. [To copy-editor: this vol has 20 authors, & appears as '(Pierre) Bourdieu et. al.' on the cover and on the spine.]
Boutang, Y. M. (2011), *Cognitive Capitalism*, Cambridge and Malden: Polity.
Braidotti, R. (2019), *The Posthuman*, Cambridge and Malden: Polity.
Brockliss, L. W. B. (2016), *The University of Oxford: A History*, Oxford: Oxford University Press.
Buckingham, H. W. and S. Finger (1997), 'David Hartley's Psychobiological Associationism and the Legacy of Aristotle', *Journal of the History of the Neurosciences*, 6 (1): 21–37.
Butler, J. (2015), *Notes Towards a Performative Theory of Assembly*, Cambridge, MA: Harvard University.
Butler, J., E. Laclau and S. Zizek (2000), *Contingency, Hegemony, Universality: Contemporary Dialogues on the Left*, London and New York: Verso.
Calabrese Barton, A., S. Menezes, R. Mayas, O. Ambrogio and M. Ballard (2018), *What Are the Cultural Norms of STEM and Why Do They Matter?*, Centre for Advancement of Informal Science Education, November 2018. Available online: https://www.informalscience.org/sites/default/files/BP-4-Cultural-Norms.pdf (accessed 13 August 2021).
Canals, L., M. Burkle and R. T. Nørgård (2018), 'Universities of the Future: Several Perspectives the Future of Higher Education', *International Journal of Educational Technology in Higher Education*, 15 (46), unpaged.
Carlson, J. and K. Stewart (2014), 'The Legibilities of Mood Work', *New Formations*, 82: 114–33.

Carvalho, L., P. Goodyear and P. de Laat (2017), *Place-Based Spaces for Networked Learning*, London: Routledge.

Casey, E. S. (1997), *The Fate of Place: A Philosophical History*, Berkeley: University of California Press.

Cassirer, E. (2000), *The Logic of the Cultural Sciences: Five Studies*, New Haven and London: Yale.

Charbonneau, B. (2018), *The Green Light: A Self-Critique of the Ecological Movement*, London: Bloomsbury.

Chomsky, N. (1968), *Language and Mind*, New York: Harcourt, Brace and World.

Clark, W. (2006), *Academic Charisma and the Origins of the Research University*, Chicago and London: The University of Chicago Press.

Code, L. (2006), *Ecological Thinking: The Politics of Epistemic Location*, Oxford: Oxford University.

Cohen, E. (2021), *The University and its Boundaries: Thriving or Surviving in the 21st Century*, London and New York: Routledge.

Collin, F. (2019), 'A New Contract is Required between Science and Society', *Danish Yearbook of Philosophy*, 52 (1): 48–60.

Collini, S. (2012), *What are Universities For?*, London: Penguin Books.

Connell, R. (2019), *The Good University: What Universities actually Do and Why It's Time for Radical Change*, Clayton: Monash University Publishing.

Connolly, W. E. (2017), *Facing the Planetary: Entangled Humanism and the Politics of Swarming*, Durham and London: Duke University Press.

Cook, J., T. Ley, R. Maier, Y. Mor, P. Santos, E. Lex, S. M. Dennerlein, C. Trattner and D. Holley (2016), 'Using the Hybrid Social Learning Network to explore Concepts, Practices, Designs and Smart Services for Networked Professional Learning', in Y. Li, M. Chang, M. Kravcik, E. Popescu, R. Huang, and N.-S. Chen (eds), *State-of-the-Art and Future Directions of Smart Learning*, 123–9, Singapore: Springer.

Cresswell, T. (2004), *Place: A Short Introduction*, Oxford: Blackwell.

Critchley, S. (2001), *Continental Philosophy: A Very Short Introduction*, Oxford: Oxford University.

Dall'Alba, G. (2012), 'Re-imagining the University: Developing a Capacity to Care', in R. Barnett (ed.), *The Future University: Ideas and Possibilities*, 112–22, London and New York: Routledge.

Darwall-Smith, R. (2008), *A History of University College Oxford*, Oxford: Oxford University Press

Davies, M. and R. Barnett, eds. (2015), *The Palgrave Handbook of Critical Thinking in Higher Education*, New York: Palgrave Macmillan.

de Bono, E. (1992), *Serious Creativity: Using the Power of Lateral Thinking to Create New Ideas*, New York: Harper Business.

de Certeau, M. (1988), *The Practice of Everyday Life*, Berkeley and London: University of California.

Delanty, G. (2001), *Challenging Knowledge: The University in the Knowledge Society*, Buckingham: Open University Press and Society for Research into Higher Education.

Delanty, G. (2018), 'Citizenship and the University: The Consequences of Globalisation', in R. Barnett and M. A. Peters (eds), *The Idea of the University, Vol 2: Contemporary Perspectives*, 333–52, New York: Peter Lang.

Delanty, G. and O'Mahony, P. (2002), *Nationalism and Social Theory*, London and Thousand Oaks, CA: Sage.

Deleuze, G. and Guattari, F. (1988), *A Thousand Plateaus: Capitalism and Schizophrenia*, London: Continuum.

Derrida, J. (1997), 'Pont de Folie: Maintenant L'architecture', in N. Leach (ed.), *Rethinking Architecture: A Reader in Cultural Theory*, 305–17, London and New York: Routledge.

Derrida, J. (2001), 'The Future of the Profession or the University without Condition (Thanks to the "Humanities," What *Could Take Place* Tomorrow)', in T. Cohen (ed.), *Jacques Derrida and the Humanities: A Critical Reader*, 24–5, Cambridge: University of Cambridge.

Descartes, R. (1966), *Essential Works*, New York: Bantam.

Descartes, R. (1999), *Meditations on First Philosophy: With Selections from the Objections and Replies*, trans. J. Cottingham. Cambridge: Cambridge University Press.

Descola, P. (2013), *Beyond Nature and Culture*, Chicago: University of Chicago.

de Sousa Santos, B. (2014), *Epistemologies of the South: Justice against Epistemicide*, London and New York: Routledge.

de Sousa Santos, B. (2018), *The End of the Cognitive Empire: The Coming of Age of Epistemologies of the South*, Durham and London: Duke University.

de Sousa Santos, B. and M. P. Meneses, eds. (2020), *Knowledges Born in the Struggle: Constructing the Epistemologies of the Global South*, New York and London: Routledge.

Dufrenne, M. (1973), *The Phenomenology of Aesthetic Experience*, Evanston: Northwestern University Press.

Dunne, A. (1999), *Hertzian Tales: Electronic Products, Aesthetic Experience and Critical Design*, London: Royal College of Art Computer Related Design Research Studio.

Dunne, A. and F. Raby (2013), *Speculative everything: Design, Fiction and Social Dreaming*, Cambridge: MIT Press.

Eagleton, T. (2000), *The Idea of Culture*, Oxford and Malden: Blackwell.

Eagleton, T. (2009), *Reason, Faith and Revolution: Reflections on the God Debate*, New Haven and London: Yale University.

Eaton, C. and M. L. Stevens (2020), 'Universities as Peculiar Organizations', *Sociology Compass*, 14 (3): e12768.

Edensor, T. and S. Sumartojo (2015), 'Designing Atmospheres: Introduction to Special Issue', *Visual Communication*, 14 (3): 251–65.

Edgerton, S., G. Holm, T. Daspit and P. Farber, eds. (2005), *Imagining the Academy: Higher Education and Popular Culture*, Abingdon and New York: RoutledgeFalmer.

Eliot, T. S. ([1948] 1962), *Notes Towards the Definition of Culture*, London: Faber and Faber.

Eliot, T. S. ([1922] 2001), *The Waste Land and Other Writings*, New York: Random House.

Elliot, D. L., S. Bengtsen, K. Guccione and S. Kobayahsi (2020), *The Hidden Curriculum in Doctoral Education*, London and New York: Palgrave Macmillan.

Ellis, R. A. and P. Goodyear (2019), *The Education Ecology of Universities: Integrating Learning, Strategy and the Academy*, London and New York: Routledge.

Englund, T. and A. Bergh (2020), 'Higher Education as and for Public Good: Past, Present and Possible Futures', in T. D. Solbrekke and C. Sugrue (eds), *Leading Higher Education as and for Public Good: Rekindling Education as Praxis*, 37–52, London: Routledge.

EUA (European University Association) (2021), *Universities Without Walls: A Vision for 2030*, Brussels: EUA, February 2021. Available online: https://www.eua.eu/downloads/publications/universities%20without%20walls%20%20a%20vision%20for%202030.pdf (accessed 13 August 2021).

Faber, G. ([1933] 1954), *Oxford Apostles: A Character Study of the Oxford Movement*, London: Pelican.

Fehrman, C., H. Westling and G. Blomqvist (2005), *Lund and Learning: The History of Lund University 1666-2004*, Lund: Lund University.

Fellows, R. and A. M. M. Liu (2013), 'Use and Misuse of the Concept of Culture', *Construction Management and Economics*, 31 (5): 401–22.

Felski, R. (2011), 'Critique and the Hermeneutics of Suspicion', *M/C Journal*, 15 (1): unpaged.

Ferraro, G. (1998), *The Cultural Dimension of International Business*, New Jersey: Prentice Hall.

Feyerabend, P. (1978), *Against Method: Outlines of an Anarchistic Theory of Knowledge*, London: Verso.

Feyerabend, P. (1982), *Science in a Free Society*, London: Verso.

Fitzpatrick, K. (2019). *Generous Thinking: A Radical approach to saving the University*, Baltimore: Johns Hopkins University Press.

Fornas, J. (1995), *Cultural Theory and Late Modernity*, London and Thousand Oaks: Sage.

Foucault, M. (1986), 'Of Other Spaces', *Diacritics*, 16 (1): 22–7.

Frank, D. J. and J. W. Meyer (2020), 'Is the Coronavirus Undermining the Intellectual Foundations of the University?', *Times Higher Education*, August 2020. Available online: https://www.timeshighereducation.com/features/coronavirus-undermining-intellectual-foundations-university (accessed 13 August 2021).

Freire, P. (2013), *Education for Critical Consciousness*, London: Bloomsbury.

Fricker, M. (2010), *Epistemic Injustice: Power & the Ethics of Knowing*, Oxford: Oxford University Press.

Friedman, T. (2005), *The World is Flat: A Brief History of the Twenty-first Century*, New York: Farrar, Straus and Giroux.

Fritzsche H. (1934), 'Dr. Goebbels und sein Ministerium', in H. H. Mantau-Sadlia (ed.), *Deutsche Führer Deutsches Schicksal. Das Buch der Künder und Führer des dritten Reiches*, 330–42, Munich: Verlag Max Steinebach.

Frodeman, R., J. T. Klein and R. C. dos Santos Pacheco, eds. (2019), *The Oxford Handbook of Interdisciplinarity*, Oxford: Oxford University.

Fukuyama, F. (1992), *The End of History and the Last Man*, London: Penguin.

Fung, D. (2017), *A Connected Curriculum for Higher Education*, London: UCL Press.

Gellner, E. (1964), 'The Crisis in the Humanities and the Mainstream of Philosophy', in J. H. Plumb (ed.), *Crisis in the Humanities*, 45–81, London: Penguin.

Gellner, E. (1969), *Thought and Change*, London: Weidenfeld and Nicolson.

Gellner, E. (1991a), *Plough, Sword and Book: The Structure of Human History*, London: Paladin.

Gellner, E. (1991b), *'The Pure Enquirer'*, chapter eight in his *Spectacles and Predicaments: Essays in Social Theory*, 148–63, Cambridge: University of Cambridge.

Gellner, E. (1992), *Reason and Culture*, Oxford and Cambridge: Blackwell.

Giannakakis, V. (2020), 'Neoliberalism and Culture in Higher Education: On the Loss of the Humanistic Character of the University and the Possibility of its Reconstitution', *Studies in Philosophy and Education*, 39 (4): 365–82.

Gibbs, P. (2004), *Trusting in the University: The Contribution of Temporality and Trust to a Praxis of Higher Learning*, Dordrecht: Kluwer.

Gibbs, P., ed. (2017), *The Pedagogy of Compassion at the Heart of Higher Education*, Cham: Springer.

Gibbs, P. (2019), 'Why Academics Should Have a Duty of Truth Telling in an Epoch of Post-truth?', *Higher Education*, 78: 501–10.

Gibbs, P. (2020), 'Martin Heidegger (1889–1976): Higher Education as Thinking', in R. Barnett and A. Fulford (eds), *Philosophers on the University: Reconsidering Higher Education*, 123–36, Cham: Springer.

Gibbs, P. (2021), 'A Pedagogy of Emergent Self-Cultivation; Why Students Should Have a "Sameness" and Why They Should Not', *Philosophy and Theory in Higher Education*, 3 (2): 43–58.

Gibbs, P. and A. Beavis (2020), *Contemporary Thinking in Transdisciplinary Knowledge: What Those Who Know, Know*, Cham: Springer.

Gieryn, T. F. (2000), 'A Space for Place in Sociology', *Annual Review of Sociology*, 26 (1): 463–96.

Gildersleeve, R. E. (2016), 'The Neoliberal Academy of the Anthropocene and the Retaliation of the Lazy Academic', *Cultural Studies: Critical Methodologies*, 17 (3): 286–93.

Gildersleeve, R. E. and K. Kleinhesselink (2019), 'Introduction: The Anthropocene as Context and Concept for the Study of Higher Education', in R. E. Gildersleeve and

K. Kleinhesselink (eds), *Special Issue on the Anthropocene in the Study of Higher Education, Philosophy and Theory in Higher Education*, 1 (1): 1–15.

Giroux, H. (2002), 'Neoliberalism, Corporate Culture, and the Promise of Higher Education: The University as a Democratic Public Sphere', *Harvard Educational Review*, 72 (4): 425–64.

Giroux, H. (2011), *On Critical Pedagogy*, London and New York: Continuum.

Giroux, H. A. (2018), 'Defending Higher Education in the Age of Barbarism', in R. Barnett and M. A. Peters (eds), *The Idea of the University: Contemporary Perspectives*, vol. 2, 37–54, New York: Peter Lang.

Goldman, C. A. and W. F. Massy (2001), *The PhD Factory: Training and Employment of Science and Engineering PhDs in the United States*, Bolton: Anker Pub. Co.

Gordon, P. E., E. Hammer and A. Honneth, eds. (2020), *The Routledge Companion to the Frankfurt School*, New York and London: Routledge.

Gramsci, A ([1973] 2005), 'The Organisation of Education and Culture', in *Selections from the Prison Notebooks*, chapter two, 26–32, London: Lawrence and Wishart.

Grant, B. (2019), 'The Future is Now: A Thousand Tiny Universities', in S. Bengtsen and R. Barnett (eds), *Special Issue on Imagining the future University, Philosophy and Theory in Higher Education*, 1 (3): 9–28.

Grant, J. (2021), *The New Power University: The Social Purpose of Higher Education in the 21st Century*, Harlow: Pearson.

Greve, J. and F. Zappe, eds. (2020), *Spaces and Fictions of the Weird and the Fantastic: Ecologies, Geographies, Oddities*, Cham: Palgrave Macmillan.

Habermas, J. ([1968] 1978), *Knowledge and Human Interests*, London: Heinemann.

Habermas, J. (1989), *The Theory of Communicative Action, Vol Two: The Critique of Functionalist Reason*, Cambridge: Polity.

Habermas, J. (1991), *The Theory of Communicative Action, Vol. One: Reason and the Rationalization of Society*, Cambridge: Polity.

Habermas, J. (1995), *Postmetaphysical Thinking: Philosophical Essays*, Cambridge: Polity.

Habermas, J. (2001), *The Liberating Power of Symbols: Philosophical Essays*, Cambridge: Polity.

Hancher, M. (1981), 'Humpty Dumpty and Verbal Meaning', *The Journal of Aesthetics and Art Criticism*, 40: 49–58.

Handy, C. B. (1985), *Understanding Organisations*, London: Penguin.

Hansen, F. T. (2020), 'Learning to Innovate in Higher Education Through Deep Wonder', in S. Bengtsen and R. Barnett (eds), *Special Issue on Imagining the Future University, Philosophy and Theory in Higher Education*, 1 (3): 51–74.

Hardy, C. (1990), 'Putting Power into University Governance', in C. Smart (ed.), *Higher Education: Handbook of Theory and Research VI*, 393–426, New York: Agathon Press.

Haraway, D. J. (2016), *Staying with the Trouble: Making Kin in the Chthulucene*, Durham and London: Duke University Press.

Harman, G. (2002), *Tool-Being: Heidegger and the Metaphysics of Objects*, Chicago and La Salle: Open Court.

Harman, G. (2005), *Guerilla Metaphysics: Phenomenology and the Carpentry of Things*, Chicago and La Salle: Open Court.
Harman, G. (2018), *Object-Oriented Ontology: A New Theory of Everything*, London: Pelican.
Harsin, J. (2015), 'Regimes of Posttruth, Postpolitics, and Attention Economies', *Communication, Culture & Critique*, 8 (2): 327–33.
Hazelkorn, E. (2015), *Rankings and the Reshaping of Higher Education: The Battle for World-Class*, New York: Palgrave Macmillan.
Hegel, G. W. F. (1977), *Phenomenology of Spirit*, trans. A. V. Miller, Oxford: Oxford University Press.
Heidegger, M. ([1962] 2000), *Being and Time*, trans. J. Macquarrie and E. Robinson, Oxford and Cambridge: Blackwell.
Heidegger, M. ([1976] 2004), *What is Called Thinking?*, trans. J. Glenn Gray, New York and London: Harper & Row.
Heidegger, M. (2008), *Basic Writings*, London and New York: Routledge.
Herbrechter, S. (2013), *Posthumanism: A Critical Analysis*, London and New York: Bloomsbury.
Higton, M. (2013), *A Theology of Higher Education*, Oxford: Oxford University.
Hilli, C., R. T. Nørgård and J. H. Aaen (2019), 'Designing Hybrid Learning Spaces in Higher Education', *Dansk Universitetspædagogisk Tidsskrift*, 15 (27): 66–82.
Hodgson, N., J. Vliege and P. Zamojski, eds. (2020), *Post-critical Perspectives on Higher Education: Reclaiming the Educational in the University*, Cham: Springer.
Hofstede, G. (1994), *Cultures and Organizations: Software of the Mind*, London: HarperCollinsBusiness.
Hofstede, G. (2002). 'Dimensions do not Exist: A Reply to Brendan McSweeney', *Human Relations*, 55 (11): 1–7.
Honneth, A. (1993), 'Max Horkheimer and the Sociological Deficit of Critical Theory', in S. Benhabib, W. Bonß and J. McCole (eds), *On Max Horkheimer: New Perspectives*, 87–214, Cambridge, MA: MIT Press.
Honneth, A. ([1992] 2005), *The Struggle for Recognition: The Moral Grammar of Social Conflicts*, Cambridge: Polity.
Hourdequin, M. (2015), *Environmental Ethics: From Theory to Practice*, London and New York: Bloomsbury.
Humboldt, W. von (2018), 'On the Spirit and the Organisational Framework of Intellectual Institutions in Berlin', in M. A. Peters and R. Barnett (eds), *The Idea of the University: A Reader*, vol. 1, 45–55, New York: Peter Lang.
Huyssen, A. (2020), 'Topographies of Culture: Siegfried Kracauer', in P. E. Gordon, E. Hammer and A. Honneth (eds), *The Routledge Companion to the Frankfurt School*, 107–20, New York and London: Routledge.
Jain, A., J. Ardern and J. Pickard (2011), 'Design Futurescaping', in M. Kasprzak (ed.), *The Era of Objects (Blowup Reader #3)*. V2_ Institute for the Unstable Media, E-book. Available online: https://v2.nl/files/2011/events/blowup-readers/the-era-of-objects-pdf (accessed 13 August 2021).

Jaspers, K. ([1946] 1960), *The Idea of the University*, London: Peter Owen.
Jessop, S. (2017), 'Adorno: Cultural Education and Resistance', *Studies in Philosophy and Education*, 36: 409–23.
Julier, G. (2005), 'Urban Designscapes and the Production of Aesthetic Consent', *Urban Studies*, 42 (5/6): 869–87.
Kagan, J. (2009), *The Three Cultures: Natural Sciences, Social Sciences and the Humanities in the 21st Century*, New York and Cambridge: University of Cambridge.
Kahn, R. (2010), *Critical Pedagogy, Ecoliteracy & Planetary Crisis*, New York: Peter Lang.
Kandlbinder, P. (2007), 'The Challenge of Deliberation for Academic Development', *International Journal for Academic Development*, 12 (1): 55–9.
Kanov, J., E. H. Powley and N. D. Walshe (2017), 'Is it Ok to Care? How Compassion Falters and is Courageously Accomplished in the Midst of Uncertainty', *Human Relations*, 70 (6): 751–77.
Kant, I. ([1929] 1982), *Critique of Pure Reason*, trans. N. K. Smith. London and Basingstoke: Macmillan.
Kant, I. (2001a), *Critique of Practical Reason*, trans. M. Gregor. Cambridge: Cambridge University Press.
Kant, I. (2001b), *Groundwork of the Metaphysics of Morals*, trans. M. Gregor, Cambridge: Cambridge University Press.
Karlsohn, T. (2018), 'Bildung, Emotion and Thought', in S. Bengtsen and R. Barnett (eds), *The Thinking University: A Philosophical Examination of Thought and Higher Education*, 103–18, Cham: Springer Publishing.
Kierkegaard, S. (1980), *The Concept of Anxiety*, trans. R. Thomte in collaboration with A. B. Anderson, Princeton: Princeton University Press.
Kierkegaard, S. (2009), *Concluding Unscientific Postscript*, trans. A. Hannay, Cambridge: Cambridge University Press.
Kidd, I. J., J. Medina and G. Jr. Pohlhaus, eds. (2017), *The Routledge Handbook of Epistemic Injustice*, London and New York: Routledge.
Knorr, C. K. (1999), *Epistemic Cultures: How the Sciences Make Knowledge*, Cambridge, MA: Harvard University.
Kohls, C., R. T. Nørgård and S. Warburton (2017), 'Sharing is Caring', *Proceedings of the 22nd European Conference on Pattern Languages of Programs (EuroPLoP '17)*. Association for Computing Machinery, New York, Article 34: 1–6.
Köppe, C., C. Kohls, A. Y. Pedersen, R. T. Nørgård and P. S. Inventado (2018), 'Hybrid Collaboration Patterns', *PLoP '18: Proceedings of the 25th Conference on Pattern Languages of Programs*, Association for Computing Machinery: 1–14.
Köppe, C., R. T. Nørgård and A. Y. Pedersen (2017), 'Towards a Pattern Language for Hybrid Education', *Proceedings of the VikingPLoP 2017 Conference on Pattern Languages of Program (VikingPLoP '17)*, Association for Computing Machinery, New York, Article 11: 1–17.
Kotler, P. (1973), 'Atmospherics as a Marketing Tool', *Journal of Retailing*, 49 (4): 48–64.

Kreber, C. (2009), *The University and its Disciplines: Teaching and Learning Within and Beyond Disciplinary Boundaries*, New York and London: Routledge.

Laclau, E. (2000), 'Constructing Universality', in J. Butler, E. Laclau and S. Zizek (eds), *Contingency, Hegemony, Universality: Contemporary Dialogues on the Left*, 281–307, London and New York: Verso.

Latour, B. (1993), *We have Never Been Modern*, Cambridge, MA: Harvard University.

Latour, B. (2016), *Is Geo-logy the New Umbrella for All the Sciences? Hints for a Neo-Humboldtian University*, Cornell University, 25 October. Available online: http://www.bruno-latour.fr/sites/default/files/150-CORNELL-2016-.pdf (accessed 13 August 2011).

Latour, B. (2017), *Down to Earth: Politics in the New Climate Regime*, Cambridge: Polity.

Lea, J. (2009), *Political Correctness and Higher Education: British and American Perspectives*, London and New York: Routledge.

Leavis, F. R. (1969), *English Literature in our Time and the University*, London: Chatto & Windus.

Leavis, F. R. ([1943] 1979), *Education and the University: A Sketch for an 'English School'*, Cambridge: University of Cambridge.

Lechner, F. J. and J. Boli (2005), *World Culture*, Malden: Blackwell.

Lefebvre, H. (1991), *The Production of Space*, Oxford: Blackwell.

Levin, M. and D. J. Greenwood (2016), *Creating a New Public Democracy and Reviving Democracy: Action Research in Higher Education*, New York and Oxford: Berghahn.

Levinas, E. (1999), *Alterity and Transcendence*, New York: Columbia University.

Levinas, E. (2000), *Otherwise Than Being or Beyond Essence*, trans. A. Lingis, Pittsburgh: Duquesne University Press.

Levinas, E. (2003), *Totality and Infinity: An Essay on Exteriority*, trans. A. Lingis, Pittsburgh: Duquesne University Press.

Lingis, A. (2000), *Dangerous Emotions*, Berkeley: University of California Press.

Lingis, A (1998), *The Imperative*, Bloomington and Indianapolis: Indiana University Press.

Lingis, A. (1989), *Deathbound Subjectivity*, Bloomington and Indianapolis: Indiana University Press.

Liyanage, M. (2020), *Miseducation: Decolonising Curricula, Culture and Pedagogy in UK Universities*, HEPI Debate Paper 23, Oxford: HEPI.

Locke, J. (1999), *Two Treatises of Government*, Cambridge: Cambridge University Press.

Loftus, S. F. and E. A. Kinsella, eds. (2021), *Embodiment and Professional Education: Body, Practice, Pedagogy*, Cham: Springer.

Løvlie, L., K. P. Mortenson and S. E. Nordenbo, eds. (2003), *Educating Humanity: Bildung in Postmodernity*, Malden and Oxford: Blackwell.

Lukens, J. and C. DiSalvo (2011), 'Speculative Design and Technological Fluency', *International Journal of Learning*, 3 (4): 23–40.

Lyotard, J.-F. (1984), *The Postmodern Condition: A Report on Knowledge*, trans. G. Bennington and B. Massumi, Minneapolis: University of Minnesota.

Lysgaard, J. A., S. Bengtsson and M. H.-L. Laugesen (2019), *Dark Pedagogy. Education, Horror, and the Anthropocene*, London: Palgrave Macmillan.

Maassen, P. A. M. (1996), 'The Concept of Culture and Higher Education', *Tertiary Education and Management*, 1 (2): 153–9.

Macfarlane, B. (2012), *Intellectual Leadership in Higher Education. Renewing the Role of the University Professor*, London and New York: Routledge.

Macfarlane, B. (2007), *The Academic Citizen: The Virtue of Service in University Life*, London and New York: Routledge.

Magna Charta Universitatum (2020), Available online: http://www.magna-charta.org/magna-charta-universitatum

Marcel, G. (2000), *The Mystery of Being. Volume 1: Reflection and Mystery*, trans. G. S. Fraser, South Bend: St. Augustine's Press.

Marginson, S. (2007), 'The New Higher Education Landscape: Public and Private Goods in Global/National/Local Settings', in S. Marginson (ed.), *Prospects of Higher Education: Globalisation, Public Goods and the Future of the University*, 29–77, Rotterdam: Sense.

Marginson, S. (2016), *Higher Education and the Common Good*, Melbourne: Melbourne University Press.

Marginson, S. (2021), *Globalisation: The Good, the Bad and the Ugly*, Working Paper 66, Oxford: Centre for Global Higher Education, University of Oxford.

Marginson, S. and X. Xu (2021), *Moving Beyond Centre-Periphery Science: Towards an Ecology of Knowledges*, Working Paper 63, Oxford: Centre for Global Higher Education, University of Oxford.

Marx, K. (1981), 'Preface to A Contribution to the Critique of Political Economy', in *Early Writings*, trans. Rodney Livingstone and Gregor Benton, 424–28, London: Penguin.

Marx, K. and F. Engels (1977), *The German Ideology*, London: Lawrence and Wishart.

Maxwell, N. (2014), *How Universities Can Help Create a Wiser World: The Urgent Need for an Academic Revolution*, Exeter: Imprint Academic.

McCarthy, E. D. (1996), *Knowledge as Culture: The New Sociology of Knowledge*, London and New York: Routledge.

Mill, J. S. ([1859] 1969), 'On Liberty' in A W. Levi (ed.), *The Six Great Humanistic Essays of John Stuart Mill*, 127–240, New York: Washington Square.

Moberly, Sir W. (1949), *The Crisis in the University*, London: SCM.

Moran, E. T. and J. F. Volkwein (1992), 'The Cultural Approach to the Formation of Organizational Climate', *Human Relations*, 45 (1): 19–48.

Morreira, S., K. Luckett, S. Kumalo and M. Ramgotra (2021), *Decolonising Curricula and Pedagogy in Higher Education: Bringing Decolonial Theory into Contact with Teaching Practice*, London: Routledge.

Murphy, P. (2018), 'The Platform University: The Destruction and Resurrection of Universities in the Auto-Industrial Age', in R. Barnett and M. A. Peters (eds), *The Idea of the University: Contemporary Perspectives*, vol. 2, 483–500, New York: Peter Lang.

Naidoo, R. (2018), 'The Competition Fetish in Higher Education: Shamans, Mind Snares and Consequences', *European Educational Research Journal*, 17 (5): 605–20.

Naidoo, R. (2016), 'The Competition Fetish in Higher Education: Varieties, Animators and Consequences', *British Journal of Sociology of Education*, 37 (1): 1–10.

Nail, T. (2019), *Being and Motion*, Oxford: Oxford University.

Nelson, H. G. and E. Stolterman (2012), *The Design Way: Intentional Change in an Unpredictable World*. Cambridge: MIT Press.

'Neoliberal Policy Context', in S. Cardoso, O. Tavares, C. Sin and T. Carvalho (eds), *Structural and Institutional Transformations in Doctoral Education: Social, Political, and Student Expectations*, 203–38, Cham: Palgrave Macmillan.

Networked Learning Editorial Collective (NLEC) (2021), 'Networked Learning: Inviting Redefinition', *Postdigital Science and Education*, 3 (2): 312–25.

Networked Learning Editorial Collective (NLEC), L. Gourlay, J. L. Rodríguez-Illera, et al. (2021), 'Networked Learning in 2021: A Community Definition', *Postdigital Science and Education*, 3 (2): 326–69.

Neumann, R. (2020), 'Leadership and Institutional Change in Doctoral Education in a Neoliberal Policy Context', in S. Cardoso, O. Tavares, C. Sin, and T. Carvalho (eds), *Structural and Institutional Transformations in Doctoral Education. Social, Political, and Student Expectations*, 203–38, Cham: Palgrave Macmillan.

Newman, J. H. ([1848] 1976), *The Idea of the University*, ed. I. T. Ker, Oxford: Oxford University.

Nikolaidis, A. C. (2021), 'A Third Conception of Epistemic Injustice', *Studies in Philosophy and Education*, 40: 381–98.

Nietzsche, F. (1968), *The Will to Power*, trans. W. Kaufmann and R. J. Hollingdale, New York: Vintage Books, Random House.

Nietzsche, F. ([1889] 2003), *Twilight of the Idols and The Anti-Christ*, London: Penguin.

Nietzsche, F. (2006), *The Gay Science*, trans. T. Common, New York: Dover Publications.

Nietzsche, F. (2010), *The Anti-Christ, Ecce Homo, Twilight of the Idols. And Other Writings*, trans. J. Norman, Cambridge: Cambridge University Press.

Nietzsche, F. (2014a), *On the Genealogy of Morality*, trans. C. Diethe, Cambridge: Cambridge University Press.

Nietzsche, F. (2014b), *Thus Spoke Zarathustra*, trans. A. Del Caro, Cambridge: Cambridge University Press.

Nixon, J. (2008), *Towards the Virtuous University: The Moral Bases of Academic Practice*, London and New York: Routledge.

Nixon, J. (2012), *Higher Education and the Public Good: Imagining the University*, London and New York: Continuum.

Norberg-Schulz, C. (1980), *Genius Loci. Towards a Phenomenology of Architecture*, London: Academy Editions.

Nussbaum, M. (2010), *Not for Profit: Why Democracy Needs the Humanities*, Princeton and Oxford: Princeton University.

Nørgård, R. T. (2021), 'Theorising Hybrid Lifelong Learning', *British Journal of Educational Technology*, 52 (4): 1709–23.

Nørgård, R. T. (2022), 'What Comes after the Ruin? Designing for the Arrival of Preferable Futures for the University', in S. Bengtsen and R. Gildersleeve (eds), *Understanding the Transformation of the University*, London: Routledge.

Nørgård, R. T. and S. Bengtsen (2016), 'Academic Citizenship beyond the Campus: A Call for the Placeful University', *Higher Education Research and Development*, 35 (1): 4–16.

Nørgård, R. T. and S. Bengtsen (2018), 'The Worldhood University: Design, Signatures, and Guild Thinking', in S. Bengtsen and R. Barnett (eds), *The Thinking University. A Philosophical Examination of Thought and Higher Education*, 167–83, Cham: Springer.

Nørgård, R. T. and S. Bengtsen, eds. (2021a), 'The Activist University: Between Practice and Policy', *Special Issue of Policy Futures in Education*, 19: 5.

Nørgård, R. T. and S. Bengtsen (2021b), 'The Activist University and University Activism: An Editorial', in R. T. Nørgård and S. Bengtsen (eds), *The Activist University: Between Practice and Policy. Special Issue of Policy Futures in Education*, 19 (5): 507–12.

Nørgård, R. T., S. Bengtsen and C. Ess (2020), 'The University of We: Value-Sensitive Design for an Ethical University', *Knowledge Cultures*, 8 (1): 48–63.

Nørgård, R. T. and C. Hilli (2022), 'Hyper-hybrid Learning Spaces in Higher Education', in E. Gil, Y. Mor, Y. Dimitriadis and C. Köppe (eds), *Hybrid Learning Spaces*, 25–41, Cham: Springer.

Nørgård, R. T., Y. Mor and S. Bengtsen (2019), 'Networked Learning in, for, and with the World', in A. Littlejohn, J. Jaldemark, E. Vrieling-Teunter and F. Nijland (eds), *Networked Professional Learning: Emerging and Equitable Discourses for Professional Development*, 71–88, Cham: Springer.

Oberdiek, H. (2001), *Tolerance: Between Forbearance and Acceptance*, Oxford: Rowman and Littlefield.

Ortega y Gasset, J. (1946), *Mission of the University*, London: Kegan Paul, Trench, Trubner and Co.

Ostling, J. (2018), *Humboldt and the Modern German University: An Intellectual History*, Lund: Lund University.

Pässilä, A., and R. Vince (2016), 'Critical Reflection in Management and Organisation Studies', in J. Fook, V. Collington, F. Ross, G. Ruch, and L. West (eds), *Researching Critical Reflection: Multidisciplinary Perspectives*, 48–62, London and New York: Routledge.

Pedersen, A. Y., R. T. Nørgård C. Köppe (2018), 'Patterns of Inclusion: Fostering Digital Citizenship through Hybrid Education', *Educational Technology & Society*, 21 (1): 225–36.

Peters, M. A. (2013), *Education, Science and Knowledge Capitalism: Creativity and the Promise of Openness*, New York: Peter Lang.

Peters, M. A. (2018), 'Renewing the Idea of the University: The Cosmopolitan and Postcolonial Projects', in R. Barnett and M. A. Peters (eds), *The Idea of the University, Vol 2: Contemporary Perspectives*, 558–74, New York: Peter Lang.

Peters, M. and R. Barnett, eds. (2018), *The Idea of the University, A Reader*, vol. 1, New York: Peter Lang.

Peters, M., S. Rider, M. Hyvönen and T. Besley, eds. (2018), *Post-Truth, Fake News. Viral Modernity and Higher Education*, Singapore: Springer.

Peters, M. A. and S. Tukeo (2010), 'Cultural Exchange, Study Abroad and Discourse of the Other' in S. Marginson, P. Murphy and M. A. Peters (eds) *Global Creation: Space, Mobility and Synchrony in the Age of the Knowledge Economy*, 266–83, New York: Peter Lang.

Peters, M. A. and P. Venkatesan (2013), 'Biocapitalism and the Politics of Life', in M. A. Peters (ed.), *Education, Science and Knowledge Capitalism: Creativity and the Promise of Openness*, 93–112, New York: Peter Lang.

Plato (2002), 'Republic', in L. Cooper et al. (trans.), *The Collected Dialogues of Plato. Including the Letters*, 575–844, Princeton: Princeton University Press.

Plumb, J. H., ed. (1964), *Crisis in the Humanities*, London: Penguin.

Plumbwood, V. (2008), *Environmental Culture: The Ecological Crisis of Reason*, London and New York: Routledge.

Popper, K. (1975), *Objective Knowledge: An Evolutionary Approach*, Oxford: Clarendon Press.

Ram, Y., P. Björk and A. Weidenfeld (2016), 'Authenticity and Place Attachment of Major Visitor Attractions', *Tourism Management*, 52: 110–22.

Readings, B. (1997), *The University in Ruins*, Cambridge and London: Harvard University.

Rebentisch, J. and F. Trautmann (2020), 'The Idea of the Culture Industry', in P. E. Gordon, E. Hammer and A. Honneth, (eds), *The Routledge Companion to the Frankfurt School*, 19–31, New York and London: Routledge.

Rickly-Boyd, J. M. (2012), 'Authenticity & Aura: A Benjaminian Approach to Tourism', *Annals of Tourism Research*, 39 (1): 269–89.

Rider, S. (2018a), 'On Knowing How to Tell the Truth', in M. A. Peters, S. Rider, M. Hyvönen and T. Besley (eds), *Post-truth, Fake News, Viral Modernity and Higher Education*, 27–42, Singapore: Springer.

Rider, S. (2018b), 'Truth, Democracy, and the Mission of the University', in S. Bengtsen and R. Barnett (eds), *The Thinking University: A Philosophical Examination of Thought and Higher Education*, 15–29, Cham: Springer.

Rider, S. S. P., M. A. Peters, M. Hyvönen and T. Besley, eds. (2020), *World-Class Universities: A Contested Concept*, Cham: Springer.

Rigby, C. (2011), 'Gernot Böhme's Ecological Aesthetics of Atmosphere', in A. Goodbody and K. Rigby (eds), *Ecocritical Theory: New European Approaches*, 139–152, Charlottesville: University of Virginia Press.

Ringer, F. K. ([1969] 1990), *The Decline of the German Mandarins: The German Academic Community*, 1890–933, Hanover and London: University Press of New England.

Robbins, Lord L. (1963), *Higher Education: Report of the Committee appointed by the Prime Minister*, London: HMSO, Cmnd. 2154.

Roggero, G. (2011), *The Production of Living Knowledge: The Crisis of the University and the Transformation of Labor in Europe and North America*, Philadelphia: Temple University.

Rosen, M. (1996), *On Voluntary Servitude: False Consciousness and the Theory of Ideology*, Cambridge: Polity.

Rosner, D. K. (2018), *Critical Fabulations: Reworking the methods and margins of design*, Cambridge, MA: MIT Press.

Rousseau, J.-J. (1968), *The Social Contract*, trans. M. Cranston, London: Penguin Books.

Rüegg, W., ed. (2003), *A History of the University in Europe*, 1–4, Cambridge: Cambridge University Press.

Ryle, M. and K. Soper (2002), *To Relish the Sublime? Culture and Self-Realization in Postmodern Times*, London and New York: Verso.

Sartre, J.-P. (2001), *Being and Nothingness: An Essay on Phenomenological Ontology*, trans. H. E. Barnes, London: Routledge.

Savin-Baden, M. (2015), *Rethinking Learning in an Age of Digital Fluency: Is being Digitally Tethered a New Learning Nexus?*, London and New York: Routledge.

Schein, E. (1990), 'Organizational Culture', *American Psychologist*, 45 (2): 109–19.

Schein, E. (2004). *Organizational Culture and Leadership*, San Francisco: Jossey-Bass.

Schildermans, H. (2019), *Making a University: Introductory Notes on the Ecology of Study Practices*, PhD Dissertation, Faculty of Psychology and Educational Sciences, Laboratory for Education and Society, KU Leuven.

Schildermans, H., M. Simons and J. Masschelein (2020), 'From Ruins to Response-Ability: Making a University in a Palestinian Refugee Camp' in N. Hodgson, J. Vliege, P. Zamojski (eds), *Post-Critical Perspectives on Higher Education: Reclaiming the Educational in the University*, 27–41, Cham: Springer.

Schopenhauer, A. ([1850] 2004), *On the Suffering of the World*, London: Penguin.

Scruton, R. ([1998] 2016), *Modern Culture*, London: Bloomsbury.

Serres, M. (2018), *The Incandescent*, London and New York: Bloomsbury.

Sewell, W. H. (1999), 'The Concept(s) of Culture', in V. E. Bonnell and L. Hunt (eds), *Beyond the Cultural Turn*, 35–62, Berkeley: University of California Press.

Shumar, W. and S. Robinson (2020), 'Agency, Risk-taking, and Identity in Entrepreneurship Education', in S. Bengtsen and R. Barnett (eds), *Special Issue on Imagining the Future University, Philosophy and Theory in Higher Education*, 1 (3): 153–73.

Singh, S., R. Bhaskar and M. Hartwig (2020), *Reality and its Depths: A Conversation Between Savita Singh and Roy Bhaskar*, Singapore: Springer.

Smyth, J. (2018), *The Toxic University: Zombie Leadership, Academic Rock Stars, and Neoliberal Ideology*, New York: Palgrave Macmillan.

Snow, C. P. ([1959] 1978), *The Two Cultures and A Second Look*, London: Cambridge University Press.

Soares, P., J. V. Rocha, M. Moniz, A. Gama, P. A. Laires, A. R. Pedro, S. Dias, A. Leite and C. Nunes (2021), 'Factors Associated with COVID-19 Vaccine Hesitancy', *Vaccines*, 9 (3): 1–14.

Spencer-Oatey, H. (2008), *Culturally Speaking: Culture, Communication and Politeness Theory*, London: Continuum.

Staley, D. J. (2019), *Alternative Universities: Speculative Design for Innovation in Higher Education*, Baltimore: John Hopkins University Press.

Standish, P. (2011), 'Teaching in the University the Day After Tomorrow', in R. Barnett (ed.), *The Future University. Ideas and Possibilities*, 152–164, London and New York: Routledge.

Stiegler, B. (2014a), *For a New Critique of Political Economy*, Cambridge and Malden: Polity.

Stiegler, B. (2014b), *The Re-Enchantment of the World: The Value of Spirit Against Industrial Populism*, London and New York: Bloomsbury.

Stiegler, B. (2015), *States of Shock: Stupidity and Knowledge in the 21st Century*, Cambridge and Malden: Polity.

Strain, J, R. Barnett and P. Jarvis, eds. (2009), *Universities, Ethics and Professions: Debate and Scrutiny*, London: Routledge.

Street, B. V. (1993), 'Culture is a Verb: Anthropological Aspects of Language and Cultural Process', in D. Graddol, L. Thompson and M. Byram (eds), *Language and Culture*, 23–44, Clevedon: BAAL and Multilingual Matters.

Stuart, M. and L. Shutt (2019), 'From Fixed to Porous: The Permeability of our Institutions', *WonkHE*, 25 January 2019. Available online: https://wonkhe.com/blogs/from-fixed-to-porous-the-permeability-of-our-institutions/ (accessed 13 August 2013).

Sum, N.-G., and B. Jessop (2013), *Towards a Cultural Political Economy: Putting Culture in its Place in Political Economy*, Cheltenham and Northampton: Edward Elgar.

Szadkowski, K. (2018), 'The Common in Higher Education: A Conceptual Approach', *Higher Education*, 78: 241–55.

Sørensen, A. (2019), 'Social Ethos and Political Mission: University on the Margins', in S. Bengtsen and A. Sørensen (eds), *Special Issue on Revising the Idea of the University, Danish Yearbook of Philosophy*, 104–38, Leiden and Boston: Brill.

Tagiuri, R. and G. H. Litwin (1968), 'Organizational Culture: A Key to Financial Performance', in B. Schneider (ed.), *Organizational Climate and Culture*, San Francisco: Jossey-Bass.

Taylor, C. (1992), *Sources of the Self: The Making of the Modern Identity*, Cambridge: University of Cambridge.

Taylor, C. (2007), *Modern Social Imaginaries*, Durham and London: Duke University.

Temple, P. (2009), 'From Space to Place: University Performance and its Built Environment', *Higher Education Policy*, 22 (2): 209–23.

Temple, P. (2019), 'University Spaces. Creating Cité and Place', *London Review of Education*, 17 (2) 223–35.

Temple, P. (2021), 'The University Couloir: Exploring Physical and Intellectual Connectivity', *Higher Education Policy*, https://doi.org/10.1057/s41307-021-00253-x.

Tharp, B. M. and S. M. Tharp (2018), *Discursive Design. Critical, Speculative and Alternative Things*, Cambridge, MA: MIT Press.

Trilling, L. (1967), *Beyond Culture: Essays on Literature and Learning*. London: Penguin, in association with Secker & Warburg.

Trowler, P., M. Saunders and V. Bamber, eds. (2014), *Tribes and Territories in the 21st Century: Rethinking the Significance of Disciplines in Higher Education*, London and New York: Routledge.

Tschumi, B. (1994), *Event-Cities (praxis)*, Cambridge, MA: MIT Press.

Tuan, Y.-F. (1974), 'Space and Place: Humanistic Perspective', in C. Board, R. J. Chorley, P. Haggett, and D. R. Stoddart (eds), *Progress in Geography*, 6, London: Edward Arnold.

Tuan, Y.-F. (1977), *Space and Place: The Perspective of Experience*, Minneapolis: University of Minnesota Press.

Ulin, R. C. (2001), *Understanding Cultures: Perspectives in Anthropology and Social Theory*, Malden and Oxford: Blackwell.

Virilio, P. (2010), *The University of Disaster*, Cambridge and Malden: Polity.

Volgger, M. (2020), 'Staging *Genius Loci*: Atmospheric Interventions in Tourism Destinations', in M. Volgger and D. Pfister (eds), *Atmospheric Turn in Culture and Tourism: Place, Design and Process Impacts on Customer Behaviour, Marketing and Branding*, 139–51, Bingley: Emerald Publishing Limited.

Voros, J. (2017), 'Big History and Anticipation: Using Big History as a Framework for Global Foresight', in R. Poli (ed.), *Handbook of Anticipation: Theoretical and Applied Aspects of the Use of Future in Decision Making*, 425–64, Singapore: Springer International.

Waddington, K. (2016), 'The Compassion Gap in UK Universities', *International Practice Development Journal*, 6 (1): 1–9.

Waddington, K. (2017), 'Creating the Conditions for Compassion', in P. Gibbs (ed.), *The Pedagogy of Compassion at the Heart of Higher Education*, 49–70, Cham: Springer.

Waddington, K. (2019), 'Understanding and Creating Compassionate Institutional Cultures and Practices', in P. Gibbs, J. Jameson and A. Elwick (eds), *Values of the University in a Time of Uncertainty*, Cham: Springer.

Walker, G. E., C. M. Golde, L. Jones, A. C. Bueschel and P. Hutchings (2008), *The Formation of Scholars: Rethinking Doctoral Education for the Twenty-first Century*, San Francisco: Jossey-Bass.

Walker, M. and C. Martinez-Vargas (2020), 'Epistemic Governance and the Colonial Epistemic Structure: Towards Epistemic Humility and Transformed South-North Relations', *Critical Studies in Education*: 1–16.

Wax, M. L. (1993), 'How Culture Misdirects Multiculturalism', *Anthropology and Education Quarterly*, 24 (2): 99–115.
Weber, M. (1991a), 'Value-judgments in Social Science', in W. G. Runciman (ed.), *Weber: Selections in Translation*, 69–98, Cambridge: Cambridge University Press.
Weber, M. (1991b), 'Science as a Vocation', in H. H. Gerth and C. W. Mills (eds), *From Max Weber: Essays in Sociology*, 129–56, London: Routledge.
Weeks, J. and C. Gulunic (2003), 'A Theory of the Cultural Evolution of the Firm: The Intra-organizational Ecology of Memes', *Organization Science*, 24 (8): 1309–52.
Wei, I. P. (2014), *Intellectual Culture in Medieval Paris: Theologians and the University, c.1100-1330*, Cambridge: Cambridge University Press.
Weidinger, J. (2018), 'Designing Atmospheres in Landscape Architecture', in J. Weidinger (ed.), *Designing Atmospheres*, 19–39, Berlin: TU Verlag.
Weil, S. (2002), *Gravity and Grace*, trans. E. Crawford and M. v. d. Ruhr, London and New York: Routledge.
Welikala, T. and R. Barnett (2021), 'Many Cultures or None? Sighting and Assessing a Post-cultural Pedagogical Paradigm', in M. Kumar and T. Welikala (eds), *Teaching and Learning in Higher Education: The Context of Being, Interculturality and New Knowledge Systems*, 275–89, Bingley: Emerald.
West, M., R. Eckert, B. Collins and R. Chowla (2017), *How Compassionate Leadership Can Stimulate Innovation in Health Care*, London: The King's Fund.
Whitchurch, C. (2012), *Reconstructing Identities in Higher Education: The Rise of 'Third Space' Professionals*, London and New York: Routledge and Society for Research into Higher Education.
Wiener, M. J. (1985), *English Culture and the Decline of the Industrial Spirit 1850–1980*, London: Pelican.
Wilkins, A. L. and W. G. Ouchi (1983), 'Exploring the Relationship between Culture and Organizational Performance', *Administrative Science Quarterly*, 28 (3): 468–81.
Williams, R. (2003), *Lost Icons: Reflections on Cultural Bereavement*, London and New York: Continuum.
Williams, R. ([1958] 2017), *Culture and Society*, London: Vintage.
Wood, D. (2015), 'Political Philosophy and the Vestiges of Colonialism: A Critical Analysis of Zizek's Leftist Plea for Eurocentricism', *Radical Philosophy Review*, 19 (3): 653–77.
Woolston, C. (2021), 'Impact Factor Abandoned by Dutch University in Hiring and Promotion Decisions', *Nature*, Career News, 25 June 2021. Available online: https://www.nature.com/articles/d41586-021-01759-5 (accessed 13 August 2021).
Worline, M. C. and J. E. Dutton (2017), *Awakening Compassion at Work: The Quiet Power that Elevates People and Organisations*, Oakland: Berrett-Koehler.
Wright, E. O. (2010), *Envisioning Real Utopias*, London and New York: Verso.
Wright, S. and C. Shore, eds. (2018), *Death of the Public University?: Uncertain Futures for Higher Education in the Knowledge Economy*, New York: Berghahn Book.

Zaman, A. (2021), 'The Puzzle of Western Social Science', *Academia Letters*, article 459, 26 March 2021. Available online: https://papers.ssrn.com/sol3/papers.cfm?abstract_id=3812894 (accessed 13 August 2021).

Zizek, S. (1999), *The Sublime Object of Ideology*, London and New York: Verso.

Zizek, S. (2000), 'Class Struggle or Postmodernism?: Yes, Please!', in J. Butler, E. Laclau and S. Zizek (eds), *Contingency, Hegemony, Universality: Contemporary Dialogues on the Left*, London and New York: Verso.

Zizek, S. (2009), *The Parallax View*, Cambridge, MA: MIT Press.

Subject Index

NB: *Book titles are italicised, and particularly significant entries are emboldened.*

academic community   78, 181, 192
academic development   111
academic freedom   110, 129, 143, 181, 199
academics   143
academic sphere   179
Academic Tribes and Territories   22
access   35, 109, 137, 189
action   191
activism   109, 191–2, 196
agency   97, 99, 178, 200
alienation   65
alien dimensions   155, 184
Alternative Universities   119
anarchy   128
anthropocene   52, 66, 146, 155, 161, 164
anxiety   197–9
architecture   71, 73, 77, 80, 90, 92–3, 102, 193
argument   63
assemblage   170
atmosphere   12–13, 82, **83–95**, 101, 105–6, 109–12, 118, 180–1, 191, 196, 204–5, *see also* design, atmospheric; university, the atmospheric
attachment   76
attunement   87, 92
audit   19
authenticity   86, 192, 205, 211

being   57, 79, 87, 120, 148, 149–51, 172, 210
belonging   76, 125, 178–9
bildung   41, 117–18, 127–8, 164
bio-science   30, 47, 155, 213
Bologna   191–2
books, *see* libraries
Brazil   189

buildings   71, 78–80, 82, 85, 92–3
built environment, *see* architecture

campus   79–80, 91, 117
capabilities   112
capitalism   45
  academic   110
  algorithmic   40, 48
  cognitive   30, 40, 56, 61, 65, 141
  economic   46
  state   44
care   9–10, 66–7, 73, 78, 99–100, 113, 117, 152, 167–8, 170, 186, 196, 207, 210–11
causation   45
China   30, 189
citizenship   3, 11, 53, 110, 112, 115, 117–18, 135, 143, 164
  academic   129
  global   22
civic engagement   110
civic society   148
civil rights   3
collaboration   142
coloniality   3–4, 18, 26, 36, 44, 53, 63, 82, 107–8, 109, 131, 181, 185
commodification   94, 110
common good   129, 131, 158, 182, 187
communication   10, 12, 51, 71, 110
community   7, 10, 52, 103, 111, 119, 127, 135, 137–41, 144–5, 151, 179, 196, 210
  academic   71, 110, 113, 128–9
  epistemic   51
  intellectual   139, 141
compassion   98–100, 104, 196, 207–8
competition   110, 127, 179, 208–9, 214
complexity   147, 184, 216
concern   57, 98–9, 207, 210, 212, 216

connectedness, *see* interconnectedness
constructivism   59
context   37
contingency   53–4, 58, 184
contract   130, 146, 170, 187, *see also* social contract
   ontological   146–8
coronavirus   3, 44
corporatism   186
cosmopolitanism   22, 159
courage   130, 134, 201
creativity   200, 202, 211
crisis   4
criticality   21, 126, **132–4**, 165
Critical Realism, *see* realism
critical thinking   100, 132
critique   6, 8–9, 23, 32, 111, 138, 209, 216
cultural
   achievement   125
   action   150
   atmosphere   91, 95 (*see also* atmosphere; university, the atmospheric)
   belonging   150
   bond   153, 157
   capital   22, 39, 47
   centre   131
   challenges   169
   clearing   211
   communities   180
   crisis   17, 27–8
   death   167
   depths   150
   dialectics   132
   diversity   169
   economy   18, 56
   ethos   126, 164–5, 171–2
   formation   13, 134, 136, 182
   glue   196
   growth   13, 152–3, 157
   hegemony   206
   horizon   150, 156
   identity   86, 97
   imperialism   23–4
   leadership   **137–48**, 182, 192 (*see also* leadership)
   margins   169
   neglect   178
   negotiation   4
   neutrality   26
   openness   150
   place   72, 75, 81, 86
   politics   170
   purposes   2, 13, 43
   relativism   58
   roles   2, 18
   schism   11
   sphere   20, 36, 183
   strategy   26
   thinking   102
   threshold   167
   tissue   206
   transformation   168
   turn   1
   unknown   169
   vacuum   150
   worlds   44
culture and university relationship   12, 20–2, 27–9, 33, 35, 55, 62–3, 67, 92, 144, 159
culture as cohesive   13
culture as foundational   1
culture-freedom   22, 25, 43, 56, 61–2, 178, 190
culture industry   44, 204
culture of debate   32, 38
culture of division   209
culture of the earth   65–8
cultures   2, 5–6, 19, 21, 24–6, 32–3, 38–40, 42–3, 46, 51–2, 56–60, 62, 67, 80, 84, 89, 92, 96, 99, 104, 107, 110, 114, 129, 149, 153, 160–1, 165, 171, 185, 189, 216, *see also* culture, universities; university cultures
   academic   71, 77, 103, 111, 126, 134, 139, 185, 190, 192–3, 196–7, 200, 202, 204, 208
   alien   153
   alternative   103, 105, 108, 110 (*see also* 'Alternative universities')
   anti-   65
   atmospheric 110 (*see also* atmosphere; cultural atmosphere; university, the atmospheric)

beyond   166, 209–10
body of   87
cancel   38
cognitive   5, 25, 45–9, 183, 206
common   12, **43–55**, 56, 193, 197
concept of   2, **7–9**, 10, 18, 20, 23, 27,
   44, 46, 52, 63, 83, 97–8, 109,
   155, 162, 172
conflicting   18, 29
corporate   71, 85
counter   11, 208
deep   208
digital   52
dominant   8, 11, 24, 32, 34, 44–5, 48,
   63, 214
ecological   13, 66, 68, 188, **212–14**
empathic   181
end of   31
epistemic   24–5, 41, 54, 57
fragile   33
future   102
general   49
hybrid   118
institutional   194
knowledge   24–5, 57, 184, 187
liberal   31
meta-   12, 23, 33–4, 42, 58, 66, 190,
   204, 210–14
networking   112–15
oppositional   214
organizational   57, 83, 106
participatory   97
placeful   **71–82**, 73, 75, 77–81, 86, 190
post-   36, 40, 42, 210
powerful   61
socio-material   72
spaces of   10–11, 72 (*see also*
   university as site of culture)
sub-   33, 51
transhuman   210
'*Two Cultures* debate'   38
universal   67–8
university   191
university for   1, 5
cultures of other species   156
culture wars   1, 3–4, 12, 18–19, 25, 27–9,
   30–42, 47, 67, 178–81
culturing   72–3, 78, 97–8, 106, *see also*
   university as culturing site

curricula   4–5, 26, 51, 128, 131, 134,
   145, 151, 155, 165, 169–71, 194,
   196–8, 212

decision-making   196, 199
decolonization   26, 74
democracy   25, 28, 32–3, 126
design   12–13, 71, 83, 93–4, 100–4, 107,
   111, 117, 191, 198, 200, 202, 212
   atmospheric   87–90, 92–3, 181
   speculative   107–8, 109
dialectics   141, 190, 208–10
dialogue   111–12, 120, 140, 156
difference   8, 111, 136, 185
digitalization   25, 27, 46–8, 51–2, 76, 109,
   113–14, 119, 200
dignity   135, 159, 171
disciplines   48, 57, 60, 62, 79, 97,
   115, 128, 130, 151, 171,
   183, 185–7, 210, 213, 215,
   see also epistemic cultures;
   'epistemicide'; epistemic
   injustice; interdisciplinarity;
   transdisciplinarity
   boundaries of   166, 183
   competing   28, 43
   cultural   21–2
   fissiparous   209
   marginalized   210
   porous   212
dispositions   87–8, 93, 125, 127
dissent   31, 216
diversity   111, 136, 169
dogma   37, 53, 130
dream   106

earth, the   5, 12, 44, 47, 56, 66, 76, 146,
   161, 165, 168, 171, 185–8,
   202–3, 209–14, 216
   culture of   65–7
Ecocene   66
ecologies   30, 47, 55, 58, 62, 96, 112,
   115, 147, 150, 154–5, 161, 163,
   165, 183, 186–7, 190, 192–3,
   195, **211–13**, *see also* culture,
   ecological
   alien   155
   knowledge   145
   learning   138

ecologies of knowledge   1, 4
economics   3
economy   6, 25, 41, 94
ecosystems   66–7, 120, 146, 186, 188, 205, 213
   knowledge   67
   learning   67
education   2, 199
elites   31–2, 146
emancipation   132–3, 141, 152, 161, 169, 180, 204
emergence   184
emotion   20, 81, 87, 91, 191, 209
empathy   98, 117–18, 209
employability   6, 11, 110
empty signifier   20
enchantment   93
energy   3, 64, 167
engagement   38, 42, 77, 109–10, 145, 153, 200
engineering, bio-   25
English   38
enlightenment, the   161, 164
entanglement   4, 26, 39, 45, 58, 74, 117–18, 120, 153, 157, 170–1, 178–9, 184, 186–7, 215
entropy   64–6, 186
epistemic
   cultures   62, 128, 130
   injustice   37, 47, 145
   narcissism   147
'epistemicide'   23
epistemology   5, 45–6, 49–50, 54, 57, 59–60, 183, 196, 209
equality   34, 109
equity   181, 189, *see also* fairness
ethics   13, 54, 66, 68, 100, 104–5, 132, 135, 137, 144, 170
ethnicity   19, 181
Europe   30, 60, 191, 192, 206, 211
European University Association (EUA)   1, 113, 119–20
'excellence'   6, 9, 35
exclusion   6, 9
experience   87

fairness   35, *see also* equity
faith   198

fear   198–9
feminism   40
fissiparousness   63, 209
flourishing   163
fragmentation   8, 11, 30, 48, 139
frameworks   6
Frankfurt School of Critical Theory   61, 204
freedom   3, 34–5, 37, 78, 110, 125, 179, 197–8, 200–1
future   98–101, 104, 106, 108, 109, 151, 165, 176, 188, 192, 200
futurescaping   **110–21**, 188

gender   3–4, 85, 181
general education   49–50
global citizens   51
Global North   5, 12, 24–5, 40, 44, 47, 51, 60, 144
Global South   5, 12, 23–4, 40, 47, 51, 144
God   162
good, the   159, *see also* public good
'Great Books'   49–50

heterogeneity   80, 109
hierarchies   113
higher education   1–2, 114, 126–7, 130, 141, 144–5, 151, 156, 163–4, 168, 179, 191
   concept of   2
   culture of   9
   future   200
   globality of   30
   hybrid   110, 117
   role of   158
   target of   150
   task of   18
higher education as cultural formation   **125–36**
higher education classroom   133
higher education ecology   165
higher learning   21, 130, 132, 135–6, 151–2, 154, 157–8, 164, *see also* learning
hope   137, 153, 164, 186, 200
hospitality   157
human being   8, 105, 162, 164, 166–7

humanism   163, 168–70
humanities   4, 24, 38–9, 47–8, 52, 54, 61, 98, 160–2, 164–5, 168–9, 171, 186–7, 203, 210, 215
   meta-   164, 202
hybridity   11–12, 40, 88, 110–11, **115–21**, 163, 176, 178, 186–8

'ideal speech situation'   4, 37, 62
The Idea of a University   207
ideas   105
identity   3, 19, 125, 139, 144, 171, 178, 184, 203, 209
ideology   6, 8, 23–4, 31–2, 34, 53, 59, 68, 107, 128, 133, 155–6, 170, 172, 190
imaginaries   106–7, 151, 180
imagination   91, 101, 106, 108, 132–3, 184–6, 202, 209
impact   210
imperialism   131
inclusion   118, 171, 181
indeterminacy   184
India   30, 189
indigenous communities   3, 12, 43, 66, 210
Indonesia   30
inquiry   57, 65
instrumentalism   8–9, 45, 47, 60, 64–5, 110, 198, 210–11, 214
integrity   28–9, **129–31**, 134–5, 137, 190, 192, 195, 207
interconnectedness   44, 55, 73, 115, 147, 184, 210
interculturality   51
interdisciplinarity   39, 50, 107, 166
internet   27, *see also* digitalization

justice   3, 53

'knowledge constitutive interests'   58
knowledge ecology   24, *see also* ecologies of knowledge
knowledge economy   138, 169
knowledge practices   145
knowledge production   120, 127, 152, 170, *see also* research
knowledge pursuits   147

knowledges   5–6, 19, 24, 45–6, 60, 67, 101, 117, 119, 125–6, 128, 132, 135, 150–1, 158–9, 184, 188, 202, 211

laboratory   105–6
labour   65
law   32
leadership   39, 72, 99, 102, 134, 138–42, 145, 180–1, 198, 200–1, 212, *see also* cultural leadership
learning   115–20, 126, 137–8, 141, 150, 196, 199–200, 203, 213, *see also* ecosystems, learning; higher learning
   networked   112
learning analytics   195
legitimacy   36, 62, 144–5, 172
liberal democracy   34–5, 37, *see also* democracy
liberty, *see under* freedom
libraries   72, 200, 202–3
life   12, 21, 57, 64, 74, 82, 110, 159, 164, 167, 203–4
lifeworld   20, 63, 72–3, 76, 79, 81, 84, 92, 94, 110, 141, 181–3

management   41, 81, 97, 99, 137, 186, 212
   performance   28
marginalization   36
margins   148, 170–1
materiality   102, 105, 118, 164
   socio-materiality   141
mathematics   25
meanings   72, 76, 147, 157
metaphysics   162, 202
meta-reality, *see under* reality
mind   41
Moebius strip   58, 68, 185
mood   88
motion   45, 59
multiculturality   18, 22, 33, 36, 40
multiplicity   178
multiverse   104, 107
music   102
mystery   156–7

nationalism 3, 131
nature 5, 44, 54, 61, 67, 163, 168, 209–10, 212–13, 216
negentropy 66
neglect 3, 18
neoliberalism 94, 107, 109, 138, 198
networks 12, 111–15, 119–20, 185
neutrality 3
NLEC 109, 112–14

ontology 4, 45–6, 49, 54, 58–9, 146, 149, 155, 167, 172, 190, 195–7, 209, 212
openness 115, 152, 185
opera 19
optimism 151
Organisation for Economic Co-operation and Development (OECD) 199
otherness 53, 57, 118, 156, 171, 185, 187, 210–12

Paris 191–2
particularity 53, 211
passion 36, 164, 200
pedagogy 4–5, 26, 36, 97, 112–13, 132, 202
performance indicators 132, 189
peripheries 147, 170–2
pessimism 161, 168–9
'pharmakon' 27, 180
philosophy 61
place 13, 72–7, 79, 81–2, 87, 89, 101, 106, 110, 112–13, 179, 191, 193, 202–4
placefulness 86, 90, 111
playfulness 117
pluralism 54, 111, 146, 160, 170
poetry 102
policy-making 24, 71
politics 131, 137, 158, 188, 213
populism 131
possibilities 2, 102, 145–6, 197–8, 209, 211
post-humanism 28, 52, 155, 163–4, 168
postmodernism 169
post-truth 126, 129
power 6, 8–9, 12, 22–3, 36, 41, 49, 61, 65, 72, 77, 81, 89, 93–4, 97–9, 126, 171, 178–9, 195, 199

practices 10, 26, 72, 77, 92, 94, 96–7, 108, 114–15, 125, 127, 145, 169, 183, 185, 187–8, 197, 202
preposterousness 101, 103–5, 107, 110–12, 121, 185–6, 188
programmes of study 2, 216
public good 12, 40, 111, 143
public sphere 19, 30, 111, 126, 134, 199, 216

race 3–4
racism 12
radicalism 31
rationality 161, *see also* reason; reasoning
realism 45
   critical 46, 54–5, 59
reality 101, 107
   meta- 162, 164
reason 6, 17, 19–20, 32, 34, 36–7, 39, 46, 53–4, 57, 59, 61, 63–4, 86, 96, 132, 161, 164, 191, 209, *see also* space of
   instrumental 110, 186
reasoning 54
relationality 184
relativism 58–9, 61–2, 68
religion 34, 181
research 4, 26, 66, 96–7, 107, 115, 118, 125, 127–8, 130–2, 135–6, 137–41, 143, 151, 154–5, 157–8, 172, 194, 196, 202
   culture 57
   universities 190
researchers 72, 114, 148, 184, 198
resilience 35
respect 113, 134, 142, 159, 170–1
responsibilities 1, 4, 11, 32, 110, 139, 147, 155, 162, 165, 171
rhizome 117–18, 170, 187
rights 30
risk 11, 25, 29, 199, 205
Robbins Report 18
Russia 189

Scandinavia 193
scholarship 128
science 3, 6, 17, 24, 30, 39, 47–9, 54, 58, 131, 172, 187

Subject Index

separateness 38
sincerity 37, 53, 63, 146
sites of culture, *see* university as culturing site
skills 41, 128, 130, 138, 154
social class 4
social contract 139, 142–3, 145
social justice 164
social science 3–4, 103, 187
society 18, 32–3, 35, 38, 42–3, 109, 113, 115, 143–4, 149, 195, 215
   knowledge 48
sociology 61–2
space of reason 32, 38, 63, 204
spaces 10, 72–80, 84, 87, 91–2, 94, 96, 108, 110, 171, 176, 179, 191, 197, 202, 213, 216
   dead 180, 186
   institutional 150
   multicultural 22
   public 32
   transcultural 7
spirit 27, 40, 64–6, 79, 86–7, 89–91, 94, 97–8, 106, 110, 118, 120, 150, 169, 180, 182–3, 186, 188
sport 25
standards 9–10, 190
state, nation 19, 32, 34, 131, 143, 148, 194
STEM 12, 22, 24–5, 28, 46–7, 215
strangeness 13, 136, 154–7, 171, 176, 184–5
strangers 32, 34, 43, 53, 208
stratification 6
students 2, 50, 62, 71–2, 91, 102, 112, 114–15, 118, 128, 138–42, 148, 151, 158, 184, 197–201, 203, 208, 211, 215
   radical students 192
suffering 98
suppression 6, 9
surveillance 198, 212, 214
sustainability 10, 66, 109, 114, 127, 147–8, 164
systems 205

teaching 4, 22, 25, 57, 66, 71–2, 102, 114–15, 117–19, 126, 137–9, 141–2, 148, 151, 158, 194, 196–201

technology 30, 49, 85, 102, 114, 210
theology 191
thinking, *see under* thought
thought 111, 125, 132–3, 151–2, 177, 191, 204, 206, 209
tolerance 33
totalitarianism 67, 79
transculturality 24
transdisciplinarity 39, 166, 213
transformation 103, 115, 126, 141, 180, 182, 187, 199
transhumanism 210
trust 129, 131, 134, 143, 170, 208
truth 130–1, 161, 196, 211
truthfulness 4, 37, 53, 63

uncertainty 161
understanding 41, 153, 207, 211
United Kingdom 38
United Nations' Sustainable Development Goals 66
United States of America 30, 189
universality 53–4, 58–9, 61–4, 66, 68, 128, 185, 206
universities 1, 31, 79, 92, 101, 129, 131, 137–8, 140, 143–5, 148–9, 151, 155–6, 158, 160, 162, 170, 172, 189, 191–4, 200, 210, 213
   actual:
      Berkeley 31
      Cambridge 38
      Colombia 31
      Harvard 31
      Lund 192
      Oxford 192–3
      Sydney 41
      Utrecht 9
   alternative **110–21**
   culture-free 19
   'world-class' 19, 176, 189–90
universities as institutions 2, 19, 71–2, 110, 148, 172, 180
Universities without Walls 113, 119–20
the university 10, 18, 26–7, 60, 62, 64, 66, 88, 90, 103, 114, 147, 154, 160, 165, 168, 178, 182, 185, 193, 199, 206, 216, *see also* universities; university

atmospheric **83–95**, 109, 113
being a 5
civic 203, 210
concept of 2
conditions of 206, 213
culture of 63, 71, 85, 87, 95, 98, 172
existential 196, 200
future 144
hybrid 118
idea of 57, 92, 109, 196
individual 194–6
living 191
mediaeval 191, 206
mode 3 112
network 112–15, 119
nomad 119
placeful 190
post-human 164
public 138
singular 189–90, 201
solidary 201
stretched 139
toxic 179
university and culture relationship, *see* culture and university relationship
university as culturing site 25, 72–3, 77, 80–2, 156, **178–9**, 184, 187
university as place, *see* cultures, placeful; place
university cultures 13, 27, 81, 102–5, 110–11, 113, 120, 179, 186, 191
university design, *see* design
The University in Ruins 1, 18
university outreach 4
unpredictability 184, 200–1
utility 41, 210–11
utopia 53, 68, 104–5, 107–8, 160, 186, 210

'validity claims' 53
value background 8
value conflicts 110
valued ends 12
valued way of life 10
value-freedom 18
value-ladenness 5
values 13, 26, 65, 89, 96, 98–102, 104–5, 107, 112, 117–18, 128, 159, 169, 182, 189, 191, 210, *see also* values
   academic 111
   civic 109
   cultural 19, 79, 125, 150, 179
   divining of 166
   institutional 194
   pedagogical 97
   public 126
value systems 147, 162
vibrant matter 118
virtues 78–9, 89, 125–9, 134, 135
vision 13, 97–100, 104–6, 108, 110, 189, 199, 202
vitality 21, 50, 81, 203
voice 95, 139, 151, 171, 177, 180, 189, 193, 199

West, the 40, 49, 161, 198
will 65
wisdom 60, 93, 176
wonder 156, 184
work 141, 145, 147, 151
world 10–11, 58–60, 78, 84, 96, 107, 109, 112, 115, 121, 178, 207–9, 215
World Bank 199

Yugoslavia 34

'zombification' 182

Name Index

Aaen, J. H.   113–14
Adorno, T.   6, 18, 56, 61, 204–5
Agnew, J. A.   76–7
Alt, P.-A.   1
Althusser, L.   23
Amin, A.   79
Anderson, B.   91–2
Anderson-Levitt, K. M.   85, 98
Appadurai, A.   71
Aristotle   125, 127, 129, 177
Arndt, S.   82, 110, 133
Arvanitakis, J.   135
Augé, M.   73–4, 76, 82
Auret, H.   90
Ayer, A. J.   20

Backhurst, D.   4, 204
Barad, K.   58
Barnacle, R.   152, 164
Barnett, R.   36, 51, 66, 68, 99, 108, 110, 112–13, 128–9, 132–3, 146–7, 153, 155–6, 158, 162, 164–5, 168–9, 177, 182, 190, 194–6, 200, 212
Bayne, S.   102
Beavis, A.   39
Becher, T.   22, 39
Bell, D.   31–2
Bendik-Keymer, J.   66
Bengtsen, S.   77, 79, 109, 129, 132, 134–5, 142, 144, 147, 151, 153, 155, 158, 165, 167, 170, 177, 182, 190, 194, 196–7, 208–10
Benhabib, S.   37
Bennett, J.   118, 146, 156
Bennett, O.   18
Bennett, T.   9, 56
Bergh, A.   110–11
Berquist, W. H.   8, 27, 40
Berry, J. W.   97
Berubé, M.   39
Bhambra, G. K.   26

Bhaskar, R.   39, 46, 52, 54–5, 59
Biesta, G. J. J.   199–200
Bille, M.   84, 87–90, 92–3
Bloom, A.   22
Boehnert, J.   52
Böhme, G.   84, 87–93, 95
Boli, J.   85
Bourdieu, P.   8, 22
Boutang, Y.-M.   40
Braidotti, R.   28, 52, 163, 168
Brockliss, L. W. B.   192
Butler, J.   53

Calabrese Barton   8
Canals, L.   113
Carlson, J.   94
Carvalho, L.   110
Casey, E. S.   72–3, 75, 78–80, 82
Cassirer, E.   7
Champagne, P.   8
Charbonneau, B.   67
Chomsky, N.   207
Clark, W.   191
Code, L.   39
Cohen, E.   24
Collin, F.   129, 143
Collini, S.   161
Connell, R.   5, 9, 110
Connolly, W. E.   169–70
Cook, J.   117
Cresswell, T.   74–6, 79
Critchley, S.   41
Cuthbert, D.   164

Dall'Alba, G.   152
Darwall-Smith, R.   193
Davies, M.   13, 22
de Bono, E.   176
De Certeau, M.   7
Delanty, G.   8, 22, 206
Deleuze, G.   79
Derrida, J.   64, 80, 206

Descartes, R.   60, 126, 130, 147
Descola, P.   66
de Sousa Santos, B.   4–5, 23, 40, 51
DiSalvo, C.   100
Disraeli, B.   11
dos Santos Pacheco, R. C.   39
Dunne, A.   100–4, 106–7
Dutton, J. E.   98

Eagleton, T.   2, 7–8, 35–6
Eaton, C.   8
Edensor, T.   92–5
Edgerton, S.   41
Eliot, T. S.   7, 36
Elliot, D. L.   139
Ellis, R. A.   138
Engels, F.   8
Englund, T.   110–11

Faber, G.   207
Fehrman, C. H.   192
Fellows, R.   71
Felski, R.   6
Ferraro, G.   85
Feyerabend, P.   24
Fitzpatrick, K.   110
Fornas, J.   7
Foucault, M.   23, 50, 75, 78
Frank, D. J.   17
Freire, P.   132
Fricker, M.   23, 47
Friedman, T.   76
Fritzsche, H.   4, 37
Frodeman, R.   39
Fukuyama, F.   32–3
Fung, D.   166

Gallagher, M.   102
Gellner, E.   6, 20, 34, 52
Giannakakis, V.   21
Gibbs, P.   39, 99, 129–30, 143, 151, 208
Gieryn, T. F.   75, 77, 79, 82
Gildersleeve, R. E.   132, 146, 155
Giroux, H.   110, 126, 132
Goebbels, J.   4
Goldman, C. A.   141
Goodyear, P.   138
Gramsci, A.   49
Grant, B.   198, 200

Grant, J.   40
Greenwood, D. J.   40
Guattari, F.   79
Gulunic, C.   97

Habermas, J.   4, 8, 37, 53–4, 58, 62–4, 111, 204
Hancher, M.   9
Handy, C. B.   97
Hansen, F. T.   156
Haraway, D.   163
Hardy, C.   83
Harman, G.   45, 146–7, 149, 154
Harsin, J.   129
Hazelkorn   189
Hegel, G. W. F.   53, 141
Heidegger, M.   64, 140, 149–52, 160, 167–8, 171, 204–5, 207
Herbrechter, S.   28
Higton, M.   6
Hilli, C.   116–19
Hodgson, N.   198
Hofstede, G.   71, 84–5
Honneth, A.   50, 53, 63
Horkheimer, M.   18, 56, 204
Hornsby, D. J.   135
Hourdequin, M.   40
Humboldt, W. von   127
Humpty-Dumpty   9
Huyssen, A.   33

Jackson, N.   164
Jain, A.   111, 120
Jaspers, K.   17
Jessop, B.   18, 56, 61
Julier, G.   94

Kagan, J.   39
Kandlbinder, P.   110–11
Kanov, J. E. H.   99
Kant, I.   51, 53, 58, 60–1, 111, 135, 152
Karlsohn, T.   128, 165
Kidd, I. J. J.   23, 47
Kierkegaard, S.   195–8
Klein, J. T.   39
Kleinhesselink, K.   146, 155, 161
Knorr-Cetina, K.   48
Kohls, C.   117, 119
Köppe, C.   117, 119

Kotler, P. 91
Kreber, C. 22

Laclau, E. 26
Latour, B. 61, 215
Lea, J. 35
Leavis, F. R. 22, 38
Lechner, F. J. 85
Lefebvre, H. 73–5, 78–9, 82
Levin, M. 40
Levinas, E. 50, 132, 149, 156, 159–60, 210, 215
Lingis, A. 136, 153, 164, 167
Litwin, G. H. 85
Liu, A. M. M. 71
Liyange, M. 1
Locke, J. 141
LØvlie, L. 41
Lukens, F. 100
Lyotard, J.-F. 34, 53, 65, 169
Lysgaard, J. A. 155, 161

Maassen, P. A. M. 83
McCarthy, E. D. 23
McDowell, J. 204
Macfarlane, B. 135, 137, 139
Marcel, G. 149, 156–7, 160
Marginson S. 30, 40, 158, 206
Martinez-Vargas, C. 23
Marx, K. 8
Massy, W. F. 142
Maxwell, N. 60
Meneses, M. P. 5
Meyer, J. W. 17
Mika, C. 133
Mill, J. S. 37
Moberly, W. 17
Moran, E. T. 97
Morreira, E. T. 109
Murphy, P. 206

Naidoo, R. 126
Nail, T. 45
Nelson, C. 39
Nelson, H. G. 104–6
Neumann, R. 138
Newman, J. H. 64, 207, 211
Nietzsche, F. 63–4, 162, 165–6, 168, 171–2

Nikolaidis, A. C. 23
Nixon, J. 73, 110, 128–9, 131, 143, 158
Norberg-Schulz, C. 90
Nørgård, R. 77, 100–1, 106, 109–10, 112–15, 117, 119, 134–5, 140, 141–2, 177, 182, 190–1, 196, 203, 205–7
Nussbaum, M. 39, 51, 53

Oberdiek, H. 33
O'Mahony, P. 8
Ortega y Gasset, J. 17, 21, 50, 63–4, 67
Ostling, J. 6
Ouchi, W. G. 97

Passeron, J.-C. 22
Pässilä, A. 99
Pawlak, K. 8, 27, 40
Pedersen, A. Y. 117
Peters, M. A. 5, 24, 36, 44, 51, 56, 129, 165
Plato 132, 159
Plumb, J. H. 38
Plumwood, V. 40, 66
Pollock, J. 152
Popper, (Sir) Karl 59

Raby, F. 100–4, 106
Ram, Y. 86
Rancière, J. 6
Readings, B. 1, 9, 18, 28, 43, 56, 61, 63–5, 67, 161, 210
Rebentisch, J. 44
Rickly-Boyd, J. M. 86
Rider, S. 110, 130–1, 165, 189–90
Rigby, K. 89
Ringer, F. K. 6
Robbins, (Sir) L. 18
Robinson, S. 133
Roggero, G. 65
Rosen, M. 8
Rosner, D. K. 104
Rousseau, J.-J. 14
Rüegg, W. 191
Ryle, M. 9

St. Augustine 126
St. Thomas Aquinas 132
Sartre, J.-P. 200

Savin-Baden, M.   52
Schein, E.   84, 97
Schildermans, H.   144
Schopenhauer, A.   207
Scruton, R.   35-6
Sellars, W.   204
Serres, M.   53, 61
Sewell, W. H.   72, 96
Shore, C.   138
Shumar, W.   133
Shutt, L.   212
Singh, S.   46
Smyth, J.   126, 138
Snow, C. P.   38
Soper, K.   9
Sorensen, A.   144-5
Spencer-Oatey, H.   84
Staley, D. J.   119
Standish, P.   166
Stevens, M. L.   8
Stewart, J.   94
Stiegler, B.   27-8, 64, 66
Stolterman, E.   104-6
Strain, J.   73
Street, B. V   71
Stuart, M.   212
Sum, N.-G.   18, 56
Sumartojo, S.   92-5
Szadkowski, K.   129

Tagiuri, R.   85
Taylor, C.   7, 20
Temple, P.   73, 75-7, 79, 203
Tharp, B. M.   104
Tharp, S. M.   104
Thrift, N.   79
Trautmann, F.   44
Trilling, L.   18
Trowler, P.   7, 22, 39

Tschumi, B.   77
Tuan, Y.-F.   74-9
Tukeo, S.   5, 36, 44

Ulin, R. C.   7

Venkatesan, P.   24
Vince, R.   99
Virilio, P.   64
Volgger, M.   85-6, 90-1, 182
Volkwein, J. F.   97
Voros, J.   101-2, 104, 184

Waddington, K.   98-9
Walker, G. E.   140
Walker, M.   23
Wax, M. L.   71
Weber, K.   26
Weeks, J.   97
Wei, I. P.   191
Weidinger, J.   89-90
Weil, S.   149, 157-8
Welikala, T.   36, 51
West, M. R.   99
Whitchurch, C.   40
Wiener, M. J.   6
Wilkins, A. L.   97
Williams, Raymond   2, 7
Williams, Rowan   19
Wood, D.   40, 206
Woolston, C.   9
Worline, M. C.   98
Wright, E. O.   103
Wright, S.   138

Xu, X.   30

Zaman, A.   40
Zizek, S.   31, 53, 61, 68, 206